What's on the Excel Screen?

Formatting toolbar

Row headings

Standard toolbar

Menu bar

Column headings

Formula bar

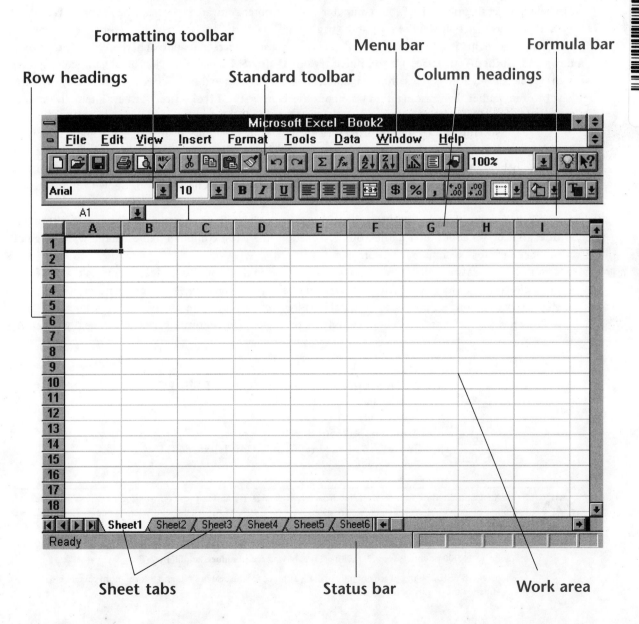

Sheet tabs

Status bar

Work area

For every kind of computer user, there is a SYBEX book.

All computer users learn in their own way. Some need straightforward and methodical explanations. Others are just too busy for this approach. But no matter what camp you fall into, SYBEX has a book that can help you get the most out of your computer and computer software while learning at your own pace.

Beginners generally want to start at the beginning. The **ABC's** series, with its step-by-step lessons in plain language, helps you build basic skills quickly. For a more personal approach, there's the **Murphy's Laws** and **Guided Tour** series. Or you might try our **Quick & Easy** series, the friendly, full-color guide, with **Quick & Easy References**, the companion pocket references to the **Quick & Easy** series. If you learn best by doing rather than reading, find out about the **Hands-On Live!** series, our new interactive multimedia training software. For hardware novices, there's the **Your First** series.

The **Mastering and Understanding** series will tell you everything you need to know about a subject. They're perfect for intermediate and advanced computer users, yet they don't make the mistake of leaving beginners behind. Add one of our **Instant References** and you'll have more than enough help when you have a question about your computer software. You may even want to check into our **Secrets & Solutions** series.

SYBEX even offers special titles on subjects that don't neatly fit a category—like our **Pushbutton Guides**, our books about the Internet, our books about the latest computer games, and a wide range of books for Macintosh computers and software.

SYBEX books are written by authors who are expert in their subjects. In fact, many make their living as professionals, consultants or teachers in the field of computer software. And their manuscripts are thoroughly reviewed by our technical and editorial staff for accuracy and ease-of-use.

So when you want answers about computers or any popular software package, just help yourself to SYBEX.

For a complete catalog of our publications, please write:

SYBEX Inc.
2021 Challenger Drive
Alameda, CA 94501
Tel: (510) 523-8233/(800) 227-2346 Telex: 336311
Fax: (510) 523-2373

Lisa Butani

TALK TO SYBEX ONLINE.

JOIN THE SYBEX FORUM ON COMPUSERVE®

- Talk to SYBEX authors, editors and fellow forum members.
- Get tips, hints, and advice online.
- Download shareware and the source code from SYBEX books.

If you're already a CompuServe user, just enter GO SYBEX to join the SYBEX Forum. If you're not, try CompuServe free by calling 1-800-848-8199 and ask for Representative 560. You'll get one free month of basic service and a $15 credit for CompuServe extended services—a $23.95 value. Your personal ID number and password will be activated when you sign up.

Join us online today. Enter GO SYBEX on CompuServe. If you're not a CompuServe member, call Representative 560 at 1-800-848-8199

(outside U.S./Canada call 614-457-0802)

SYBEX
Shortcuts to
Understanding

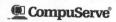

THE PUSHBUTTON GUIDE™ TO

MICROSOFT® OFFICE

Peter G. Aitken

SYBEX ®

San Francisco · Paris · Düsseldorf · Soest

PUSHBUTTON GUIDE BOOK CONCEPT: David Kolodney
ACQUISITIONS EDITOR: Joanne Cuthbertson
DEVELOPMENTAL EDITOR: Sarah Wadsworth
EDITOR: Abby Azrael
TECHNICAL EDITOR: Ellen Ferlazzo
BOOK DESIGNER: Claudia Smelser
PRODUCTION ARTIST AND SCREEN GRAPHICS: Lisa Jaffe
TYPESETTERS: Ann Dunn and Dina F Quan
PROOFREADER/PRODUCTION ASSISTANT: Kate Westrich
INDEXER: Ted Laux
COVER DESIGNER: Joanna Kim Gladden

Screen reproductions produced with Collage Complete.

Collage Complete is a trademark of Inner Media Inc.

SYBEX is a registered trademark of SYBEX Inc.

TRADEMARKS: SYBEX has attempted throughout this book to distinguish pro-prietary trademarks from descriptive terms by following the capitalization style used by the manufacturer.

Every effort has been made to supply complete and accurate information. How-ever, SYBEX assumes no responsibility for its use, nor for any infringement of the intellectual property rights of third parties which would result from such use.

Library of Congress Card Number: 94-66852
ISBN: 0-7821-1543-8

Manufactured in the United States of America
10 9 8 7 6 5 4 3

Acknowledgments

My thanks go to my editors at SYBEX, Sarah Wadsworth and Abby Azrael, who were instrumental in bringing this book from idea to completion. Thanks also to the SYBEX production team.

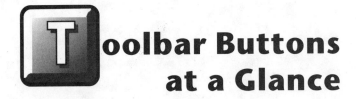 # oolbar Buttons at a Glance

Office Manager toolbar

Microsoft Word   **5,22**

Microsoft Excel   **5**

Microsoft PowerPoint   **6**

Microsoft Mail   **6**

Microsoft Office   **10,12**

Word Tools

Align Left   **63**

Align Right   **64**

AutoFormat   **73**

Bold   **59**

Border   **69, 118**

Word Tools

Bottom Border **70–71, 118**

Bullets **66–67**

Center **63, 137**

Columns **125**

Copy **45, 121, 138**

Cut **45, 121, 138**

Decrease Indent **64**

Full Screen **160**

Help **51**

Increase Indent **64**

Insert Table/Rows/Columns **106, 112–113**

Inside Border **70, 118**

Word Tools

Italic **60**

Justify **63**

Left Border **70, 118**

Magnifier **161**

Microsoft Excel **5**

Microsoft PowerPoint **6**

Multiple Pages **161**

New **36, 58**

No Border **70–71, 118**

Numbering <_> **66–67**

One Page **161**

Open **34–35**

Word Tools

Outside Border **69, 118**

Save **30–31**

Paste **45, 122–123, 138, 141, 143**

Show/Hide ¶ **77**

Print **50, 53, 161–162**

Shrink to Fit **160**

Print Preview **159**

Spelling **148, 150**

Redo **45**

Switch between Header and Footer **95**

Right Border **70, 118**

Top Border **70, 118**

Word Tools

Underline **60**

Undo **44, 73, 81**

Excel Tools

Align Left **138**

Align Right **138**

AutoSum **248**

Bold **221**

Borders **221–222**

Center **218**

ChartWizard **264**

Chart Type **276**

Color **223**

Excel Tools

Comma Style **216**

Format Painter **229**

Copy **122, 141, 198**

Function Wizard **244**

Currency Style **216**

Increase Decimal **217**

Cut **198, 278**

Italic **221**

Decrease Decimal **217**

Legend **278**

Font Color **222**

Microsoft Mail **6, 388**

Excel Tools

Microsoft Word **5**

New Workbook **189**

Open **122, 187**

Paste **199, 270**

Percent Style **216**

Print **286**

Print Preview **301**

Save **182**

Underline **221**

Undo **201**

PowerPoint Tools

Arc **339**

PowerPoint Tools

Autoshapes **338**

Bold **337**

Center **334**

Copy **143**

Decrease Font Size **336**

Demote (Indent More) **334, 358, 368**

Ellipse **338**

Freeform **339**

Increase Font Size **336**

Insert Clip Art **340**

Insert Graph **344**

Italic **337**

PowerPoint Tools

Line **339**

Microsoft Excel **5**

Microsoft Word **5**

New **309**

Open **143, 328**

Paste **335**

Print **384**

Promote (Indent Less) **334, 358, 368**

Save **327**

Spelling **370**

Text **334**

Text Color **337**

PowerPoint Tools

Text Shadow **337**

Underline **337**

Undo **338**

Microsoft Mail Tools

Compose **397**

Forward **395**

Next **391**

Previous **391**

Reply **394**

Reply All **394**

Contents at a Glance

Table of Contents

CHAPTER 4 **Formatting Fundamentals** **55**

CHAPTER 9 **Proofing and Printing** 147

CHAPTER 13 Formulas and Functions 231

CHAPTER 14   **Creating Charts of Your Data**   **255**

CHAPTER 17   **Working with Slides**   **329**

CHAPTER 18 **Enhancing Your Presentations** 357

Introduction

Welcome to *The Pushbutton Guide to Microsoft Office*. As you may already know, Office is the fastest selling (and I believe the best) office suite product, which combines all the programs that most busy people in business and technical fields need for their day-to-day work. Office includes:

- Microsoft Word, a word processing program
- Microsoft Excel, a spreadsheet program
- Microsoft PowerPoint, a presentation program
- Microsoft Mail, an electronic mail program

Each of these programs is a market leader in its own right. Put them together and you have a great deal of power and flexibility at your fingertips.

These are not, however, simple programs. Each one has a wide array of features and capabilities, and new users often find it difficult to get up to speed on their own. You could buy a 600 page book on each of the four programs, but now you don't need to. In a single volume I have combined all the information you need to use Office for the real-world tasks you face every day. I don't cover *every* detail of the programs, but rather have concentrated on those features people need the most.

The Approach

The title of this book, *Pushbutton Guide*, indicates the approach I have taken. All of the Office programs have a graphical user interface that makes good use of buttons you can "push" with your mouse to carry out many program tasks. Each button has a picture or some text on it to remind you of its function. Rather than trying to remember some obscure key sequence, or hunting through the menus for the right command, you can usually find the needed button simply by looking at your screen.

This book is a visual tour of the Office programs that *shows* you what to do. Throughout the book you'll see each button (as well as other graphical screen elements) next to clear, concise, step-by-step explanations of the tasks at hand. Of course, I also mention keyboard shortcuts and menu commands for tasks when needed, but the emphasis is on the buttons in each program.

The Structure

Chapter 1 introduces you to Office and shows you how to start and switch between the various Office programs. I suggest that everyone read this chapter first. The remainder of the book is divided into four sections: eight chapters on Word, six on Excel, four on PowerPoint, and one on Mail. You can start with whichever section interests you most, but within each section I suggest that you read the chapters in order. If you need to find out about a specific task *right now,* you can use the index to find the corresponding pages.

Conventions Used in This Book

Many instructions in this book tell you to click on an item on your screen. This means to move your mouse until the mouse pointer on your screen is over the item, and then quickly press and release the left mouse button. When selecting menu commands, you'll usually have to select two or three items in sequence. I'll use the following shortcut notation for menu commands: if I say

> Select File ➤ Open

It means select File, then select Open.

While the Office applications are designed to be used with the mouse, you can also perform most functions using the keyboard. The underlined characters in commands tell you which keys to press, together with the Alt key. To pull down the File menu, for example, you could press Alt+F.

Microsoft Office also provides shortcut key combinations for many functions (such as Ctrl+S for Save). You'll see these shortcut keys listed next to options on pull-down menus.

The Poster

The various applications in Microsoft Office have literally hundreds of buttons and menu options, so don't worry about trying to remember them all. Instead, pull out and open the poster that you'll find at the back of this book. This poster illustrates the most important toolbars of

Microsoft Office, along with a description of each button and any corresponding menu options or shortcut keys.

Use the poster as a quick and easy reference. If you forget how to perform a task, scan the poster to find the toolbar button or command you need. The top of the poster shows buttons that are common to many of the toolbars. The remaining buttons are grouped according to each application's toolbars. So once you locate the button you need, you'll know which toolbar to use.

1

MICROSOFT OFFICE

Up and Running
with Office

WHAT IS MICROSOFT OFFICE? Microsoft Office is the most popular of a relatively new breed of computer software—the *office suite*. An office suite provides, in a single package, the major computer applications that are needed in a typical business or technical office. In Microsoft Office you get the following programs:

- Microsoft Word, a word processing program for creating documents of all kinds

- Microsoft Excel, a spreadsheet program for analysis and graphical display of numerical data

- Microsoft PowerPoint, a presentation graphics program for creating visual presentations

- Microsoft Mail, an electronic mail program for sending and receiving mail over a network

NOTE

If you have the Professional version of Microsoft Office you also get Microsoft Access, a database management program. Access is not covered in this book, however.

Many people use the individual programs that make up Microsoft Office, because they are full-featured applications. When combined into a suite, the programs are even more powerful, because the suite is designed so that all of its parts work well together. For example, sharing data between applications in Microsoft Office is particularly easy.

Starting Office Applications

Office itself is not a program that needs to be started (but see the section "The Office Manager"). Rather, you must start the individual applications (Word, Excel, PowerPoint, and Mail) that you wish to use. You can have one, two, three, or all four of these programs running at the same time.

> ### N O T E
>
> **Of course, Office must be installed on your computer for you to be able to use it. See the appendix for installation instructions.**

One method for starting programs is from the Windows Program Manager. Another method utilizes the Office Manager toolbar, which you may find displayed on your screen when Windows starts. The Office Manager is covered later in the chapter. The Program Manager is the first screen that you see when you start Windows. You will see one or more windows, or rectangular regions, each with a number of small graphical images, or *icon*s, in it. The exact number and appearance of these windows will depend on how your computer is set up. To activate the Microsoft Office window, press Ctrl+F6 until you see a blue bar titled "Microsoft Office." Figure 1.1 shows the Program Manager screen with the Microsoft Office window active.

You'll note that the Microsoft Office window has numerous icons in it, representing the various components of Microsoft Office that were installed. There will be icons for the main applications (Word, Excel, PowerPoint, and Mail) as well as for a variety of utility programs. Don't worry about these other programs—we're just interested in the "big 4."

Microsoft
Word

Microsoft
Excel

FIGURE 1.1

You start Office programs from the Microsoft Office window on the Program Manager screen

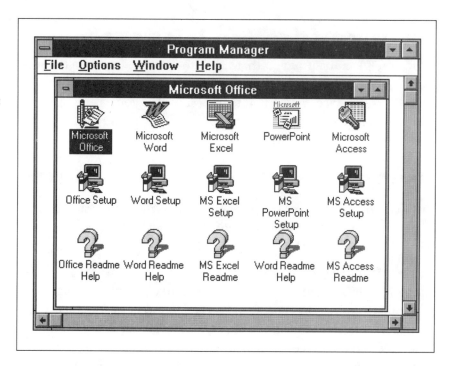

Microsoft
PowerPoint

Microsoft
Mail

To start an Office application, just double-click on its icon (position the mouse pointer over the icon, and then press and release the left mouse button twice). The program will start and you can turn to the relevant section of this book and get to work.

Starting One Application from Another

One of the major advantages of using Windows programs is that you can have more than one program running at the same time. You will often want to start one Microsoft Office application while you are

working in another—for example, start Excel while you are using Word. There are several ways to do this. One involves switching from the current application to the Program Manager, and then starting the new application from there:

1. Press Ctrl+Esc to display the Task List. This list includes the name of every Windows application that is currently running.

2. Click the Program Manager entry in the list, and then click the Switch To button. The Program Manager screen will be displayed.

3. Locate the Microsoft Office window and start the desired application, as was described earlier in this chapter.

Another method of starting one Microsoft Office application while working in another is to use the Microsoft toolbar. This toolbar is available in each of the Microsoft Office applications. To display it in any Microsoft Office application:

1. Select <u>V</u>iew ➤ <u>T</u>oolbars from that application's menu.

2. Select Microsoft from the list of toolbars that is displayed.

3. Click the OK button.

Note that this toolbar displays an icon for every Microsoft Office application as well as some other Microsoft programs, such as Microsoft Schedule and Microsoft Publisher. These icons are displayed regardless of whether the corresponding application is actually installed on your system. If you try to start an application that is not installed, you will see a message telling you the application is not installed.

To move the Microsoft toolbar, point to its title bar, click the left mouse button, and drag it to the desired location. If you drag it near the left or right edge of the screen it becomes a vertically-oriented toolbar.

To close the toolbar, click the box in its upper-left corner.

Switching between Applications

If you have more than one Microsoft Office application running, you'll often want to switch from one to the other. You can do so using the Microsoft toolbar, as described in the previous section. If you click an icon on the Microsoft toolbar, and the application is running, Windows will switch to it.

You can also switch applications using the Task List. Press Ctrl+Esc to display the Task List. Click the name of the desired application (if it is not displayed on the Task List, it is not running).

Then, click the Switch To button.

The third and, in my opinion, fastest way to switch between applications is with the keyboard. Here's how it works:

1. Press and hold down the Alt key, and then press the Tab key (do not release Alt). Windows will display a small box on-screen with the name of another running Windows application.

2. Tap the Tab key one or more times; as you tap, Windows will cycle through the names of all running applications.

3. When the name of the desired application is displayed, release the Alt key.

The Microsoft Office Manager

The Microsoft Office Manager is a component of Microsoft Office that can be used to start applications and switch between them. The default setup is for Office Manger to start automatically when Windows is started. Using Office Manager is optional.

NOTE

If Office does not start automatically and you would like it to, drag the Office icon from the Microsoft Office group to the Startup group on your Windows Program Manager screen. To disable automatic starting, drag the Office icon out of the Startup group back to the Office group. See your Windows documentation if you need help with these procedures.

On other systems you must start it manually by double-clicking its icon in the Microsoft Office window. You can tell if Office Manager starts automatically because it will display its logo when Windows starts, and the Office Manager toolbar will be displayed. It normally includes icons for the installed Office applications as well as two icons of its own.

In the Office Manager toolbar (see top of page), the Word, Excel, Mail, and PowerPoint icons, as well as the two Office Manager icons, are displayed. The Office Manager toolbar always stays "on top"—it is always displayed no matter which application you are using.

To start or switch to any Office application, click its icon on the Office Manager toolbar. If you can't remember which program a particular icon

starts, position the mouse pointer over the icon for a moment (don't click), and the program name will be displayed next to the pointer.

Customizing the Office Manager Toolbar

You have several options for customizing the Office Manager toolbar. You can change its position on-screen by pointing to its title bar and dragging it to the new location. If you find that the Office Manager toolbar is getting in your way, you can minimize it to a small icon by clicking the downward pointing triangle in its upper-right corner. To restore the minimized toolbar, double-click on its icon.

You can also customize its appearance. To change which applications are displayed on the toolbar, their relative positions, and the size of the toolbar buttons:

1. Click the Microsoft Office button on the Office Manager toolbar.

2. Select Customize from the menu that is displayed. Office Manager displays the Customize dialog box.

3. If necessary, click the Toolbar tab to display the toolbar options, as shown in Figure 1.2.

4. The list gives names of all Microsoft applications, in the order in which they are displayed on the toolbar. Those whose icons are displayed on the toolbar have an X in the box before the name.

5. To add an application to, or remove it from, the toolbar, click on its name to select it, and then click on its box to add or remove the X.

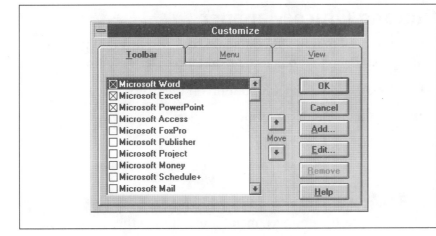

FIGURE 1.2

The Office Manager Customize dialog box lets you specify which Microsoft applications are displayed as icons on the Office Manager toolbar.

6. To change the display position of an application's icon on the toolbar, click its name to select it, and then click the up or down arrow to change its position.

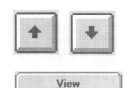

7. To change the display size of the toolbar buttons, click the View tab in the dialog box to display the View options.

8. In the Toolbar Button Size section, select the desired size

N O T E

To quickly change toolbar button size, click on the Office Manager toolbar with the right mouse button, and then select the desired button size from the shortcut menu that is displayed.

9. Once the Office Manager toolbar is customized to suit your preferences, click the OK button.

Quitting Office Manager

You do not need to quit Office Manager before quitting Windows or turning your computer off. You *can* quit, however, as follows:

1. Click the Microsoft Office button on the Office Manager toolbar.

2. From the menu that is displayed, select Exit.

The various Microsoft Office applications are each specialized for a specific task. There are, however, many similarities in the way you use them. Because commands, menus, and screen layout all follow similar patterns, much of what you learn about one Microsoft Office application is relevant to other applications.

Menus

Every Microsoft Office application—and indeed every Windows application—relies heavily on menus. Menus provide a way for the user to select the various commands that tell the program what to do. The *menu ba*r is displayed near the top of the screen, just below the program's title bar. Each item on the menu bar represents a menu. For example, File represents the File menu, Edit represents the Edit menu, and so on. To display a menu:

E<u>dit</u>

- With the mouse, click the menu's name.

- With the keyboard, press Alt+*letter*, where *lette*r is the single letter that is underlined in the menu name.

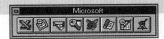

Figure 1.3 shows Word's Edit menu. Each line of the menu lists a specific command that Word can carry out. You should note several features of this menu.

- An underlined letter in a command indicates the key you can press to select the command when the menu is displayed.

- A shortcut key, listed only for some commands, indicates the key or keys you can use to issue the command without using the menus. For example, you can see that pressing Ctrl+G is the same as displaying the Edit menu and then selecting Go To.

- Grayed text indicates that the command is not available at present.

- Ellipses following a command indicate that the command leads to a dialog box in which you must enter additional information that the program needs to execute the command.

G̲o To...   Ctrl+G

O̲bject

B̲ookmark...

FIGURE 1.3

The Edit menu in Word shows the various special features that are shared by all of the Office programs.

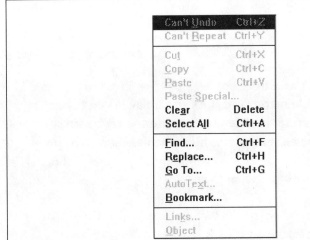

Clear   Delete

- The highlight bar, which displays a command as white letters on a dark background, marks the command that will be executed if you press ↵ (you can press ↑ or ↓ to move the highlight bar up and down the menu).

Once a menu is displayed, there are three ways to select a command from it:

- Press the key corresponding to the underlined letter in the command.

- Click the command with the mouse.

- Press ↑ or ↓ to highlight the command and press ↵.

One useful feature of the menu system is that, when a menu is displayed, the status bar along the bottom edge of the screen displays a brief description of the currently highlighted command. If you display a menu and change your mind, press Esc twice to close the menu without executing a command.

N O T E

Remember that the instruction "select File ➤ Save" means to first display the File menu, and then select Save from the menu commands. The underlined letters indicate the keyboard shortcut for issuing the command. In this example, you would press Alt+F followed by S to select the command. You can, of course, use the mouse if you prefer.

Toolbars and Buttons

All Office applications except Mail make excellent use of *toolbar*s. A toolbar contains a number of buttons, each of which has a small picture, or icon, displayed on it. Each button corresponds to a command, and clicking the button executes the command.

> **NOTE**
>
> **Mail does make use of buttons for selecting commands with the mouse. It's just that the buttons are not organized into toolbars.**

The benefits of toolbars are twofold:

- Clicking a button is usually faster than selecting the corresponding command from the menus.

- The icons on the toolbar buttons serve as a reminder of which button does what, making it easier to select the proper button.

> **TIP**
>
> **If you move the mouse pointer over a button and leave it there for a second or two (don't click!), the program will display a brief description of the button, called a *ToolTip*, next to the mouse cursor.**

Of course, toolbars are most beneficial for people who like to use the mouse. If you are a really fast typist you may find the menus faster and

easier. It's up to you—use whichever system, or combination of systems, suits you best.

An application typically has one or two toolbars displayed at a given time, and their usual position is immediately below the menu bar. Some specialized toolbars "float" at a variable screen location.

Most Office applications have a number of different toolbars available. Which toolbars are displayed depends on exactly what you're doing and on the program's option settings. To control toolbar display from any Microsoft Office application:

1. Select <u>V</u>iew ➤ <u>T</u>oolbars. The Toolbars dialog box is displayed. Figure 1.4 shows Word's Toolbars dialog box.

FIGURE 1.4

The Toolbars dialog box in Word

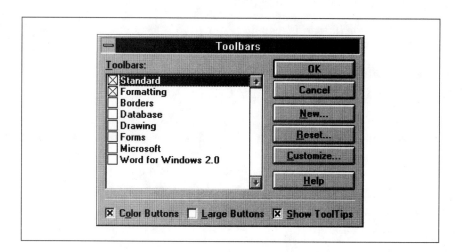

2. All of the available toolbars are listed, with an X in the box next to those that are currently displayed. Click the name of a displayed toolbar or the box next to it to turn its display off (the X will disappear from the box). Click it again to redisplay that toolbar.

3. When the toolbar display options are set as you desire, click OK.

> ### N O T E
>
> **You can also control toolbar display by right-clicking on any toolbar to display its shortcut menu. On the menu are listed all the application's toolbars, with a checkmark next to those that are currently displayed. Click the name of a toolbar to turn its display on or off.**

What Next?

You now know the basics of Microsoft Office—starting the programs, switching between them, and using menus and toolbars. You are ready to start working through the book, learning the details of how each program can be used to accomplish your daily tasks.

2 WORD FOR WINDOWS

Getting Started
with Word

NOW YOU'RE READY to create and edit documents using Word. You learned the first step, how to *start* Word for Windows, in Chapter 1. In this chapter we'll begin by taking a look at the Word screen. Then you'll learn how to enter text; move around the document; save, close, and open documents; and exit the program.

The Word for Windows Screen

To start Word, double-click the Word icon in the Program Manager window. Even easier, click the Word icon on the Microsoft Office toolbar. When it starts, Word displays a blank document for you to work with.

The Word screen may seem complicated, but once you get used to it you'll find it easy to use. It displays all of the elements you need to create and edit documents, as shown in Figure 2.1. You'll learn how to use these elements throughout the book.

- The *title bar* displays the name of your document. If a document has not yet been named, Word displays default names in the form *Document1*, *Document2*, and so on. The term *default* refers to the way Word will do things if you don't specify otherwise.

- The *menu bar* allows you to access menus from which you select Word's various commands.

- The *Standard toolbar* displays buttons that you can click with the mouse to perform commonly needed tasks.

- The *Formatting toolbar* displays buttons and lists that you use to format your document.

- The *ruler* allows you to set margins, tabs, and indents.

FIGURE 2.1

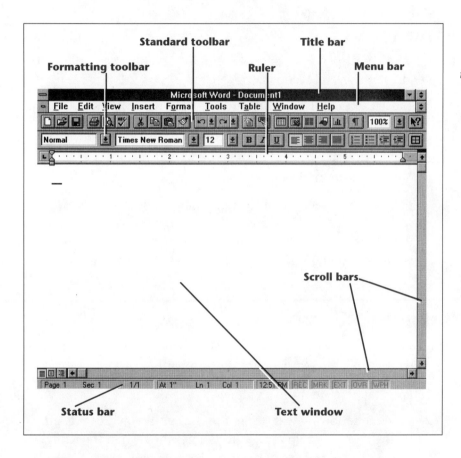

The main elements of the Word screen as they appear when you first start the program

- The *status bar* displays information about your document.

- The *scroll bars* allow you to move around in your document.

- The *text window* is where your document is displayed (it is empty in the figure).

The Status Bar

The status bar displays a variety of useful information (see Figure 2.1). It is divided into several sections:

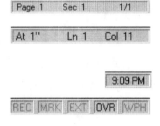

- The left section displays the current page number in the document.

- The next section displays the position of the cursor on the current page.

- The next section displays the current time.

- The five small sections at the right make up the *mode display*, which provides information about Word's operating mode. If the letters in a section are gray, the corresponding program mode is turned off. If the letters are black, the mode is on.

Entering Text

Now that you know the basics of the Word screen, you can start entering text. Let's practice with a sample document:

1. Press Tab to indent the first line.

2. Type the following text. Do not press ↵ until you are through typing. Word automatically starts a new line when the text reaches the right edge of the page. If you make an error, press Backspace to erase it.

> Our meeting with Ms. Watkins that was scheduled for today at noon has been postponed. Her plane was delayed by bad weather and she will not arrive until this evening.

3. Press ↵ to end the first paragraph, and then press ↵ again to add a blank line.

4. Press Tab to indent the first line of the second paragraph, and then type the following text followed by ↵ to end the paragraph:

> The meeting is tentatively rescheduled for tomorrow at 10:00 AM.

Your screen should now appear as in Figure 2.2.

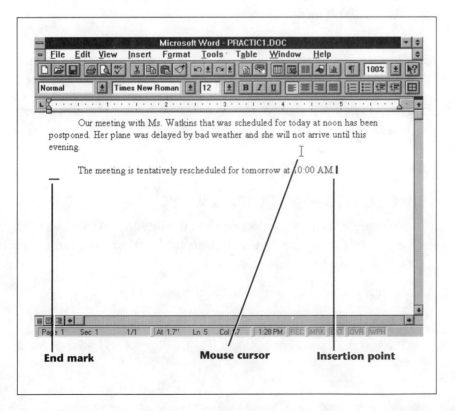

End mark　　　　　**Mouse cursor**　　　　**Insertion point**

FIGURE 2.2

The sample document on-screen, showing the insertion point, the end mark, and the mouse pointer

Figure 2.2 shows three more screen elements that you need to know about:

- The *insertion point* is a vertical line that indicates where text you type will appear.

- The *end mark* is a horizontal line that marks the end of the document.

- The *mouse pointer* moves on the screen as you move your mouse. It appears as a vertical I-beam or an arrow, depending on where it is located.

N O T E

If the mouse pointer displays as an hourglass, the program is busy and you must wait for the pointer to resume its I-beam or arrow shape before you can continue to work.

Moving around in Word

When you are working on a document you'll often need to move the insertion point to add or delete text at different locations. You can use the keyboard to move the insertion point short distances.

- To move left or right one character, press ← or →.

- To move up or down one line, press ↑ or ↓.

- To move to the end or beginning of the line, press End or Home.

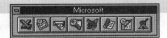

- To move left or right one word, hold down the Ctrl key and then press ← or →.

NOTE

Computer keys automatically repeat their function if you hold them down. For example, press and hold down ← to move continuously to the left.

Moving Larger Distances

When you are working with longer documents you'll often need to move more than a few lines up or down. Here's how:

- To move up or down one entire screen, press PgUp or PgDn.
- To move to the beginning of a document, press Ctrl+PgUp, and to move to the end of the document, press Ctrl+PgDn.

NOTE

If your document is longer than one printed page, Word will automatically start new pages as needed. An *automatic page break* is indicated by a dotted line across the screen. To add a manual page break, press Ctrl+↵.

Moving with the Mouse

You can also use the mouse to move around in your document. If the location where you want to place the insertion point is visible, simply move the mouse pointer there and click. If the location is not visible on the current screen, you'll need to *scroll* to the desired location:

- To scroll up or down one line, click the up or down arrow on the vertical scroll bar.

- To scroll up or down one screen, click on the vertical scroll bar between the scroll box and the up or down arrow.

- To scroll a variable distance, point at the scroll box and drag it up or down with your mouse.

NOTE

To move the insertion point, first scroll to the desired location, and then click on the point where you want to insert text.

Inserting Text

Let's try moving the insertion point and inserting some text in the middle of our practice document:

1. Use the mouse or the arrow keys to move the insertion point to the right of the period at the end of the first sentence ("...been postponed.").

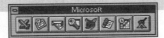

2. Type the additional sentence below.

She called and told me that they have 10 inches of snow!

Your document should now appear as shown in Figure 2.3.

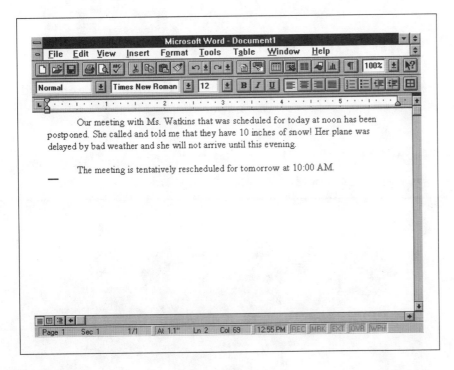

FIGURE 2.3

*The sample document
after adding a sentence*

Insert and Overstrike Modes

Word normally operates in *insert mode*. This means that if there is text to the right of the insertion point, it moves over to make room for new text that you type.

You can also use *overstrike mode*, in which text you type replaces existing text, character for character. Overstrike mode is indicated by the OVR indicator on the status bar. To switch between insert and overstrike mode, press Ins or double-click the OVR indicator.

Saving Your Document

Save

You need to save your document to have it available the next time you use Word. To save a document, click the Save button on the Standard toolbar, or press Shift+F12. One of two things will happen:

- If the file has been saved before, and already has a name, Word will save the file and return you to the document.

- If the file has not been saved before, Word will display the Save As dialog box, which is shown in Figure 2.4.

FIGURE 2.4

The Save As dialog box

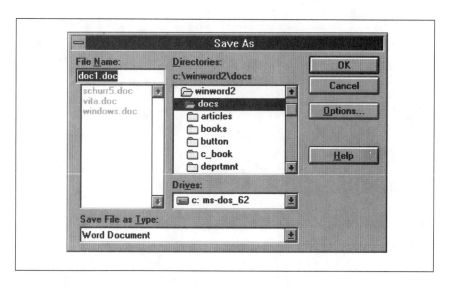

You can assign a name that is one to eight characters long to your document. The name must start with a letter, and can contain letters, numbers, and the underscore character. Word automatically adds a period and the extension DOC to the document's file name.

It's a good idea to use descriptive names for your documents. Creativity can be difficult when you're limited to a maximum of eight characters, but give it a try! Here are some examples:

Document contents	File name
Letter to Jane	JANE_LET
Sales report for 1993	SALES_93
Chapter 5 of the employee handbook	EHB_CH05
Employee evaluations	EMP_EVAL

To assign a name to your document:

1. Type the name into the File Name box. The highlighted text that is displayed there will be replaced by what you type. If the File Name box is not highlighted, press Alt+N before typing in the name.

2. Click the OK button or press ↵.

You should now save your practice document with the name PRACTIC1. Here are the steps to follow:

1. Click the Save button on the Standard toolbar or press Shift+F12. Word will display the Save As dialog box.

2. Type PRACTIC1. Your screen will appear as shown in Figure 2.5.

Save

FIGURE 2.5

*Saving the practice
document with the
name PRACTIC1.*

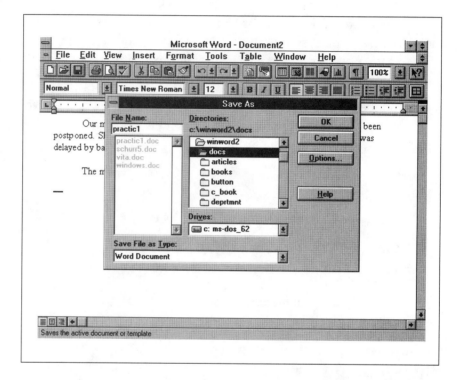

3. Click the OK button or press ↵. The document will be saved.
Note that Word now displays the newly assigned document
name in the title bar.

TIP

It's a good idea to save a document at regular intervals—say
every ten minutes—as you work on it, and also whenever you
take a break from your computer.

Closing a Document

When you have finished working on a document and have saved it, you may want to *close* it and then work on another document. Closing a document removes it from the screen. To close a document, double-click on the document control box at the left end of the menu bar. Don't double-click the box at the left end of the title bar by mistake—doing so will close the entire Word program!

If you haven't changed the document since you last saved it, it will close immediately. Otherwise, Word will display a dialog box asking if you want to save the changes to the document:

- Click the Yes button to save the changes, and then close the document.

- Click the No button to close the document without saving the changes. You will lose any changes that you made to the document since the last time you saved it.

- Click the Cancel button to return to the document without closing it.

Go ahead and close your sample document. Once the document is closed, Word displays a blank screen. You can now exit Word, open an existing document, or start a new document. These procedures are explained next.

Opening a Document

If you want to work on an existing document—one that has been saved previously—you must *open* it. When you open a document, Word reads

Open

it from disk and displays it ready for editing. To open a document, click the Open button on the Standard toolbar or press Ctrl+O. Word will display the Open dialog box, shown in Figure 2.6.

FIGURE 2.6

You use the Open dialog box to open an existing document for editing.

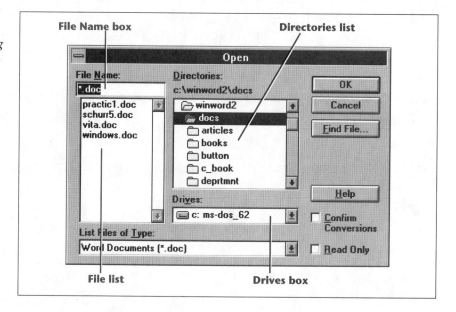

These are the components of the Open dialog box:

- The *File Name box* displays the name of the document to be opened.

- The *File list* displays the names of all the Word documents in the current directory.

- The *Directories list* displays the names of the current directory at the top, and other directories in the box.

- The *Drives box* displays the letter and label of the current disk drive.

Follow these steps to open a document file:

1. Click the Open button on the Standard toolbar or press Ctrl+O to display the Open dialog box.

Open

2. Highlight the desired file name in the file list, or type it into the File Name box.

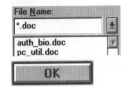

3. Click the OK button or press ↵.

What if the document you want to open isn't listed? It's probably been saved to a different drive or directory. Here's what to do:

- To list files on a different disk, open the Drives box and select the desired drive.

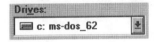

- To list files in a different directory, double-click the directory name in the Directories list.

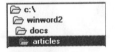

Now go ahead and open your sample document:

1. Click the Open button on the Standard toolbar or press Ctrl+O.

2. Type **PRACTIC1** in the File Name box.

Open

3. Click the OK button or press ↵.

The document will be displayed on-screen, just as it was when you saved it. The insertion point will be positioned at the beginning of the document.

Starting a New Document

New

When you start Word it displays a new, empty document on-screen, ready for you to start entering text. There may also be times when you want to start a new document while you're working in Word. To do so, simply click the New button on the Standard toolbar.

Using Templates

Documents are based on *templates*. A template may contain boilerplate text, such as a company letterhead, or styles for formatting (you'll learn about styles in Chapter 5). When you click the New button on the Standard toolbar, Word creates a new document based on the Normal template.

The Normal template is the most basic Word template, and is fine for most documents. Word comes with many other templates, however, designed for specific kinds of documents, such as FAX cover sheets, inter-office memos, and manuscripts. I don't have the space to describe all of these templates, but here's how you can find out for yourself. To open a new document based on a specific template:

1. Choose File ➤ New. Word displays the New dialog box, which is shown in Figure 2.7.

2. Scroll through the Template list and highlight the name of the desired template.

3. Click the OK button. Word creates a new document based on the selected template.

OK

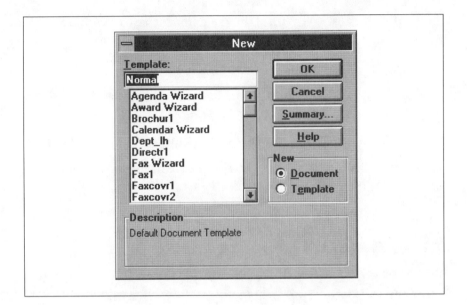

FIGURE 2.7

*In the New dialog box
you can select the
template for a new
Word document to be
based on.*

Using Wizards

Some of Word's templates are called *Wizards*. You'll see them identified
on the Template list by the Wizard name—for example, Calendar Wizard, FAX Wizard, and so on. A Wizard is simply a template that auto-
mates part of the task of creating a document. When you create a new
document with a Wizard, Word will prompt you to enter certain information about the document's contents and/or formatting. For example,
the FAX Wizard asks for your name and phone number. Each Wizard is

different. When using a Wizard, just remember these rules and you'll have no problems:

- Click the Next button to go on to the next step.

- Click the Back button to return to the previous step and change your entries.

- Click the Finish button when you're finished using the Wizard.

When the Wizard is done, you can continue editing your document, save it, print it, and so on.

Exiting Word

When you're done using Word, you should exit the program. You must exit Word before exiting Windows or turning your computer off. To exit Word, double-click the application control menu box (at the left end of the title bar), choose File ➤ Exit, or press Alt+F4.

If you have not changed the document since you last saved it, Word will exit immediately. Otherwise Word will display a dialog box asking if you want to save the changes to the document:

- Click the Yes button to save the changes before Word exits.

- Click the No button to exit without saving the changes. You will lose any changes that you made to the document since the last time you saved it.

- Click the Cancel button to return to the document without exiting or saving.

CHAPTER THREE

Basic Editing
Tasks

MUCH OF THE TIME that you spend with Word will be devoted to editing tasks— deleting unwanted items, moving sections of text around, and so on. In most cases you'll also need to print your document. In this chapter, you will learn how to edit your documents, print them, and use Word's on-line Help system.

Selecting Text

Many of Word's editing commands require that you *select* text first. By selecting text, you tell Word what text your command should be applied to. Selected text is highlighted. With the standard black text and white background, this displays as white letters on a black background. In Figure 3.1, for example, the first two words of the second sentence are selected.

You can select text with either the mouse or the keyboard. Here's how to select text with the mouse:

1. Move the pointer to the beginning of the text to be selected.

2. Press and hold the mouse button and drag to the end of the text.

3. Release the mouse button.

WARNING

If you type while text is selected, whatever you type will replace the selected text.

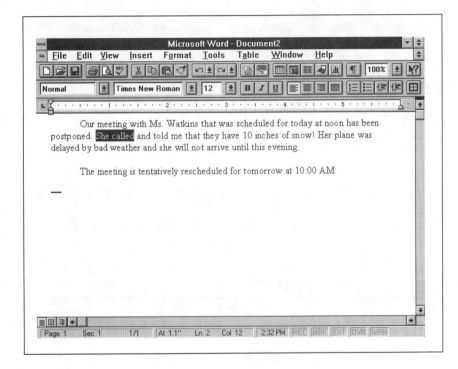

FIGURE 3.1

Selected text is displayed as white letters on a black background.

To select text using the keyboard, use the movement keys (arrows, Home, End, PgUp, PgDn) that you learned about in Chapter 2:

1. Move the insertion point to the start of the text to be selected.

2. Press and hold down the Shift key.

3. Move the insertion point to the end of the text and release the Shift key.

> ### N O T E
>
> Changed your mind? You can *deselect* any text by pressing ←.

Text Selection Shortcuts

Here are several mouse shortcuts for selecting text:

> ### N O T E
>
> Some of these shortcuts use the *selection bar*, the area to the left of the document text. The selection bar is not marked; it is simply the white area, or margin, to the left of your text. You can tell when the mouse pointer is in the selection bar because the pointer changes to an arrow.

To select this...	Do this...
One word	Double-click the word.
One sentence	Hold down the Ctrl key and click anywhere in the sentence.
One line	Click in the selection bar.
One paragraph	Double-click in the selection bar.

> ### N O T E
>
> To select the entire document, press Ctrl+A or triple-click in the
> selection bar.

Using Extend Mode

Word has a nifty feature called *extend mode* that can be very useful when
you are selecting text. Extend mode is indicated by the EXT indicator on
the status bar. To turn extend mode on, press F8 or double-click the EXT indicator on the status bar. While in extend mode you can select the next
unit of text (word, sentence, paragraph) by pressing F8 one or more times.
Select the next occurrence of a character by pressing that character Shrink
the selection to the next smaller unit of text by pressing Shift+F8.

To turn extend mode off, press Esc or double-click the EXT indicator again.

Deleting Text

Let's face it, we all make mistakes! You'll often need to delete text from
your document. Deleting characters is easy:

- Press Backspace to delete the character to the left of the insertion point.

- Press Del to delete the character to the right of the insertion point.

Entire words can be deleted as follows:

- Press Ctrl+Backspace to delete the word to the left of the insertion point.

- Press Ctrl+Del to delete the word to the right of the insertion point.

For larger sections of text, first select the text you want to delete, and then press Del.

The Undo Feature

What if you mistakenly delete some text that you really wanted to keep? No problem! Word's Undo feature lets you undo almost any editing action, including typing new text, deleting text, and changing formatting. Word "remembers" most of your actions during a work session and lets you undo one or more of them. Here's how to use Undo:

Undo

- To undo your most recent action, click the Undo button on the Standard toolbar or select Edit ➤ Undo.

Undo

- To undo several editing actions, click the arrow next to the Undo button to display a list of actions, and then click the first action you want undone. Word will undo the selected action and all actions since.

WARNING

Some actions—such as saving or printing a document—cannot be undone.

Reversing Your Undo Commands

While the Undo feature can be a life-saver, you will sometimes find that you've undone something that you wanted to keep. The Redo command "undoes" the Undo command. In other words, you can reverse the effects of one or more Undo commands.

Redo

- To redo your most recent Undo command, click the Redo button on the Standard toolbar, or select Edit ➤ Redo.

- To reverse several Undo commands, click the arrow next to the Redo button to display a list of undone actions, and then click the first undo action that you want reversed. Word will reverse the selected undo action and every subsequent undo.

Redo

Moving and Copying Text

The ability to move and copy text can greatly simplify many word processing procedures. To move or copy text, do the following:

1. Select the text that you want to move or copy.

2. The next step depends on whether you want to move or copy:

Cut

- To *move* the text, click the Cut button on the Standard toolbar, select Edit ➤ Cut, or press Ctrl+X.

- To *copy* the text, click the Copy button on the Standard toolbar, select Edit ➤ Copy, or press Ctrl+C.

Copy

3. Move the insertion point to the new location for the text.

4. Click the Paste button on the Standard toolbar, select Edit ➤ Paste, or press Ctrl+V.

Paste

Mouse Shortcuts

To move or copy relatively small amounts of text short distances, you may find the mouse convenient:

1. Select the text to be moved or copied.

2. Move the mouse pointer to the selected text; the pointer will change from an I-beam to an arrow.

3. To copy the text, press and hold down the Ctrl key. To move the text, don't press any key.

4. Press and hold down the left mouse button. The mouse pointer changes to an arrow with a small box (and, if you're copying, a plus sign).

5. As you move the mouse cursor, a dotted vertical line moves in the text. Position this dotted line at the new location for the text.

6. Release the mouse button (and the Ctrl key, if you were copying text).

Searching for Text

If you need to locate a specific word or section of text in your document, you don't have to search for it manually, thanks to Word's Find command.

1. Choose Edit ➤ Find to display the Find dialog box (shown in Figure 3.2).

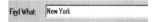

2. In the Find dialog box, enter the text you want to locate in the Find What box.

FIGURE 3.2

The Find dialog box

3. Select any needed options, as described in the section below.

4. Click the Find Next button or press ↵. Word will highlight the first occurrence of the text in the document, leaving the Find dialog box on-screen.

5. Click the Find Next button or press ↵ again to search for the next occurrence of the text.

6. Click the Cancel button or press Esc to close the dialog box.

If Word reaches the end of the document before searching all the text, it displays the dialog box shown in Figure 3.3, asking if you want to continue the search at the beginning of the document. Click the Yes button to continue searching, or click the No button to end searching and return to your document.

Once the entire document has been searched, Word displays a message to that effect. Click the OK button to return to the document.

FIGURE 3.3

Word displays this dialog box when the search reaches the end of the document.

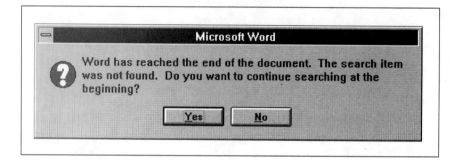

Text Search Options

In most situations, you will not need to use any of the options available in the Find dialog box. But at times these options can be very useful:

- Pull down the Search list to specify the direction of the search: Down or Up from the insertion point. Select All to search the entire document.

- Select the Match Case option if you want to match uppercase and lowercase letters exactly.

- Select the Find Whole Words Only option if you don't want Word to match partial words. For example, with this option turned on, a search for *profit* would not match *profitable* or *profits*. This option is available only if you have entered a single word in the Find What box.

- Use the Sounds Like option to locate words that sound similar to the one in your search. For example, *Kathy* would match *Cathy*.

Replacing Text

Not only can you search for text in a document, but you can also re-place it with new text automatically. For example, you could change every occurrence of *Nebraska* to *Kentucky* in a flash. Here's how:

1. Choose <u>E</u>dit ➤ <u>R</u>eplace. Word displays the Replace dialog box, shown in Figure 3.4.

Replace
Fi<u>n</u>d What: ▢	<u>F</u>ind Next
	Cancel
Re<u>p</u>lace With: ▢	<u>R</u>eplace
	Replace A<u>l</u>l
	<u>H</u>elp
<u>S</u>earch: Down ▢	▢ Match <u>C</u>ase ▢ Find Whole Words Only ▢ Use Pattern <u>M</u>atching ▢ Sounds Li<u>k</u>e
Find
No Formatting	For<u>m</u>at ▼	Sp<u>e</u>cial ▼

FIGURE 3.4

The Replace dialog box

2. Type the text to be replaced in the Fi<u>n</u>d What box.

3. Type the replacement text in the Re<u>p</u>lace With box.

4. Click the <u>F</u>ind Next button. Word highlights the first occur-rence of the search text in the document.

Find What: Nebraska

Re<u>p</u>lace With: Kentucky

<u>F</u>ind Next

You now have several options:

- Click the Replace button to replace the highlighted text with the replacement text and then highlight the next occurrence of the search text.

- Click the Replace All button to replace the highlighted text and all other occurrences of the search text with the replacement text.

- Click the Find Next button to leave the highlighted text unchanged and then highlight the next occurrence of the search text.

Printing

Print

Printing a single copy of your document is easy. Of course, you must have a printer attached to your system, either directly or through a network, and the printer must be turned on and loaded with paper. Once these preliminaries are out of the way, just click the Print button on the Standard toolbar.

NOTE

Word offers a number of printing options, such as printing multiple copies or a single page. I'll cover these options in Chapter 9.

The Help System

Word has a sophisticated Help system that can display useful information on-screen as you work. There are several ways you can access on-line Help:

- Click the Help button on the Standard toolbar (the mouse cursor will change to a question mark), and then click on the screen element of interest (for example, a menu item or a toolbar button).

- Click the Help button that is displayed in many dialog boxes.

- Press F1 while working in your document.

The main Help screen is shown in Figure 3.5. You can scroll around on the Help screen using PgUp and PgDn or the scroll bar.

The information displayed on the Help screen varies depending on how you accessed Help. However, the way you use the Help system is standardized.

- Click on an underlined topic heading to move to that topic.

- To view the main Help table of contents, click on the Contents button.

- To search for Help on a specific topic, click the Search button. Word displays a list of all Help topics. Scroll through the list to the desired topic, or scroll automatically by typing the first few letters of the topic. Double-click a topic to see a list of related entries in the lower part of the dialog box, and then double-click the desired entry to read more about it.

FIGURE 3.5

The Word Help Table of Contents screen lets you find the Help topic you need.

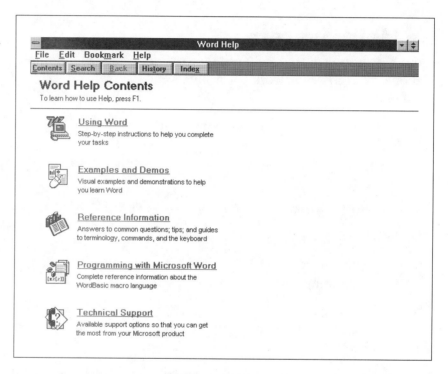

- Click the Index button to display an alphabetic list of all Help topics. Scroll through the list and click the item of interest to display related Help information.

- Click the History button to see a list of Help subjects you have viewed. Double-click an item in the list to display it.

- Click the Back button to display the last Help topic you viewed.

- Click the << or >> button to move forward or backward through related Help topics. These buttons are grayed if there are no related topics.

- Double-click the Help window's control box at the left end of the title bar (or press Alt+F4) to close the Help window.

How To Help

When you select some Help topics, Word displays a "How To" Help box, shown in Figure 3.6.

- Click the Print button to print a copy of the information in the box.

- Click the Index button to display the main Help index (as described above).

- Click the On Top button to have the How To box remain displayed when you return to your document, so you can view the How To information as you work.

- Click the Close button to close the How To box.

FIGURE 3.6

A How To Help box

CHAPTER FOUR

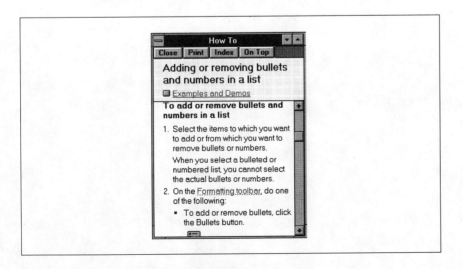

Formatting
Fundamentals

WHILE THE CONTENTS of your documents are of primary concern, their appearance is important too. This chapter shows you some of the tools that Word provides for enhancing the visual impact of your documents.

Using Different Fonts

Word provides a wide variety of fonts from which you can choose. The term *font* refers to the appearance, or style, of the letters and numbers in your document. Each font is available in many different sizes. Font size is measured in *points* (there are 72 points in an inch). The most common font sizes used in regular document text are 10, 11, and 12 points. Figure 4.1 shows a document that uses different fonts to good effect.

N O T E

The Font box and Font Size box on the Formatting toolbar display the name and size of the font in effect at the location of the insertion point.

You can change the font and/or the size of existing text or of text you are about to type:

1. To change existing text, select the text. To change new text, move the insertion point to the location of the text.

2. Click the arrow next to the Font box on the Formatting toolbar to display a list of available fonts. The most recently used fonts are at the top of the list, and the other available fonts are listed alphabetically below.

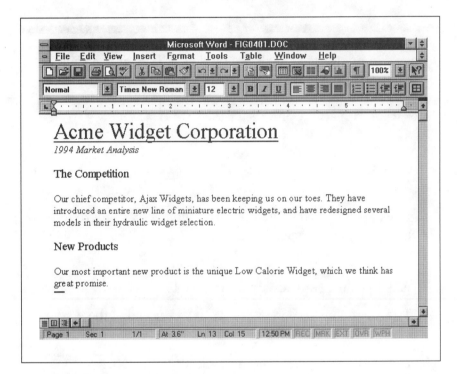

FIGURE 4.1

*Using different fonts
and font sizes can
improve the clarity and
impact of your
documents.*

3. Select the desired font from the list.

4. Click the arrow next to the Font Size box.

5. Select a point size from the Font Size list.

N O T E

If your Formatting toolbar is not displayed, right-click on any toolbar, and then select Formatting from the shortcut menu. If no toolbar is displayed, select View ➤ Toolbars. In the dialog box, click Formatting, and then click OK.

Let's try out some different fonts and font sizes now. If Word isn't running, start it.

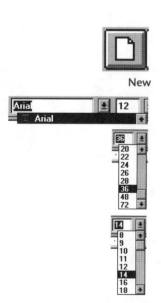

New

1. If necessary, click the New button on the Standard toolbar to start a new, empty document.

2. Pull down the Font list and select Arial.

3. Pull down the Font Size list and select 36.

4. Type the following and press ↵ twice at the end of the text:

IMPORTANT NOTICE

5. Pull down the Font Size list and select 14.

6. Type the following text:

There will be a safety inspection next Monday at 10:00 AM. Let's try to have a perfect scorecard this time! If you have any questions please see Mr. Watkins.

When you're done, your document should appear as in Figure 4.2.

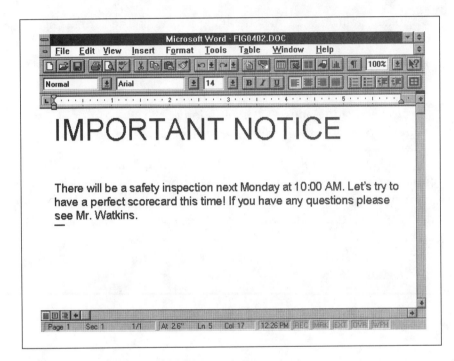

FIGURE 4.2

When you're done with your sample document, it will look like this.

Bold, Italic, and Underline

Any of Word's fonts can be displayed and printed in bold, italic, or underline format (or any combination of these). You can apply these attributes to existing text or to new text.

1. To change existing text, select the text. To add a format to new text, move the insertion point to the location for the text.

2. To add bold format, click the Bold button on the Formatting toolbar or press Ctrl+B.

Bold

Italic

Underline

3. To add italic format, click the Italic button on the Formatting toolbar or press Ctrl+I.

4. To add underline format, click the Underline button on the Formatting toolbar or press Ctrl+U.

After activating one or a combination of the above buttons, type your text. It will appear in the format you chose.

When the insertion point is in text that has bold, italic, or underline format applied to it, the corresponding button on the Formatting toolbar will appear *depressed*, or pushed in. To turn off any one of these attributes, click the corresponding button or press the appropriate key combination (Ctrl+B, Ctrl+I, Ctrl+U) again. Features such as these, which are activated and deactivated by pressing the same button, are called *toggles*.

Changing Letter Case

Word can quickly and easily change the case of letters in your document—changing uppercase letters to lowercase and vice-versa. This feature can be very useful in a variety of situations, such as when you've accidentally hit the Caps Lock key and everything comes out backwards: tHIS IS WHAT i MEAN! To change case:

1. Select the text to be changed.

2. Choose Format ➤ Change Case to display the dialog box shown in Figure 4.3.

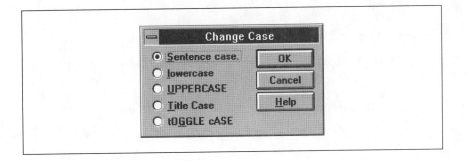

FIGURE 4.3

The Change Case dialog box lets you change the case of letters in several different ways.

3. Select the desired option:

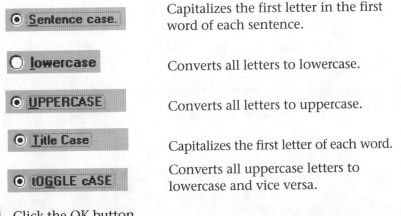

Capitalizes the first letter in the first word of each sentence.

Converts all letters to lowercase.

Converts all letters to uppercase.

Capitalizes the first letter of each word.

Converts all uppercase letters to lowercase and vice versa.

4. Click the OK button.

Line Spacing

Line spacing controls the amount of space between lines of text in your document. You have complete control over the way lines are spaced in Word.

1. To change spacing for a single paragraph, move the insertion point to the paragraph. For multiple paragraphs, select them.

2. Choose Format ➤ Paragraph to display the Paragraph dialog box, shown in Figure 4.4.

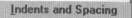

3. Click the Indents And Spacing tab if it is not already foremost in the dialog box.

4. Pull down the Line Spacing list and select the desired spacing:

- Select Single, 1.5 Lines, or Double to set line spacing to 1, 1.5, or 2 lines.

- Select At Least to specify a minimum spacing in the At box that Word can increase if necessary to accommodate larger fonts and graphics.

FIGURE 4.4

The Paragraph dialog box with the Indents And Spacing tab displayed

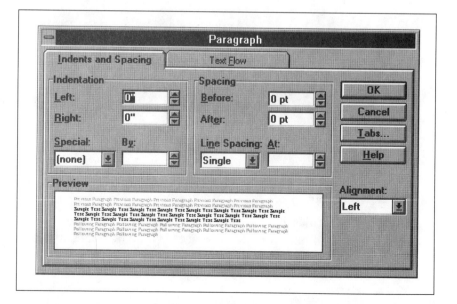

- Select Exactly to specify an exact spacing in the At box that Word will not modify.

- Select Multiple to enter a custom spacing value in the At box. For example, a value of 2.5 will space text 2.5 lines apart.

5. Click the OK button to apply the selected line spacing.

Changing Text Justification

Word's default is to use left justification of text. In left-justified text, the left ends of all lines in a paragraph are aligned at the left margin, while the right edges are ragged.

Align Left

To change justification for a single paragraph, first place the insertion point anywhere in the paragraph. For multiple paragraphs, select the paragraphs to be changed. Then click the Formatting toolbar button corresponding to the desired justification. (The Align Left button is shown in the margin above.)

- The Center button on the Formatting toolbar centers each line on the page, placing equal distances between the left and right edges of the text and the margins.

Center

- The Justify button on the Formatting toolbar aligns both the left and right edges of text with the margins.

Justify

N O T E

Fully justified text contains extra space between words and letters (except for the last line of a paragraph). Full justification looks better with some fonts than with others.

Align Right

- The Align Right on the Formatting toolbar button aligns the right edges of text while leaving the left edge ragged.

Changing Indents

The term *indent* refers to the distance between the left or right edge of a paragraph and the left or right page margin. Word's default is not to indent paragraphs, but you can change this to suit your needs.

Increase Indent

To change the indent of a single paragraph, first move the insertion point to any location in the paragraph. For multiple paragraphs, select them. Then click the Formatting toolbar's Increase Indent button one or more times. Each click of the Increase Indent button moves the entire paragraph to the right by one tab stop (1/2-inch by default).

Decrease Indent

To move the text back to the left, click the Decrease Indent button on the Formatting toolbar. Each click of the Decrease Indent button moves the paragraph to the left by one tab stop.

N O T E

To indent just the first line of a paragraph, press Tab at the start of the first line.

Using the Ruler

You can also change indents using the ruler, which provides greater flexibility than the Indent buttons. You are not limited to 1/2-inch increments when using the ruler, and you can indent the first line of the paragraph a different amount from the other lines. You can also change the indent of the right edge of the paragraph.

Start by moving the insertion point to the desired paragraph, or by selecting multiple paragraphs. If your ruler is not displayed, choose View ➤ Ruler. Then:

- To change the left indent of the first line in the paragraph, point at the First Line Indent Marker and drag it to the desired position on the ruler.

- To change the left indent of all lines in the paragraph *except* the first line, point at the Left Indent Marker and drag it to the desired position.

- To change the left indent of all lines in the paragraph, point at the All Lines Indent Marker and drag it to the desired position.

- To change the right indent of all lines in the paragraph, point at the Right Indent Marker and drag it to the desired position.

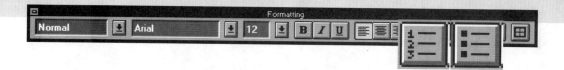

> **NOTE**
>
> The indent markers on the ruler display the indent settings of the paragraph containing the insertion point.

Hanging Indents

To create a *hanging indent,* in which the first line begins to the left of the rest of the paragraph, place the insertion point in the paragraph and press Ctrl+T. To reduce a hanging indent, press Ctrl+Shift+T.

Bulleted and Numbered Lists

Word makes it easy to organize text into bulleted or numbered lists. Word can automate the creation of these lists, and even renumber items automatically if you add or remove items from a numbered list. Figure 4.5 shows examples of bulleted and numbered lists.

In a bulleted or numbered list, each paragraph gets its own number or bullet character. (Remember, you end one paragraph and start a new one by pressing ↵.) To create a bulleted or numbered list as you type:

Numbering

1. Click the Numbering button or the Bullets button on the Formatting toolbar. (The button will appear depressed when activated.)

Bullets

2. Type the paragraphs that you want numbered or bulleted.

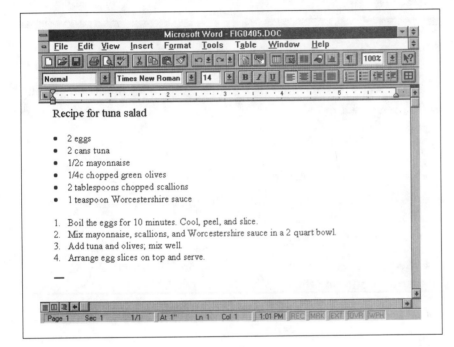

FIGURE 4.5

*A sampling of bulleted
and numbered lists*

3. When the list is complete, toggle the Numbering button or the Bullets button off.

To convert existing paragraphs to a numbered or bulleted list, select the paragraphs and then click the corresponding button on the Formatting toolbar.

N O T E

When the insertion point is in a numbered or bulleted list, the corresponding button on the toolbar will be depressed. If you add one or more new paragraphs, Word will number or bullet them automatically.

Changing Bullet and Numbering Style

Word's default bullets and numbers are fine for many purposes, but there are other styles that you can use. Here's how to change the style of bullets and numbers in lists:

1. Select Format ➤ Bullets and Numbering to display the Bullets and Numbering dialog box.

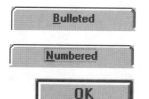

2. Click the Bulleted or the Numbered tab to display the appropriate section of the dialog box.

3. Click on the bullet or number style you want.

4. Click the OK button.

The new bullet or numbering style you select will apply only to new lists unless you selected a list before following these steps.

Borders and Shading

Borders and shading can be useful for calling attention to important information, or simply for improving the visual appeal of a document. Figure 4.6 shows a document with borders and shading applied.

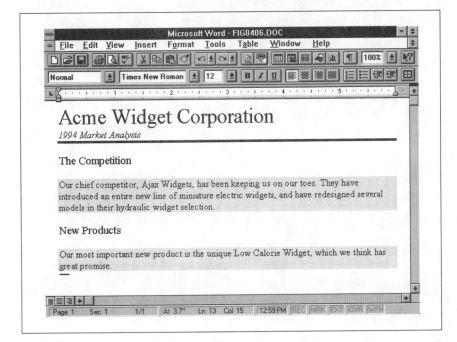

FIGURE 4.6

A document that uses borders and shading

You can apply borders and shading using buttons on the Borders toolbar. To display this toolbar, click the Border button on the Formatting toolbar. Click the button again to hide the Border toolbar.

Border

Applying Borders

To apply borders to a single paragraph, first move the insertion point to any location in the paragraph. For multiple paragraphs, select the paragraphs. Then click one of these buttons on the Borders toolbar:

- Click the Outside Border button on the Border toolbar to apply borders to all four edges of the paragraph.

Outside Border

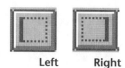

Left **Right Border**

Top Border **Bottom Border**

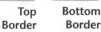

Inside Border

No Border

- To apply a border to one, two, or three edges of the paragraph, click the appropriate buttons: Left, Right, Top, or Bottom border on the Border toolbar. For example, to apply left and right borders, click the Left Border and Right Border buttons. To remove a single border from a paragraph, click the corresponding button again. The buttons that correspond to a paragraph's assigned borders appear depressed on the Border toolbar.

- To apply inside borders, click the Inside Border button on the Border toolbar. This option, which is applicable only when you have more than one paragraph selected, will place a border between paragraphs in the selection.

- Click the No Border button to remove existing borders from the paragraph.

Changing Line Style

Word normally uses a single, thin solid line for borders. A variety of other line styles are available, including thicker lines, double lines, and dotted and dashed lines.

To change the border style, pull down the Line Style list on the Borders toolbar and select a new style before applying borders to the document.

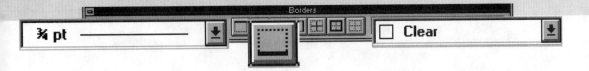

> ## N O T E
>
> To change the style of borders you already applied, first re-move the old borders by clicking the No Border button on the Borders toolbars, and then change the line style and reapply the border.

We can improve the appearance of our sample document with a border. Here are the steps to follow:

1. Select the first paragraph (the heading "IMPORTANT NOTICE").

2. Pull down the Line Style list on the Borders toolbar and select the solid line labeled 6 pt.

3. Click the Bottom Border button on the Border toolbar. The document should now appear as in Figure 4.7.

Adding Shading

The Shading command permits you to change the color of the background behind your text. You can use various shades of gray as well as different patterns.

To apply shading to a single paragraph, first move the insertion point to any location in the paragraph. For multiple paragraphs, select the paragraphs.

Next, pull down the Shading list on the Borders toolbar and select the desired shading. To remove shading, select Clear from the list.

FIGURE 4.7

The sample document with a bottom border added to the first paragraph.

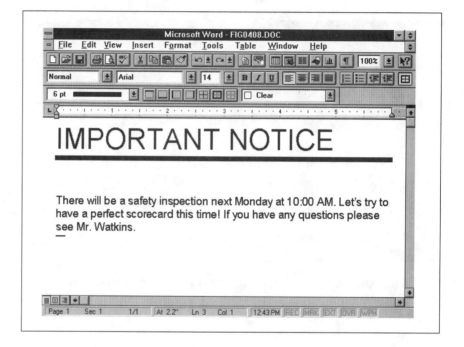

AutoFormat

Word's AutoFormat command can automatically format a document that contains various standard elements. When you use AutoFormat, Word looks through your document, recognizing design elements such as headings and lists, and then applies appropriate and consistent formatting to those elements. These are the specific actions AutoFormat takes:

- Formats document headings

- Replaces asterisks or other characters used for bulleted lists with "real" bullets (•)

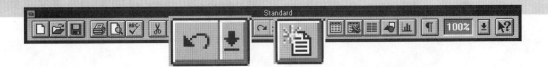

- Replaces (C), (R), and (TM) with the copyright, registered trade-mark, and trademark symbols (©, ®, ™)

- Replaces straight, single, and double quotation marks with more professional looking curly ones

- Removes extra and unnecessary line spaces (↵)

- Replaces indents created with Tab and the spacebar with "real" indents

If you want to AutoFormat an entire document, the insertion point can be anywhere in that document. To restrict AutoFormat changes to a part of the document, you must select the section to be affected. Then click the AutoFormat button on the Standard toolbar.

AutoFormat

What if you don't like the way AutoFormat changed your document? No problem! To reverse the effects of AutoFormat, just click the Undo button on the Standard toolbar straightaway.

Undo

Customizing AutoFormat

You can customize the way AutoFormat works to suit your personal preferences. Word's default is to have all of AutoFormat's capabilities turned on, but you can modify these settings as follows:

1. Choose Format ➤ AutoFormat to display the AutoFormat dialog box.

2. In the AutoFormat dialog box, click the Options button to display the AutoFormat Options dialog box (Figure 4.8).

3. In the AutoFormat Options dialog box, click the various option settings to turn them on or off.

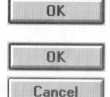

4. When the options are set as desired, click the OK button to return to the AutoFormat dialog box.

5. In the AutoFormat dialog box, click the OK button to apply Auto-Formatting (with the new options) to your document. Or click the Cancel button to save the new options without AutoFormatting your document.

FIGURE 4.8

The AutoFormat Options dialog box

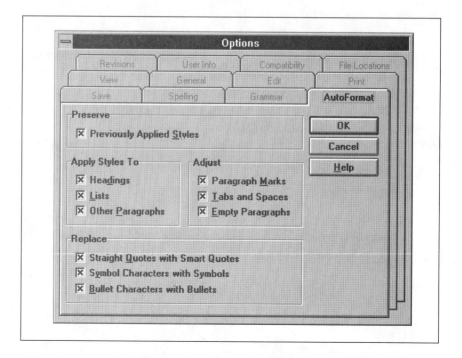

CHAPTER FIVE

Using Styles

STYLES ARE ONE of Word's most powerful formatting features. In this chapter, you will learn how to save yourself a great deal of time and effort by using styles.

What Is a Style?

A *style* is a set of formatting specifications that has been saved under an assigned name. For example, a style could specify:

- Arial 12 point font
- Double line spacing
- One-half inch indents
- A single border

If you want to use a particular kind of formatting, all you need to do is apply the style that specifies that formatting to text in your document. Using a style is a lot faster than issuing all those formatting commands individually!

In addition, if you later modify the style, then the new formatting is automatically applied to all parts of the document that have that style assigned to them. This feature makes it easy to maintain consistent formatting throughout your documents, and greatly simplifies the task of changing formatting.

For example, let's say you have applied a style that specifies 14-point underlined Times Roman to several dozen headings in a document. You later decide that headings should be in 16-point italic Times Roman. It's a lot easier to edit the one style than it is to go through the document and change the headings one by one.

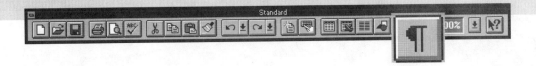

Types of Styles

Word has two different types of styles. A *paragraph style* is applied to entire paragraphs. A *character style* can be applied to any amount of text from a single character to an entire document. Usually, however, character styles are used to format small sections of text within paragraphs.

> **TIP**
>
> Remember that you end one paragraph and begin another by pressing ↵ (thus adding a hard return to your document). If you're not sure where the hard returns are in your document, click the Show/Hide ¶ button on the Standard toolbar. Word will display a nonprinting paragraph symbol (¶) at the end of each paragraph. Other nonprinting characters will be marked as well—tabs by → and spaces by a dot. To hide these symbols, toggle the Show/Hide ¶ button off.

Show/Hide

Applying a Style

Word's default paragraph style is called Normal. To apply a different style, you must first tell Word what part of the document is to be changed:

- To apply a paragraph style to a single paragraph, place the insertion point anywhere in the paragraph.

- To apply a paragraph style to multiple paragraphs, select them.
- To apply a character style, select the text to be affected.

Next, follow these steps:

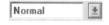

1. Pull down the Style list on the Formatting toolbar (click on the down arrow at the right edge of the box).

2. Select the desired style from the list that is displayed. In this alphabetical list, paragraph styles are listed in boldface format and character styles are listed in plain text. When you select a style, it will immediately be applied to the document.

N O T E

Formats in character styles are added to the text's existing formatting. For example, if you apply a character style that specifies italics to text that is boldfaced, the result will be bold italics.

Displaying Paragraph Style Names

The Style box on the Formatting toolbar usually displays the name of the style assigned to the current paragraph. The only exception is when the insertion point is in text that has a *character* style applied; then the Style box displays the character style name.

You may find it convenient to display the style names of *all* paragraphs on-screen, in the *Style Area* in the left margin, as shown in Figure 5.1.

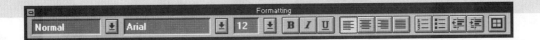

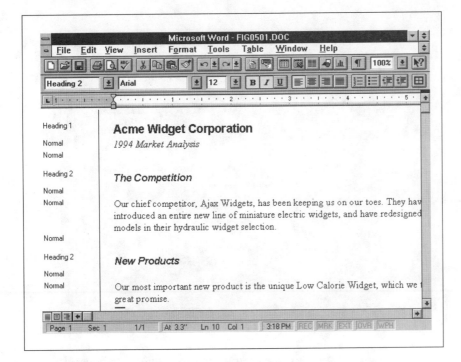

FIGURE 5.1

*The Style Area displays
paragraph style names
in the left margin.*

To display the style names of all paragraphs on-screen:

1. Choose <u>T</u>ools ➤ <u>O</u>ptions to display the Options dialog box.

2. If necessary, click the View tab to display the View options, as
shown in Figure 5.2.

3. In the Style Area Width box click the up and down arrows or enter a value for the width of the Style Area in inches. Depending

FIGURE 5.2

The View options in the Options dialog box let you control various apects of your screen display.

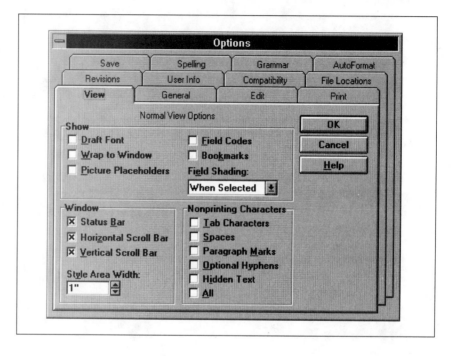

on the size of your monitor, you may find values between 0.5 and 1 inch suitable.

4. Click the OK button or press ↵.

When the Style Area is displayed, you can change its width by pointing at the Style Area's right border (the mouse pointer will change to a vertical line with left- and right-pointing arrows) and dragging to the desired width. To hide the Style Area, repeat the above steps and enter a value of 0 in the Style Area Width box, or drag the Style Area border all the way to the left edge of the screen.

Creating Your Own Styles

Word comes with a few predefined styles that you may find useful. But the real power of styles comes from *custom* styles that you can create to suit your own specific needs.

Creating a Paragraph Style

To create your own paragraph style, follow these steps:

1. Format a paragraph with the formatting that you want in the new style.

2. With the insertion point in the paragraph, click the Style box on the Formatting toolbar. The current style name will be selected.

3. Type the new style name, which will replace the old name.

4. Press ↵.

Be sure to assign descriptive names to your styles. Otherwise, you may not remember what the style is for! Style names can be up to 253 characters long, and can include letters, numbers, spaces, commas, colons, and most other characters, such as % and ^. The characters that are forbidden in style names are the backslash (\), braces ({}), and semicolon (;). If you mistakenly enter a name that contains a character that is not allowed, Word will display an error message and let you re-enter the name.

If you enter the name of an existing style, Word will assign that style to the paragraph instead of creating a new style. Click the Undo button on the Standard toolbar to reverse the change, and then repeat the steps above to enter an unused name for the new style.

Undo

Creating a Character Style

Creating a new *character* style is a bit more complicated than creating a paragraph style, because you cannot do it by example. Rather, you must use dialog boxes to specify the contents of the new style.

1. Choose Format ➤ Style to display the Style dialog box.

2. In the Style dialog box click the New button to display the New Style dialog box, shown in Figure 5.3.

3. Pull down the Style Type list and select Character.

4. Type the new style name in the Name box.

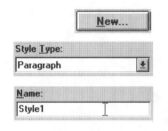

FIGURE 5.3

You must use the New Style dialog box to define a character style.

5. Click the Format button and select Font from the list that is displayed. Word will display the Font dialog box, shown in Figure 5.4.

6. Select options in the Font dialog box to specify the appearance of the new character style. As you make changes, the Preview box shows you what the style will look like.

7. Click the OK button to return to the New Style dialog box, and then click OK again to return to the Style dialog box.

8. Click the Apply button to apply the new style to the document; it will be applied to any text that was selected prior to step 1 above, or if no text was selected, to new text you type. Or, click the Close button to save the new style without applying it to any text.

FIGURE 5.4

You use the Font dialog box to specify the font in a character style.

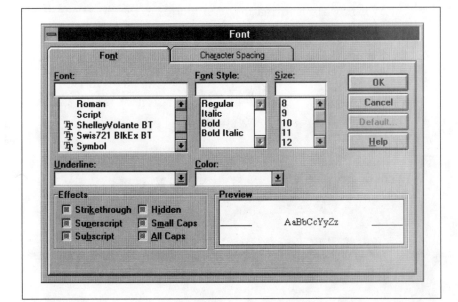

Modifying a Style

You can modify a style at any time. When you do so, the new formatting is automatically applied to all parts of the document that have been assigned that style. The steps for modifying paragraph and character styles are similar. Generally speaking, you should not modify Word's predefined styles, particularly the Normal style. Doing so can have unexpected effects.

1. To modify a paragraph style, select a paragraph that has been assigned that style. To modify a character style, select at least one character of text that has been assigned the style.

2. Verify that the name of the style you want to modify is displayed in the Style box on the Formatting toolbar.

3. Use Word's various formatting commands to modify the format of the selection as desired.

4. Click the Style box on the Formatting toolbar and then press ↵.

5. Word displays the Reapply Style dialog box, shown in Figure 5.5. Be sure the option "Redefine the style..." is selected, and then click the OK button or press ↵.

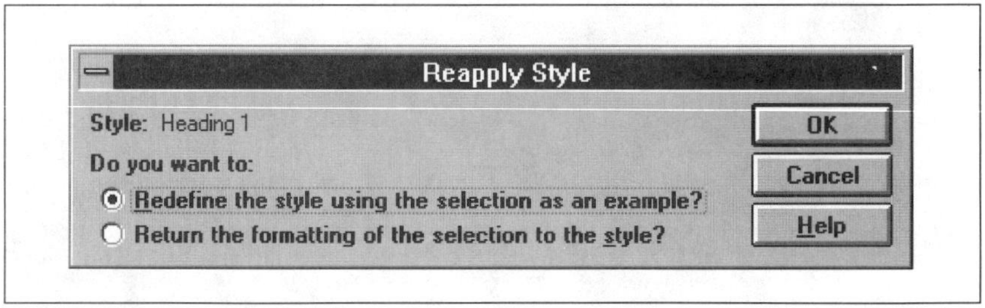

FIGURE 5.5

*You use the Reapply
Style dialog box
when changing
the formatting
associated with a style.*

Deleting a Style

If you won't be using a style any more, you can delete it from the document. When you delete a paragraph style, paragraphs formatted with
that style will be assigned the Normal style (Word's default paragraph
style). When you delete a character style, affected text will be displayed
in the format specified by its paragraph style.

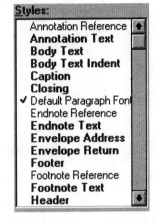

1. Choose F<u>o</u>rmat ➤ <u>S</u>tyle to display the Style dialog box, shown
in Figure 5.6.

2. Open the List box and select the styles to be displayed:

> **Styles in Use** Lists only those styles actually used in the
> document.

> **All Styles** Lists all styles available in the document.

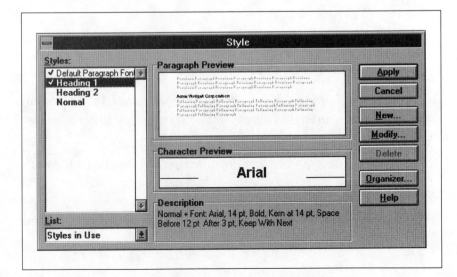

FIGURE 5.6

*The Style dialog box is
used to delete styles you
no longer need.*

User-Defined Styles Lists only user-defined styles, not Word's built-in styles.

3. In the Styles list click the name of the style that you want to delete.

4. Click the Delete button.

5. Word asks for confirmation. Click the Yes button to delete the style.

6. Repeat Steps 3 through 6 to delete other styles.

7. Click the Close button to return to your document.

N O T E

You cannot delete some of Word's built-in styles. If you select one of these styles in the Styles list, the Delete button will be grayed.

Using Styles in Other Documents

When you create or modify a style, the new or modified style is available only in the current document. If you want to use the new or modified style in other documents, you must copy it.

If you copy a style to an existing document, it will be available for use the next time you open that document for editing. If you want to use the style in documents that you start in the future, you must copy it to the NORMAL template (the template that Word bases new documents on).

This is true both for the blank document that Word displays when you start the program, and for new documents created when you click the New button on the Standard toolbar.

To copy styles, you must first open a document that contains the styles. Then:

1. Choose Format ➤ Style to display the Style dialog box.

2. Click the Organizer button to display the Organizer dialog box, shown in Figure 5.7.

3. To copy styles to another document, click the Close File button on the right side of the dialog box. If you want to copy styles to the NORMAL template, skip to step 7.

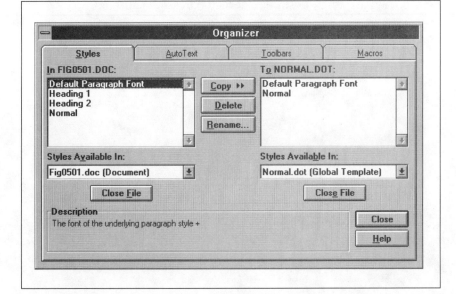

FIGURE 5.7

The Style section of the Organizer dialog box. The list on the left shows the names of the styles in the current document, and the list on the right shows the names of the styles in the NORMAL template.

Open File...

OK

4. The Close File button changes to an Open File button. Click it.

5. Word displays a dialog box listing your documents. Select the document you want to copy styles to, and then click the OK button. You are returned to the Style Organizer dialog box. The list on the right now displays the styles in the document you just opened.

Copy ▸▸

6. In the Styles list on the left side of the dialog box, click the style you want to copy, and then click the Copy button.

Yes

7. If you tried to copy a style with a name that is already used in the destination document, Word displays a dialog box asking for confirmation. Click the Yes button.

8. Repeat steps 7 and 8 for any other styles that you want to copy.

Close

9. When all styles have been copied, click the Close button.

Formatting Your Pages

WORD'S PAGE FORMATTING commands affect the overall appearance of pages in your document. You need to be familiar with *page formatting* in order to create many types of documents. In this chapter you will learn how to add page numbers, use headers and footers, change page margins, and more.

Page Numbers

Word provides complete flexibility in displaying page numbers in your documents.

> **N O T E**
>
> Page numbers can be added by themselves or as part of a header or footer, as covered later in this chapter.

To display page numbers in your document:

1. Choose Insert ➤ Page Numbers to display the Page Numbers dialog box (see Figure 6.1).

FIGURE 6.1

The Page Numbers dialog box lets you specify the format and placement of page numbers in your document.

Page Numbers	
Position: Bottom of Page (Footer)	**OK**
Alignment: Right	**Cancel**
☒ Show Number on First Page	**Format...**
	Help

2. Pull down the Position list by clicking the arrow at the right side of the box and specify whether you want the page numbers displayed at the top or bottom of the page. The Preview box shows you the appearance of the selected option.

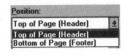

3. Pull down the Alignment list and select the horizontal position of the page numbers. Your choices are Left, Center, and Right. The Inside and Outside choices are relevant only if you are printing a two-sided document. If you choose the Inside option, the page number will print on the right side of even-numbered pages and the left side of odd-numbered pages; if you choose the Outside option, the page number will print on the left side of even-numbered pages and the right side of odd-numbered pages.

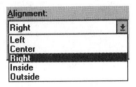

4. Click the Show Number On First Page option to turn it off (clear the *X* from the box) if you do not want the page number displayed on the first document page.

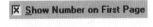

5. Click the OK button or press ↵.

Changing the Page Number Value and Format

Word normally starts page numbers at 1 and displays them as standard numbers (1, 2, 3, etc.). But you can start numbering with a value other than 1, and you can use different numbering formats. The available formatting includes uppercase and lowercase Roman numerals (i, ii, iii or I, II, III, etc.) and uppercase or lowercase letters (A, B, C or a, b, c, etc.).

Formatting
Normal
Arial
12
B
I
U

NOTE

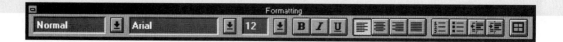

When you change the format and/or starting value for page numbers, the entire document is affected—no matter where the insertion point is located.

To change the page number value or format:

1. Choose Insert ➤ Page Numbers to display the Page Numbers dialog box.

Format...

2. In the dialog box, click the Format button. The Page Number Format dialog box (shown in Figure 6.2) will appear.
3. To change format, pull down the Number Format list and select the desired format.

FIGURE 6.2

The Page Number Format dialog box

Page Number Format
Number Format:
1, 2, 3, ...
OK
Cancel
Help
Include Chapter Number
Chapter Starts with Style
Heading 1
Use Separator:
- (hyphen)
Examples: 1-1, 1-A
Page Numbering
Continue from Previous Section
Start At:

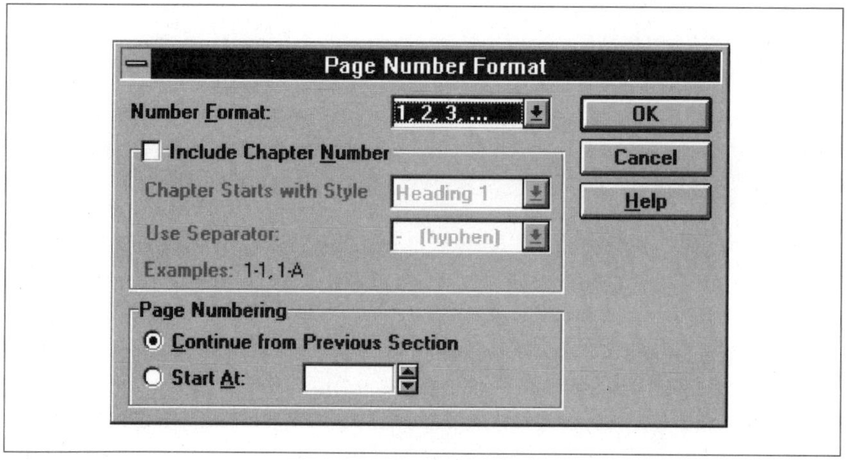

4. To specify a different starting number, turn on the Start At option and then enter the desired starting value in the box (or click the arrows to increase or decrease the value).

5. Click the OK button or press ↵ to return to the Page Numbers dialog box, and then click OK again to return to your document.

Headers and Footers

A *header* is information that is displayed at the top of every page, and a *footer* is information that is displayed at the bottom. Headers and footers can contain text and other document elements, such as graphics and lines. Headers and footers are useful for displaying information such as the document title, chapter and author name, page number, date, time, and so on.

In many documents, you will want the same header or footer on all pages of the document. You can also specify that there be one header/footer on the first page and a different header/footer on other pages, or a different header/footer on odd- and even-numbered pages.

Headers and footers are not displayed on screen in Normal view. You can see them in Print Preview, which is explained in Chapter 9. You can also see them (but not directly edit them) in Page Layout view. To switch to Page Layout view, click the Page Layout View button at the bottom-left of the screen just above the status bar.

To switch back to Normal view, click the Normal View button at the bottom-left of the screen just above the status bar.

To add or modify headers and footers, start by choosing <u>V</u>iew ➤ <u>H</u>eader and Footer. Word displays the current page's header in a dotted box on-screen along with the Header And Footer toolbar, as shown in Figure 6.3.

FIGURE 6.3

You use the Header And Footer toolbar to edit headers and footers.

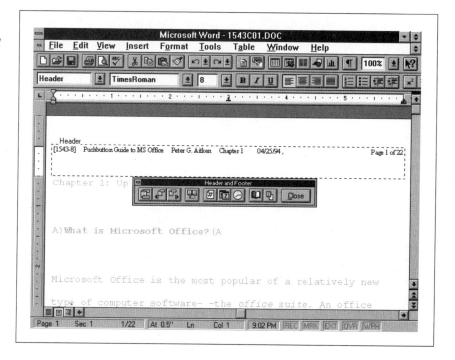

If you're working in Page Layout view, and you want to edit a header or footer, double-click it. The header or footer will be displayed in the dotted box on the screen. To add or modify the header or footer text, type in text and use Word's usual editing and formatting commands. Here are some of the things you can do:

- Change font and font size.

- Add bold, underline, or italic format.

- Start a new line by pressing ↵.

- Center or justify text.

Switch back to editing the document by double-clicking the document text.

Using the Header and Footer Toolbar

You can use the buttons on the Header And Footer toolbar for special tasks. To move the toolbar, point at its title bar and drag it to another screen location.

Click the Switch Between Header And Footer button to edit the footer. Click the Switch Between Header And Footer button again to switch back to editing the header.

Click the Page Number button to insert the page number at the cursor location.

Click the Date button to insert the current date at the cursor location.

Click the Time button to insert the current time at the cursor location.

Click the Close button to return to normal document editing.

NOTE

When you insert the date or time in a header or footer, Word inserts a code that updates to show the current date or time according to your computer's system clock—not the date or time when the header or footer was created. To ensure that the current date and time are displayed, press Ctrl+5 (on the numeric keypad) to select the entire document, and then press F9.

Different Header/Footer on Different Pages

Use the techniques described above if you want to display and print the same header/footer on each page of your document. But, as I mentioned earlier, you can have a different header/footer on the first page of the document, or on odd and even pages. You specify this in the Layout part of the Page Setup dialog box, which is shown in Figure 6.4.

There are two ways to display this dialog box:

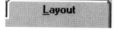

- Choose File ➤ Page Setup and, if necessary, click the Layout tab to display the Layout section.

- If you are editing a header or footer, click the Page Layout button on the Header And Footer toolbar.

FIGURE 6.4

The Layout section of the Page Setup dialog box

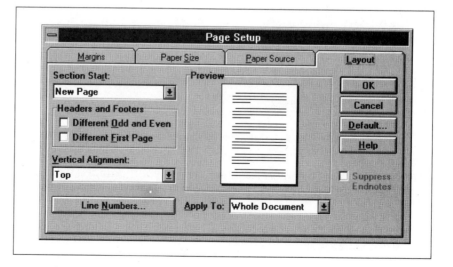

Once the Page Setup dialog box is displayed, turn on the Different Odd And Even and/or the Different First Page options as desired, and click OK or press ↵. Then, move the insertion point to the desired page and choose <u>V</u>iew ➤ <u>H</u>eader And Footer to add or edit header/footer text, as described earlier in this chapter.

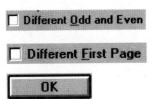

> **N O T E**
>
> See the next section, "Page Margins," for information on how to specify the position of headers and footers on the page.

Page Margins

Page margins control the amount of space between text and the edges of the paper. There are four margins on every page, and you can control them independently. You can change the margins for the entire document, for selected text, or from the location of the insertion point onward:

- To change the margins for the whole document, position the insertion point anywhere.

- To change the margins for a portion of the document, select the text.

- To change the margins from a specific location to the end of the document, move the insertion point to that location.

Then, follow these steps:

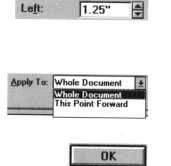

1. Choose File ➤ Page Setup to display the Page Setup dialog box. If necessary, click the Margins tab to display the margins section of the dialog box, as shown in Figure 6.5.

2. Select the Top, Bottom, Left, or Right box depending on the margin you want to set. Enter the margin width in the box, or click the up and down arrows next to the box to change the current value.

3. Repeat step 2 as needed to set all margins.

4. Pull down the Apply To list and select the desired scope of the margin change.

5. Click the OK button or press ↵.

FIGURE 6.5

You set margins in the Page Setup dialog box.

Changing Margins with the Ruler

You can change the margins for an entire document using the ruler. The ruler allows you to work visually rather than by entering measurements. You can use the ruler to change margins in Print Preview (see Chapter 9 for details), or you can use Page Layout view, as described below. If your ruler is not displayed, choose View ➤ Ruler to display it.

To change margins in Page Layout view:

1. If necessary, click the Page Layout View button at the bottom-left of the screen just above the status bar to switch to Page Layout view (see Figure 6.6).

FIGURE 6.6

In Page Layout view, you can change margins using the ruler.

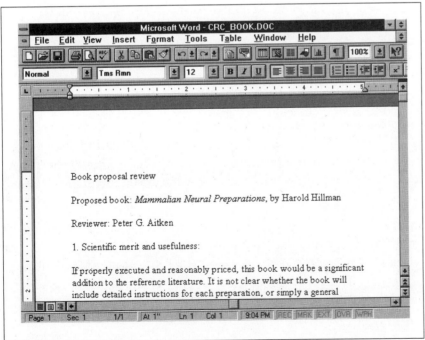

2. Point at the left or right margin indicator on the ruler. The mouse pointer will change to a horizontal two-headed arrow.

3. Press and hold down the mouse button. A vertical line is displayed down the page at the current margin position.

4. Drag the margin to the desired location and release the mouse button.

> **N O T E**
>
> It can be difficult to find the margin indicator on the ruler, particularly at the left margin if the indent markers get in the way. Be sure that the mouse pointer has changed to a two-headed arrow or you may end up changing the indents instead of the margin!

Paper Size and Orientation

Word can format your document for just about any size of paper you can imagine. There are situations in which you'll want to change paper size even if you are not printing a document. For example, selecting a wide paper size permits you to display wide tables and graphics on-screen.

In addition to selecting paper size, you can also select the paper orientation. *Portrait* orientation, which prints lines of text parallel to the short edge of the paper, is used most often. *Landscape* orientation, which prints lines of text parallel to the long edge of the paper, is useful for certain special kinds of documents.

You can change the paper size and orientation for the entire document, in which case the insertion point can be located anywhere in the document. You can also change it for selected text, or from the location of the insertion point onward.

1. If you're not changing paper size or orientation for the entire document, select the text to be affected or move the insertion point to the location at which you want the changes to take effect.

2. Choose <u>F</u>ile ➤ Page Set<u>u</u>p to display the Page Setup dialog box. If necessary, click the Paper Size tab to display the paper size options, as shown in Figure 6.7.

3. Pull down the Paper Size list and select the desired size. This list includes most common paper sizes. If the desired size is not listed, select Custom and then enter the paper dimensions in the Width and Height boxes.

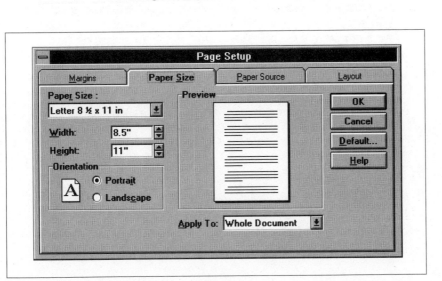

FIGURE 6.7

Set paper size options in the Page Setup dialog box.

4. Select the Portrait or Landscape option.

5. Pull down the Apply To list and select the portion of the document to which the new settings should apply.

6. Click the OK button or press ↵.

When you apply a different paper size or orientation to a portion of the document, Word inserts a section break at each location where the paper size or orientation changes. Section breaks are marked on-screen by a double horizontal line and an "End of Section" label. A *section* is a part of the document where certain formatting is in effect. Other than paper size, sections can be defined by column definitions and headers and footers. Please refer to the Word documentation for more information on sections.

NOTE

A few older printers, particularly dot matrix printers, do not have the ability to print in Landscape orientation.

Let's try changing the paper orientation for one of your documents. You can use any document—one of your "real" ones or a practice document from earlier in the book. Once the document is displayed on-screen, follow these steps:

1. Choose File ➤ Page Setup to display the Page Setup dialog box. If necessary click the Paper Size tab.

2. Click the Landscape option.

3. Be sure that the Whole Document option is selected in the Apply To box.

4. Click the OK button or press ↵ to return to your document.

Note that in Landscape orientation each line of text in multi-line paragraphs is longer. Likewise, there are fewer lines per page. This makes perfect sense, of course, because when you switch from Portrait to Landscape orientation the paper width increases from 8.5 to 11 inches, and its length decreases from 11 to 8.5 inches. Word automatically adjusts the text on each page to fit the page size and the margin settings.

When you're finished looking at the document, repeat the steps above, selecting the Portrait option, to return the document to its original settings.

CHAPTER SEVEN

Creating Tables and Multicolumn Documents

THE ABILITY TO create tables is one of Word's most useful features. Using tables, you can organize words or numbers in a row and column format that is ideal for certain kinds of information. You can add attractive formatting to tables, too. Word also makes it easy to create documents that format text in columns, such as newsletters and brochures.

Creating a Table

When you create a table you must specify how many rows and columns it should have. You can always add or delete rows and columns later, but you have to start somewhere!

1. Move the insertion point to the location at which you wish to place the table.

Insert
Table

2. Click the Insert Table button on the Standard toolbar. Word displays a grid below the button, as shown in Figure 7.1.

3. Point to the box in the upper-left corner of the grid and press and hold down the mouse button. Drag down and to the right until you highlight the desired number of rows and columns. (If you reach the lower-right corner the grid will expand as needed.)

4. Release the mouse button. Word inserts the table in the document at the location of the insertion point.

NOTE

A table can contain a maximum of 31 columns.

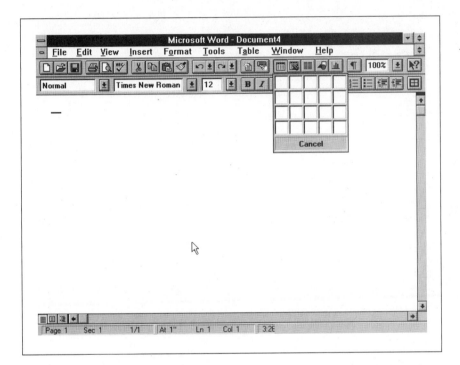

FIGURE 7.1

After clicking the Insert Table button, you specify dimensions for the table on this grid.

When a table is first created all of its cells are empty, and all columns have the same width. Figure 7.2 shows an example, in which a 3-row by 4-column table was just inserted in the document. The borders between cells are marked by dotted lines. The remainder of this chapter shows you how to add and edit table data and how to modify table formatting.

FIGURE 7.2

A newly inserted table contains empty rows and columns ready for you to enter data.

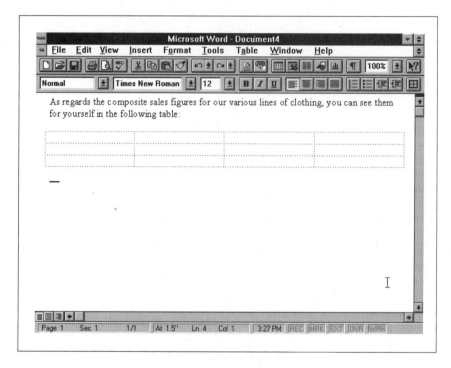

Moving around in a Table

When you're working in a table—that is, when the insertion point is in a table cell— there are some special movement keys you use to move from cell to cell:

To move the insertion point...	**Press**...
To the next cell in a row	Tab
To the previous cell in a row	Shift+Tab

To move the insertion point...	Press...
To the first cell in the current row	Alt+Home
To the last cell in the current row	Alt+End
To the top cell in the current column	Alt+PgUp
To the bottom cell in the current column	Alt+PgDn

If the insertion point is at the edge of a cell, use ← and → to move to the next cell. You can use the mouse to move to any cell by simply pointing to it and clicking.

N O T E

Since pressing Tab moves to the next cell, how do you insert an actual tab in a table? Simple—press Ctrl+Tab.

Adding and Editing Table Data

When the insertion point is in a table cell, you add, delete, and edit data in the usual way. If text reaches the right edge of the cell it automatically wraps to a new line in the same cell. The editing and formatting tools available to you in a table include (but are not limited to):

- Selecting text for copying and moving

- Changing line spacing

- Using left, center, right, and full justification

- Applying paragraph and character styles
- Changing font and font size

As with normal document text, you will often need to select text in a table to apply formatting. To select part of the text in a cell you use the usual techniques:

- Point and drag with the mouse.
- Press Shift and use the arrow keys.

In a table there are some additional methods you can use to select one or more cells:

- To select one entire cell, click in the left margin of the cell, between the text and the cell border. The mouse pointer changes from an I-beam to an arrow when it's in this area.
- To select a rectangular block containing two or more cells, point at the first cell and drag to the last cell.
- To select the entire row or column containing the insertion point, choose Table ➤ Select Row or Table ➤ Select Column.
- To select the entire table, position the insertion point anywhere in the table and press Alt+5 (the 5 on the numeric keypad).

Deleting Rows and Columns

If your table is too big or too small, you can add or delete columns and rows as needed. To delete a row or column:

1. Move the insertion point to any cell in the row or column to be deleted.

2. Choose Table ➤ Delete Cells to display the Delete Cells dialog box, shown in Figure 7.3.

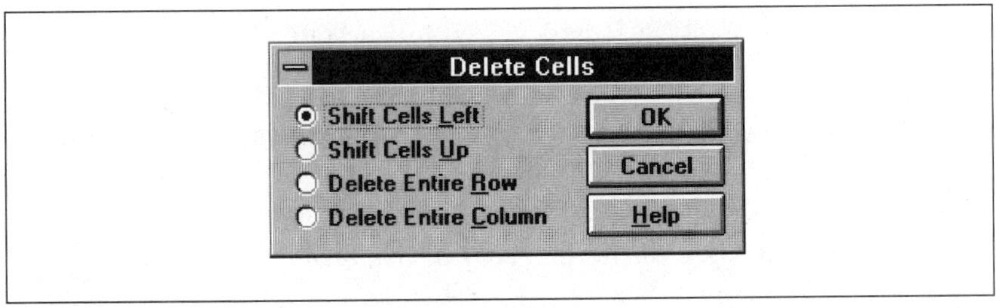

FIGURE 7.3

The Delete Cells dialog box provides several options for deleting cells from a table.

3. Select either the Delete Entire Row or the Delete Entire Column option.

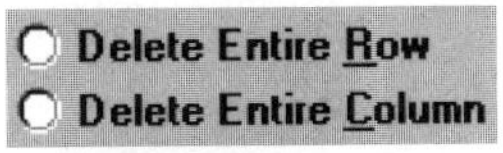

4. Click the OK button or press ↵.

There is a difference between deleting the contents of a row or column and deleting the row or column itself. If you delete the contents of a row by selecting the entire row and pressing Del, the row remains in the table but all of its cells are now empty. If you delete the row as described above, the cells and their contents are deleted and the table ends up with one fewer row.

Adding Rows and Columns

You can add new rows or columns at any location in a table. To insert a new row:

1. Move the insertion point to a cell below the location at which you want the new row or column.

Insert Rows

2. Choose T<u>a</u>ble ➤ Select <u>R</u>ow.

3. Click the Insert Rows button on the Standard toolbar. The Insert Rows button is the same as the Insert Table button. Its function depends on whether the insertion point is in a table.

> ### NOTE
>
> **To add a new row at the bottom of the table, move the insertion point to the last cell of the last row of the table and press Tab.**

To add a new column:

1. Move the insertion point to any cell in the column that you want to be to the right of the new column.

2. Choose T<u>a</u>ble ➤ Select <u>C</u>olumn.

Insert Column

3. Click the Insert Column button on the Standard toolbar. The Insert Column button is the same as the Insert Table button. Its function changes to Insert Column when you are working in a table and have selected a column.

To add a column at the right edge of a table:

1. Move the insertion point to any cell in the rightmost column of the table. If necessary, press End to move the insertion point to the end of any text in the cell.

2. Press → to move the insertion point to the right margin outside of the table cell.

3. Choose Table ➤ Select Column.

4. Click the Insert Column button on the Standard toolbar.

Insert
Column

Adjusting Column Width

When you first create a table, Word automatically makes all the columns the same width so that the table fills all the space between the page margins. You can adjust the width of individual columns with the mouse:

1. Point at the right border of the column. The mouse pointer changes to two vertical lines with sideways pointing arrowheads.

2. Drag the border to the desired position.

3. Release the mouse button.

You can also change column widths using a dialog box. This method has the advantage that you can specify an exact width measurement, control the amount of space left between columns, and even have Word automatically adjust column widths to fit their contents.

1. Move the insertion point to any cell in the column to be adjusted.

2. Choose Table ➤ Cell Height And Width to display the Cell Height And Width dialog box. If necessary, click the Column tab to display the column width options, as shown in Figure 7.4.

3. The current column width is displayed in the Width Of Column *n* box, where *n* is the number of the current column. Enter the desired column width, in inches, or click the up and down arrows to increase or decrease the displayed value by one-tenth inch per click.

FIGURE 7.4

Click the Column tab in the Cell Height And Width dialog box when you want to set column widths.

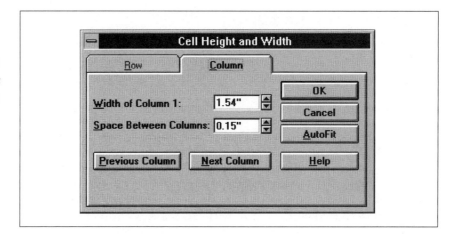

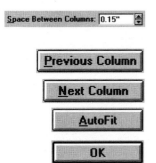

4. In the Space Between Columns box enter the value, or click the arrows, to specify the amount of space between columns.

5. If desired, click the Previous Column or Next Column button to select a different column for changing, and then repeat step 3.

6. Click the AutoFit button to have Word automatically adjust the width of all columns in the table on the basis of the cell contents.

7. Click the OK button or press ↵.

Adjusting Row Height

Word's default is to automatically adjust the height of each table row to fit the "tallest" data in the row. In most situations this is fine, but there

may be times when you want to adjust the height of one or more rows manually.

1. To set the height of all rows in the table, position the insertion point in any cell. To set the height of a single row, select the row.

2. Choose Table ➤ Cell Height And Width to display the Cell Height And Width dialog box. If necessary, click the Row tab to display the row settings, as shown in Figure 7.5.

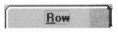

3. Open the Height Of Row list and select one of the following options:

> **Auto** Word automatically adjusts the row height to fit the tallest cell.
>
> **At Least** The row height is at least the value you specify. Word will increase the height if necessary to accommodate tall cells.

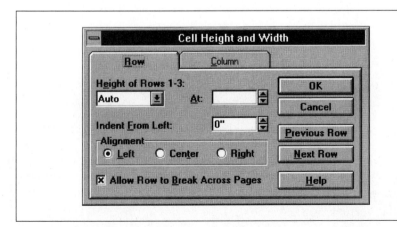

FIGURE 7.5

You set row height in the Cell Height And Width dialog box, with the Row tab displayed.

Exactly   The row height is exactly the value you specify. If a cell's contents exceed the row height, only a portion of the contents is displayed.

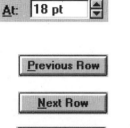

4. If you selected either the At Least or Exactly option, enter the desired row height in the At box, or click the arrows to increase or decrease the displayed value.

5. If you're setting the height of a single row, you can click the Previous Row or Next Row button and then repeat steps 3 and 4 to set the height of other rows.

6. Click the OK button or press ↵.

Formatting a Table

You can make your tables more attractive and easier to read with some formatting. Table formatting consists of applying borders, lines, and shading to various parts of the table. The Table AutoFormat command makes formatting your tables a breeze.

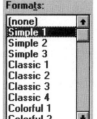

1. Move the insertion point to any location in the table.

2. Choose Table ➤ Table AutoFormat to display the Table Auto-Format dialog box, shown in Figure 7.6.

3. In the Formats list select a table format. The Preview box shows you what the selected format looks like.

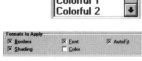

4. In the Formats To Apply section, click to turn individual options on or off to apply or remove specific elements of the predefined table format. Some of the options do not apply to all formats. The AutoFit option changes the table size to fit its contents.

FIGURE 7.6

The Table AutoFormat dialog box. The Preview box shows you how the selected options will appear.

5. In the Apply Special Formats To section, click to turn options on or off to control whether Word applies special formats to the first and last row and column in the table.

6. When the sample table has the desired appearance, click the OK button or press ↵.

N O T E

To remove all formatting from a table, select the (none) option in step 3 above.

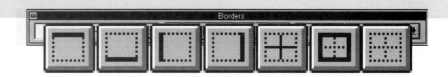

Doing Your Own Table Formatting

While the AutoFormat feature can produce a wide variety of attractive table formats, there may be times when you wish to "roll your own."

Borders

You can use Word's Borders And Shading feature to create a customized table format. Borders and shading are best applied using the Borders toolbar, as explained in Chapter 4. To display the Borders toolbar, click the Borders button on the Formatting toolbar. Click the button again to hide the Borders toolbar.

Outside Border

The procedures for adding borders and shading to a table are very similar to those for regular text that you learned in Chapter 4. If you want to format a single table cell, position the insertion point in the cell. For multiple cells you must first select the cells. This could be a block of cells, an entire row or column, or the entire table. Then:

Left Border

Right Border

- To apply borders to the four outer edges of the selected table region, click the Outside Border button on the Borders toolbar.

Top Border

Bottom Border

- To apply a border to one edge of the selected cells, click the Left, Right, Top, or Bottom Border button on the Borders toolbar. To apply two or three borders, click each button in turn. For example, click the Top Border button followed by the Bottom Border button to add borders above and below the cells.

Inside Border

- To place a border between cells in a selection, click the Insider Border button on the Borders toolbar. (This is applicable only when you have more than one cell selected.)

No Border

- To remove existing borders from the selection, click the No Border button on the Borders toolbar.

To change the style of lines used for borders, pull down the Line Style list on the Borders toolbar and select the desired style. To change the style of borders you have already applied, remove the old borders by clicking the No Border button, change the line style, and then reapply the border.

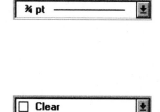

To add shading to the selected cells, pull down the Shading list on the Borders toolbar by clicking the down arrow to the right of the Shading box and selecting the desired shading. To remove shading, select Clear from the list.

Using the Table Wizard

Word's Table Wizard feature can help you create tables that are customized to your exact needs. The Table Wizard leads you through a series of dialog boxes, asking questions about the size, format, and contents of your table. When you are finished it creates the table for you. You can then add data to the table, modify its formatting, and so on. Here's how it works:

1. Position the insertion point at the location in the document at which you want to place the table.

2. Choose Table ➤ Insert Table to display the Insert Table dialog box.

3. Click the Wizard button. Word displays the Table Wizard dialog box, shown in Figure 7.7.

4. Select the table style you want, and then click the Next button to display the next Table Wizard dialog box.

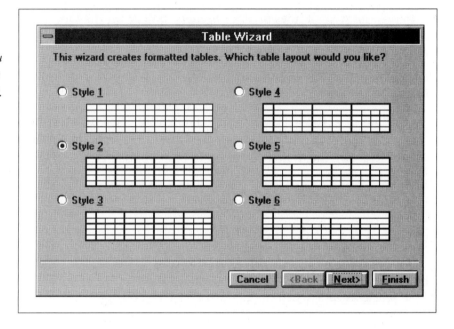

5. In each dialog box select the table options you want. In each of the dialog boxes you have the following choices (if a choice is not available its button will be grayed):

Accepts the selected options and goes to the next Wizard dialog box

Returns to the previous Wizard dialog box where you can modify the settings

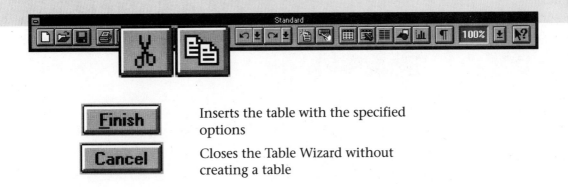

Finish	Inserts the table with the specified options
Cancel	Closes the Table Wizard without creating a table

Deleting or Moving a Table

You can delete the contents of a table while leaving the table and its formatting intact. You can also delete the entire table along with its contents.

1. Move the insertion point to any cell in the table.

2. Press Alt+5 (the 5 on the numeric keypad) to select the table.

3. Press Del to delete the contents only. Press Alt+A followed by D to delete the entire table.

To move or copy a table to another document location:

1. Move the insertion point to any cell in the table.

2. Press Alt+5 (the 5 on the numeric keypad) to select the table.

3. Click the Copy button on the Standard toolbar (to copy the table) or the Cut button on the Standard toolbar (to move the table).

Copy   Cut

4. Move the insertion point to the new location for the table.

Paste

5. Click the Paste button on the Standard toolbar. The table will appear in the chosen location.

Creating a Table from an Excel Worksheet

You may find that the data you want to place in a table in your Word document already exists in an Excel workbook. Do you have to retype everything? Not on your life! You can copy data right from Excel and drop it directly into a Word document, and it will automatically be placed in a table.

Excel

1. Start Excel, or if it is already running, switch to it, by clicking the Excel button on the Microsoft toolbar or on the Office Manager toolbar.

Open

2. Click the Open button on Excel's Standard toolbar to open the workbook that contains the data you want in a table.

Copy

3. Select the cells to be placed in the table. Figure 7.8 shows an Excel worksheet with a group of cells selected.

4. On Excel's Standard toolbar, click the Copy button.

Word

5. Switch back to Word by clicking the Word button on the Microsoft toolbar or on the Office Manager toolbar.

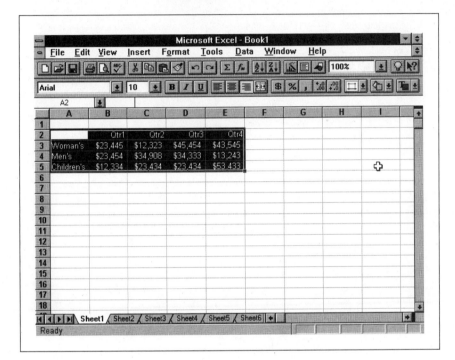

FIGURE 7.8

To place Excel data in a Word table, you must first switch to Excel and select the workbook data.

6. Position the insertion point where you want the table to go.

7. Click the Paste button on the Standard toolbar. A new table is created, with one cell for each Excel cell that was copied. The pasted table is shown in Figure 7.9.

You can now format the table as desired.

Paste

FIGURE 7.9

The Excel data after it is pasted into a Word document

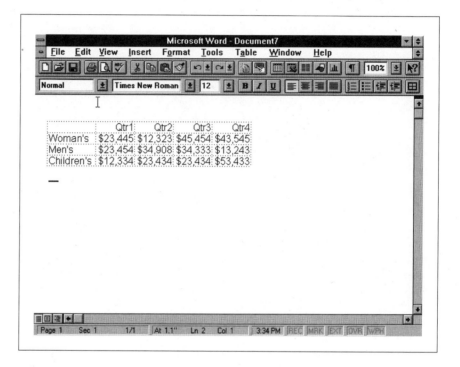

Multicolumn Documents

Certain kinds of documents, such as newsletters and brochures, lend themselves to a multicolumn layout. Figure 7.10 shows an example of a two column document. Word makes multicolumn documents easy to create. The most useful kind of columns are called *newspaper* columns, in which text snakes down the first column to the bottom of the page and then continues at the top of the second column.

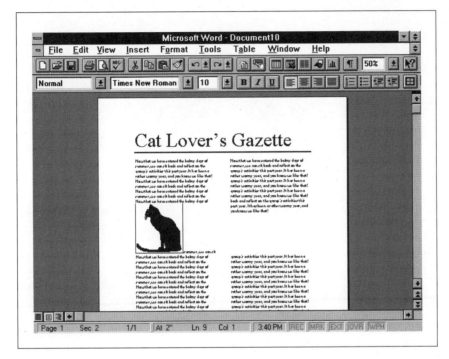

FIGURE 7.10

A two column layout is appropriate for various kinds of documents, such as this newsletter.

Equal-Width Columns

Here are the steps to follow to create two or more columns of equal width.

1. To apply the columns to the entire document, the insertion point can be positioned anywhere. To apply the columns to part of the document, select the text.

2. Click the Columns button on the Standard toolbar.

Columns

3. Word displays a graphic of small columns. Drag over the graphic to highlight the desired number of columns.

4. Release the mouse button.

N O T E

To remove columns from the document, follow the above steps and select one column.

In Normal view Word displays only a single column at a time, although columns will be printed properly. To view multiple columns on-screen you must work in Page Layout view.

Remember, to switch to Page Layout view, click the Page Layout View button on the left end of the horizontal scroll bar.

Columns of Unequal Width

You can also create a layout consisting of two columns of unequal width. The narrower column can be on either side of the page.

1. To apply the columns to part of the document, select the text. Otherwise the insertion point can be positioned anywhere.

2. Select Format ➤ Columns to display the Columns dialog box, shown in Figure 7.11.

3. In the Presets section of the dialog box click either Left or Right depending on where you want the narrower of the two columns.

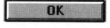

4. Click the OK button.

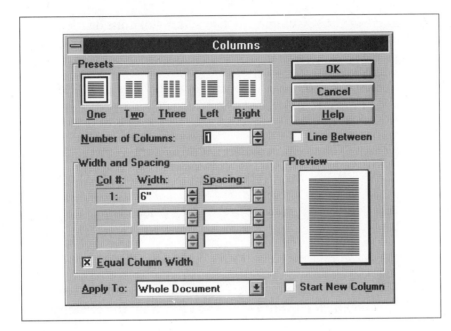

FIGURE 7.11

You can use the Columns dialog box to create columns of unequal width.

Changing Column Format

While the defualt columns discussed above are fine for many documents, you may want to customize your column format. You can change individual column widths, change the space between columns, and display a vertical line between columns.

1. Move the insertion point to any location in the document where you wish to customize the column.

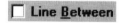

2. Select Format ➤ Columns to display the Columns dialog box (shown earlier in Figure 7.11). The Width And Spacing section of the dialog box will display the current column settings.

3. To change the width of a column, change the value in the corresponding Width box, or click the up and down arrows to change the setting.

4. To change the spacing to the right of a column, change the value in the corresponding Spacing box, or click the up and down arrows to change the setting.

5. To display a vertical line between each pair of columns, turn on the Line Between option.

6. Click the OK button or press ↵.

When you change column width or spacing, Word always makes adjustments to make the total width of the text fit within the page margins. In a two column layout, for example, increasing the width of the left column results in an automatic corresponding decrease in the width of the right column.

CHAPTER EIGHT

Working with Graphics

ONE OF WORD'S most useful features is its ability to include graphics, or pictures, in documents. While not every picture is worth a thousand words, there's no doubt that graphics can greatly improve the appearance and effectiveness of many documents. In this chapter I'll show you how to use graphics in your Word documents.

Sources of Graphics

Where do you get the graphics to include in your document? The answer is "just about anywhere!" Word can use computer graphics from most graphics programs. For example, you can use graphics created with Lotus 1-2-3, Micrographx Designer, AutoCAD, Paintbrush, and many other programs. Word also comes with its own collection of graphics.

Graphics can be divided into two general categories. The first category, which can be called *custom graphics*, includes pictures that have been specially created for a specific purpose. Examples include a bar graph of your firm's sales figures, an engineering diagram of one of your products, or a scanned photograph of an employee. The second category, *clip art*, consists of predesigned images intended for general-purpose uses. The graphics supplied with Word are clip art images.

There are two ways to insert a graphic into a document. In the first method, you use a graphic that is stored on your disk in its own file. This is the method you usually use for clip art images and for custom graphics created with programs that are not part of Microsoft Office. I'll cover this method first. In the second method, discussed later in the chapter, you copy the graphic directly from the source application to your Word document. This is the method you'll most often use with graphics created in Excel and PowerPoint.

Adding a Graphic

To add a graphic to your document, start by moving the insertion point to the location where you wish to place the graphic. Then:

1. Choose Insert ➤ Picture to display the Insert Picture dialog box, shown in Figure 8.1.

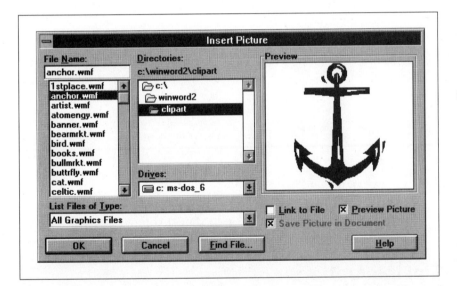

FIGURE 8.1

The Insert Picture dialog box lets you select a graphics file to insert in your document.

2. If you want Word to list only a specific type of graphics file, pull down the List Files Of Type list and select the desired file type. The type of file will depend on the original source of the graphic. For example, some graphics programs store their data in bitmap files with the .BMP extension, while some others use the .PCX extention.

3. If necessary, use the Drives and Directories lists to select a different drive and/or directory where your graphics files are located.

4. Click on a graphics file name in the File Name list, using the scroll bar to scroll through the list if necessary. If the Preview Picture option is checked, then the highlighted graphic will be displayed in the Preview box.

5. Select other options as desired (these are explained in more detail below):

Select the Link To File option if you want the picture in the document to be updated when the original graphics file changes.

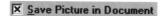

Turn off the Save Picture In Document option to minimize the document file size.

6. When the desired file name is highlighted, click the OK button. Word inserts the graphic in the document at the location of the insertion point. Figure 8.2 shows a document with an inserted graphic.

Linking Options

Word offers some options when inserting a graphic in a document. You select these options in the Insert Picture dialog box.

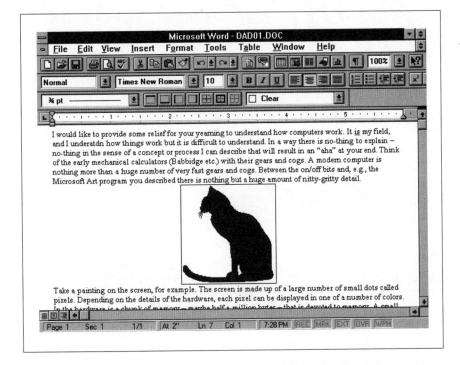

FIGURE 8.2

An inserted graphic can improve the appearance and impact of a document.

The first option, Link to File, controls whether the picture in your document will be updated to reflect changes in the original graphics file:

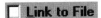

- If you select the Link To File option the picture in the document will be *linked* to the original graphics file. If you make changes to the graphics file, those changes will show up in the document.

- If the Link To File option is not selected, no link is established. The picture in the document will always remain as it was when first inserted, regardless of any changes to the original graphics file.

Use the Link To File option when you think you may modify the original file and these changes need to be reflected in the document. You would usually not use this option for clip art graphics, because clip art images generally are not modified, so there's no need to update them.

> ### N O T E
>
> **If you do not specify the Link To File option but you do change the graphics file, the only way to have the changes reflected in the document is to delete the graphic from the document and then reinsert the modified file.**

☒ Save Picture in Document

The second option, Save Picture in Document, is applicable only if you have selected the Link To File option, as just described.

- If you select this option, a copy of the linked graphic is stored as part of the document file. The file becomes larger, but the graphic can still be displayed and printed even if the original graphics file has been deleted.

- If you do not select this option, a copy of the linked graphic is not stored as part of the document. The file size is reduced, but the graphic will not be displayed or printed if the original file is not available.

> ### N O T E
>
> **If you insert a graphic from an Encapsulated PostScript (EPS) file, it will not display on-screen but it *will* print properly.**

Updating Links

When you insert linked graphics, the updating of the links is not neces-
sarily automatic. You control the updating of links as follows:

1. Choose Edit ➤ Links to display the Links dialog box (Figure 8.3).
   The Links command will not be available if your document
   does not contain any links.

2. The list displays the document's links. Click on the link with
   which you are working to highlight it. To highlight more than
   one link, hold down the Shift key while clicking.

3. To update the selected link(s) click the Update Now button.

FIGURE 8.3

*The Links dialog box
lets you control the
updating of links
between your document
and other files.*

4. To specify the link's update mode, select an option under Update:

  The link is automatically updated whenever new source data becomes available.

⊙ **Manual** The link must be updated manually.

Note that the Update options are not available for all types of links.

5. Click the OK button.

OK

T I P

To update a single graphic, select it and press F9. To update all links in the document, press Ctrl+5 (on the numeric keypad) to select the entire document, and then press F9.

Editing a Graphic

Before editing a graphic you must click on it to *select* it. When a graphic is selected it is surrounded by a box with small black rectangles, called *handles*, on the corners and edges. Figure 8.4 shows a selected graphic with its handles displayed.

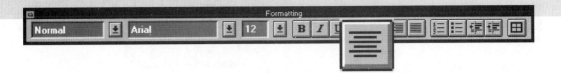

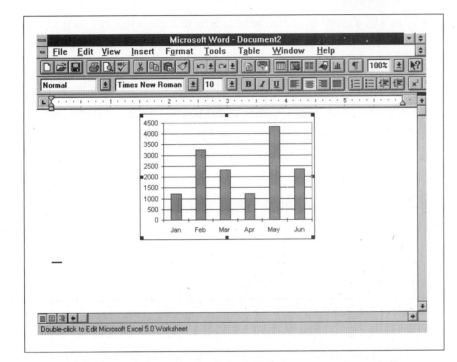

FIGURE 8.4

When selected, a graphic appears in a box with handles.

N O T E

When you point to a graphics handle with the mouse, the mouse pointer changes to a two-headed arrow.

You have several editing options for inserted graphics. You can change a graphic's left-right position and modify its size as follows:

- To center a graphic left-to-right on the page, click the Center button on the Formatting toolbar.

Center

Align Left **Align Right**

- To align a graphic at the left or right margin, click the Align Left or Align Right button on the Formatting toolbar.

- To change a graphic's height, point at the handle in the center of the top or bottom edge and drag to the desired height.

- To change a graphic's width, point to the handle in the center of the left or right edge and drag to the desired width.

- To change a graphic's size, point to one of the corner handles and drag to the desired size.

- To delete a graphic, press Del.

Moving or Copying a Graphic

To move or copy a selected graphic to another location in the document:

1. Select the graphic.

Copy **Cut**

Paste

2. To copy the graphic, click the Copy button on the Standard toolbar or press Ctrl+C. To move it, click the Cut button on the Standard toolbar or press Ctrl+X.

3. Move the insertion point to the new location for the graphic.

4. Click the Paste button on the Standard toolbar or press Ctrl+V.

Cropping a Graphic

When you insert a graphic file in your document, the default is for the entire graphic to be displayed, but there may be times when you would like to *crop* a graphic. Cropping moves the boundaries of the graphic in

to hide part of the graphic. You can also move the boundaries outward to increase the amount of white space around the graphic. To crop a graphic:

1. Select the graphic.

2. Press and hold down the Shift key.

3. Point at one of the graphic's handles and drag to the desired cropping position.

4. Release the Shift key.

Returning a Cropped and Resized Graphic to Its Original State

After experimenting with cropping and resizing a graphic you may decide that you prefer it the way it was. But can you remember its exact original size and cropping? No problem—Word can! To return a cropped graphic to its original state:

1. Select the graphic.

2. Choose Format ➤ Picture to display the Picture dialog box.

3. In the dialog box click the Reset button.

4. Click the OK button.

Adding an Excel Graph

Excel is the spreadsheet component of Microsoft Office, and will be covered in Chapters 10 through 15. One of Excel's strengths is its ability to

create terrific-looking charts from data in the spreadsheet. If you want to use an Excel chart in your Word document, you'll be glad to know that it's really easy (that's one of the advantages of Office, after all!).

1. Switch to Excel by clicking the Excel button on the Microsoft toolbar.

2. Click on the chart that you want in your Word document to select it. Figure 8.5 shows Excel with a selected chart.

FIGURE 8.5

Microsoft Excel with a selected chart to be copied to a Word document

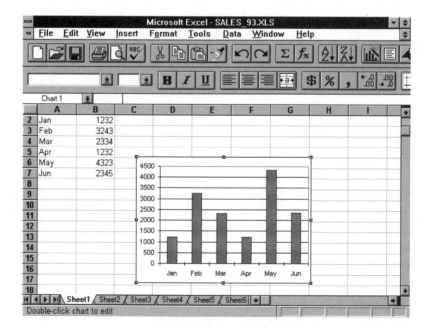

3. Still in Excel, click the Copy button on the Standard toolbar or press Ctrl+C.

4. Click the Word button on the Microsoft toolbar to return to Word.

5. In Word, position the insertion point at the location in the document at which you want the Excel chart to appear.

6. Click the Paste button on the Standard toolbar or press Ctrl+V. The chart will be inserted in the document. Figure 8.6 shows a Word document with the Excel chart inserted.

Copy

Word

Paste

FIGURE 8.6

A Word document with an inserted Excel chart

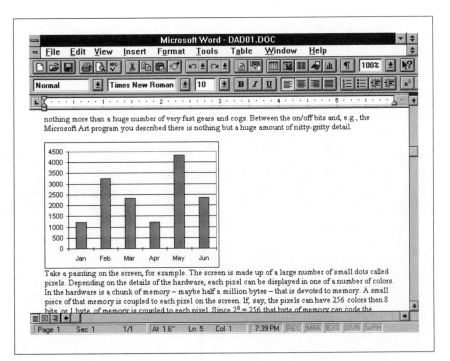

Once the Excel chart has been inserted you can move it, resize it, etc., as described earlier in this chapter.

Linking an Excel Chart

The procedure that I just described inserts a copy of an Excel chart in your document, but does not establish a link between the document and the chart, so the chart in the document will not be updated if the Excel chart is changed. If you want to insert a *linked* Excel chart the procedure is a bit different. Start by following steps 1 through 5 above. Then, once you are back in Word:

7. Choose Edit ➤ Paste Special to display the Paste Special dialog box (shown in Figure 8.7).

FIGURE 8.7

*The Paste Special
dialog box*

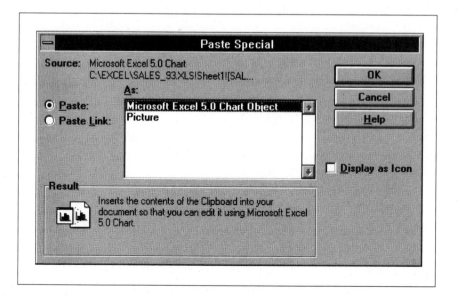

8. Select the Paste Link option.

9. Click the OK button.

Once a linked Excel chart has been inserted, you control its updating as described earlier in the chapter for other links.

Adding a PowerPoint Graphic

Another component of Microsoft Office is PowerPoint, a presentation graphics package. You'll learn how to use PowerPoint to create presentations in Chapters 16 through 19. Once you've created a presentation, you may wish to add individual PowerPoint pictures, called *slides*, to a Word document. The procedure is similar to that for adding an Excel chart:

1. Start or switch to PowerPoint by clicking the PowerPoint button on the Microsoft toolbar.

PowerPoint

2. In PowerPoint, click the Open button on the Standard toolbar to open the presentation that contains the slide you want in your document.

Open

3. Choose View ➤ Slide Sorter to display the presentation's slides in thumbnail sketches.

4. Click the slide you want in your Word document.

Copy

5. Click the Copy button on the Standard toolbar.

6. Switch back to Word by clicking the Word button on the Microsoft toolbar.

Word

7. Click the Paste button on the Standard toolbar or press Ctrl+V. The slide will be inserted in the document.

Paste

Figure 8.8 shows a Word document with the PowerPoint slide inserted. Once the slide has been inserted you can move it, resize it, etc., as described earlier in this chapter. You can also control its linking with the source file (see "Linking an Excel Chart" above).

FIGURE 8.8

A Word document with an inserted PowerPoint slide

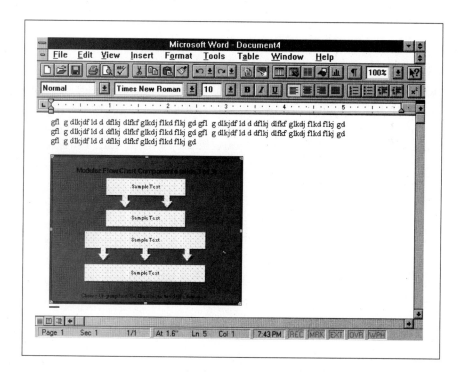

Placing a Box around a Graphic

Inserted graphics are normally displayed without any sort of border (unless of course the imported picture includes its own border). Figure 8.9

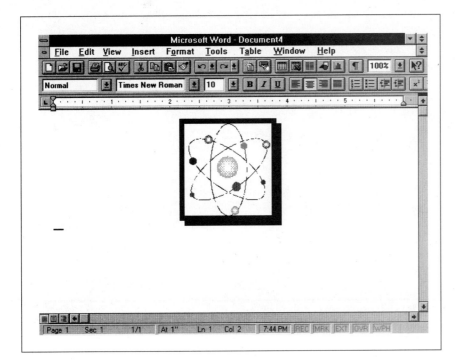

FIGURE 8.9

A graphic with a drop shadow

shows a graphic that has a drop shadow added. Here's how you can place a border or a drop shadow around any imported graphic:

1. Select the graphic.

2. Select Format ➤ Borders And Shading to display the Picture Borders dialog box, shown in Figure 8.10.

3. Click the Box icon to add four even borders to the graphic.

FIGURE 8.10

*The Picture Borders
dialog box*

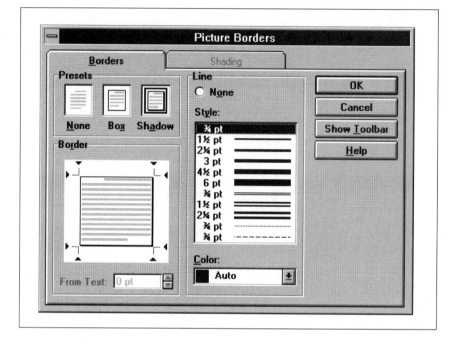

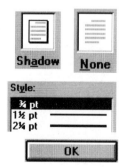

4. Click the Shadow icon to add a drop shadow box to the graphic. Click the None icon to remove a box or shadow from the graphic.

5. In the Style list, select the line style to be used for the box or shadow.

6. Click the OK button.

CHAPTER NINE

Proofing and Printing

MOST DOCUMENTS eventually need to be printed. You learned about basic printing in an earlier chapter, but here I'll explain some of your extra printing options. I'll also explain how you can use Word's proofing tools to ensure that your documents are error-free.

Checking Your Spelling

Everyone makes spelling errors from time to time. Even when you know perfectly well how to spell a word, a slip of the finger while typing can result in a spelling mistake. There are few tasks more boring than proofreading a document—and few things more embarrassing than turning in a final document with a speeling erorr (see what I mean!). Fortunately, Word's spell checker can save you from both boredom and embarrassment. The spelling checker is quite clever. Not only can it find misspelled words and add new words to its dictionary, but it can usually suggest one or more replacements for a misspelled word and then make the change for you automatically.

Spelling

To check the spelling of an entire document, click the Spelling button on the Standard toolbar. Word starts looking through the document from the location of the insertion point. If it encounters a word that is not in its dictionary, it displays the Spelling dialog box, which is shown in Figure 9.1.

In this dialog box, the Not In Dictionary box displays the word that Word thinks is misspelled. The word is highlighted in the document as well. The Suggestions list shows one or more suggested replacements for the word. The Change To box displays the word that is highlighted in the Suggestions list; if Word has no suggestions, the original word is displayed.

Spelling: English (US)

Not in Dictionary:	thier
Change To:	their
Suggestions:	their / there / Thai / thinner / thief / theirs

Ignore   Ignore All
Change   Change All
Add   Suggest

Add Words To: CUSTOM.DIC

AutoCorrect   Options...   Undo Last   Cancel   Help

FIGURE 9.1

The Spelling dialog box is used to find and correct misspelled words in your document.

In the Spelling dialog box you can take the following actions:

- Click the Ignore button to skip the highlighted word and continue the spelling check. Word will find other instances of the word, if any, in the document.

- Click the Ignore All button to skip the highlighted word and other instances of the word, if any, in the document.

- Click the Change button to replace the highlighted word with the contents of the Change To box.

- Click the Change All button to replace all instances in the document of the highlighted word with the contents of the Change To box.

- Click the Add button to add the highlighted word to the dictionary.

- Click the Cancel button to end the spelling check.

Ignore

Ignore All

Change

Change All

Add

Cancel

When the spelling check is finished, or if Word does not find any misspelled words in your document, it will display a dialog box informing you that the spelling check is complete. Click the OK button to return to your document.

Checking a Single Word

You can check the spelling of a single word at any time:

1. Select the word. (Remember, you can select a word by double-clicking it.)

Spelling

2. Click the Spelling button on the Standard toolbar.

3. If the selected word is not found in the dictionary, Word displays the Spelling dialog box, which you use as described above.

4. When the word has been checked or corrected, Word asks you if you want to check the spelling of the remainder of the document. Click the Yes button to continue the spelling check; click the No button to return to editing the document.

To quickly select the word that you just typed, press Ctrl+Shift+←.

Using the AutoCorrect Feature

If you're like me, there are a few words that you consistently mis-type. My favorites are typing "don;t" for "don't" and "teh" for "the." You may wish to use Word's AutoCorrect feature to correct these mistakes on the fly. You can also use AutoCorrect to speed your work by entering long words or phrases to replace abbreviations you type. For example, you could specify that every time you type "cz" it be replaced with "Czechoslovakia." Pretty handy if you're writing a book on Eastern European history!

Once you have defined an AutoCorrect entry, whenever you type the abbreviation or the misspelling in the document (followed by a space or punctuation mark) it will be replaced immediately and automatically.

To define a plain (unformatted) AutoCorrect entry:

1. Choose Tools ➤ AutoCorrect to display the AutoCorrect dialog box, shown in Figure 9.2.

2. In the Replace box enter the abbreviation (for example cz) or misspelling (for example, teh).

3. In the With box enter the expanded or corrected word or phrase (e.g., Czechoslovakia or the).

4. Click the Add button.

5. Repeat steps 2 through 4 as needed to define other AutoCorrect entries.

6. Click the OK button.

FIGURE 9.2

The AutoCorrect dialog box lets you define abbreviations and misspellings that will automatically be replaced as they are typed.

AutoCorrect

☒ Change 'Straight Quotes' to 'Smart Quotes'
☒ Correct TWo INitial CApitals
☐ Capitalize First Letter of Sentences
☒ Capitalize Names of Days

☒ Replace Text as You Type

Replace: With: ● Plain Text ○ Formatted Text

teh   the

occurence	occurrence
recieve	receive
seperate	separate
synaptoc	synaptic
teh	the
ttt	the

OK
Cancel
Help
Replace
Delete

AutoCorrect

NOTE

In the Spelling dialog box you may have noticed the AutoCorrect button. If you click this button, the misspelled word and its suggested replacement are added to the AutoCorrect list automatically, and the word is replaced in the document as well.

AutoCorrect has some other neat features as well. In the AutoCorrect dialog box, you can turn the following options on or off:

- The **Change Straight Quotes to Smart Quotes** option automatically changes regular single and double quotation marks with the more professional looking "curly" type.

- The **Correct TWo INitial CApitals**, **Capitalize First Letter of Sentences**, and **Capitalize Names of Days** options are self-explanatory.

- The **Replace Text as You Type** option determines whether defined AutoCorrect abbreviations will be replaced automatically.

N O T E

To remove an AutoCorrect definition, highlight it in the list and click the Delete button.

> **Delete**

Formatted AutoCorrect Entries

A plain AutoCorrect entry, as described above, enters unformatted text in the document. The text will take on whatever formatting (font, etc.) is in effect at the cursor location. You can also define a formatted Auto-Correct entry. When inserted in the document, a formatted AutoCorrect entry retains its original assigned formatting. Thus, for example, you could define an entry that is in boldface italics and it will always be inserted that way.

To create a formatted AutoCorrect entry:

1. Type the text in your document and apply all desired formatting.

2. Select the text. If it is an entire paragraph, be sure to include the end-of-paragraph mark in the selection.

3. Choose Tools ➤ AutoCorrect to display the AutoCorrect dialog box (Figure 9.2 above). The highlighted text will already be entered in the With box.

4. Click the Formatted Text option.

5. Type the desired abbreviation in the Replace box.

6. Click the Add button.

7. Click the OK button.

The Thesaurus

A *thesaurus* is used to find words that have a meaning identical to or similar to a given word. It can also be used to find *antonyms*—words with a meaning opposite to a given word. Judicious use of a thesaurus can help provide variety in your writing. For example, rather than using the word *interesting* 20 times in a sales brochure, you could add a little variety by replacing it with *fascinating, absorbing, entertaining, attractive, intriguing,* etc.

To use Word's thesaurus, place the insertion point on the word of interest and press Shift+F7. Word displays the Thesaurus dialog box, shown in Figure 9.3.

- The Looked Up box displays the word of interest.

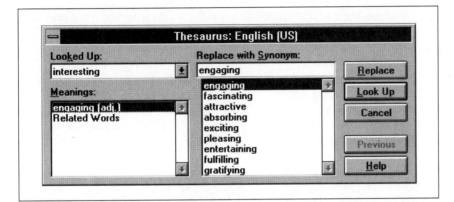

FIGURE 9.3

The Thesaurus dialog box can help you find just the right word for the meaning you're trying to communicate.

- If the word was not found in the thesaurus, the Looked Up box changes to the Not Found box.

- The Meanings list shows one or more possible meanings for the word. This is necessary because many words have more than one meaning. For example, *sink* could refer to something you have in your kitchen or to what the *Titanic* did. The term *antonyms* may appear in the list as well.

- If the word was not found, the Meanings list changes to an Alphabetic List of similar words.

- The Replace With Synonym list displays suggested synonyms for the meaning that is highlighted in the Meanings list.

When the Thesaurus dialog box is displayed, these are the actions you can take:

- To display synonyms for a specific meaning, click on the desired meaning in the Meanings list to highlight it.

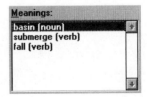

Look Up

- To look up a different word, type the word into the Looked Up box and click the Look Up button.

Replace

- To replace the word in the document with one of the words in the Replace With Synonym list, highlight the word and then click the Replace button.

Cancel

- To close the dialog box without replacing the word in the document, click the Cancel button.

N O T E

Unlike the spelling dictionary, you cannot add words and meanings to the thesaurus.

Previewing Your Document

To minimize wasted paper and unnecessary trips to the printer, it's ideal to print your document as few times as possible. Ideally, only the final copy will require printing. This is possible with Word because it has several features that permit you to see exactly how your document will look when printed. You can make your final layout and formatting changes completely on-screen without having to resort to the old print-edit-print-edit cycle.

Page Layout View

Page Layout view shows your document on-screen just as it will look when printed. Multiple columns, headers, footers, footnotes, and so on are all displayed in the exact positions in which they will be printed.

You can perform all the usual editing tasks and see their effects immediately. To switch to Page Layout view, click the Page Layout View button at the left end of the horizontal scroll bar. Figure 9.4 shows a document displayed in Page Layout view.

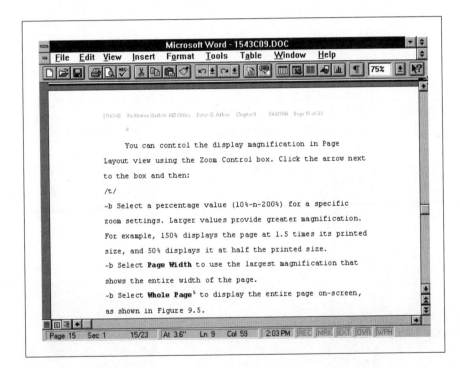

FIGURE 9.4

Displaying a document in Page Layout view lets you see multiple columns, headers, footers, and other document elements in their final positions.

You can control the display magnification in Page Layout view using the Zoom Control box on the Standard toolbar. Click the arrow next to the box and then:

- Select a percentage value (10%–200%) for a specific zoom setting. Larger values provide greater magnification. For example,

150% displays the page at 1.5 times its printed size, and 50% displays it at half the printed size.

- Select **Page Width** to use the largest magnification that shows the entire width of the page.

- Select **Whole Page** to display the entire page on-screen, as shown in Figure 9.5.

- Select **Two Pages** to view two adjacent pages at once.

FIGURE 9.5

A document displayed in Page Layout view at the Whole Page zoom setting

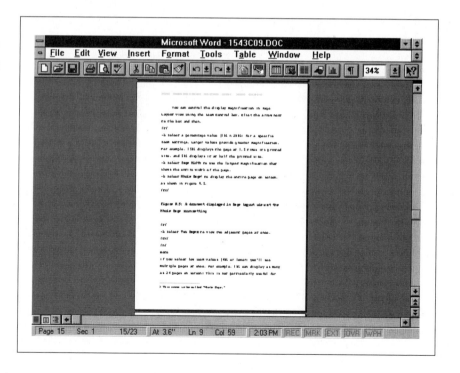

If you select low zoom values (40% or lower) you'll see multiple pages at once. For example, 10% can display as many as 24 pages on-screen! This shrinkage is not particularly useful for text editing (although it can be done) but could be useful for layout adjustments.

To return from Page Layout view to Normal view, click the Normal View button at the left end of the horizontal scroll bar.

Print Preview

You can also preview your document using Word's Print Preview feature. While similar in concept to Page Layout view, Print Preview has some differences that make it more suitable for some tasks. Although you'll rarely use Print Preview to edit document text, it's very useful for adjusting margins and indents, positioning graphics, and so on. To activate Print Preview, click the Print Preview button on the Standard toolbar. Figure 9.6 shows a document displayed in Print Preview.

Print Preview

Note that the Print Preview screen displays both vertical and horizontal rulers. You can use these rulers to adjust document margins, tabs, and indents as you learned in Chapter 6.

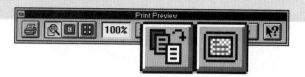

FIGURE 9.6

Print Preview mode lets you see exactly how a document will appear when printed.

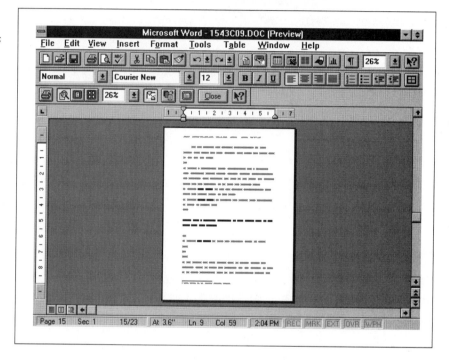

Print Preview has its own special toolbar. You can use the buttons on this toolbar as follows:

Full Screen

Shrink to Fit

- Click the Full Screen button to display the document full-screen, hiding all other screen elements except the toolbar. Click the button again to cancel Full Screen view.

- Click the Shrink To Fit button if there is only a small amount of text on the last page of the document and you want Word to attempt to rearrange the document so this "leftover" text fits on the previous page.

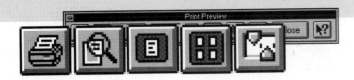

- Click the View Ruler button to hide or display the vertical and horizontal rulers.

- Pull down the Zoom Control list to change the display magnification.

- Click the Multiple Pages button and then drag over the page grid to specify the number of pages you want to see at once.

- Click the One Page Button to return to a single-page display.

- Click the Print button to print the entire document using the default print settings.

While text editing is not what Print Preview mode is intended for, you may want to edit in Print Preview mode if, for example, you notice a minor change that needs to be made. Here are the steps to follow:

1. In Print Preview mode the mouse pointer displays as a small magnifying glass with a + symbol in it. Point to the document location to edit, and then click. The display will enlarge to show the document at 100% magnification. (If you decide not to edit the text, click again to return to the original magnification.)

2. Click the Magnifier button. The mouse cursor changes to the standard I-beam editing pointer.

3. Click in the document at the location for editing, and then add, delete, and modify text as needed.

4. When you're finished editing, click the Magnifier button again. The mouse cursor changes to a magnifying glass with a – symbol in it.

View Ruler

26%

Multiple Pages

One Page

Print

Magnifier

Magnifier

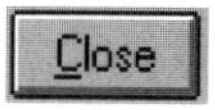

5. Click anywhere on the document to return to the original magnification.

When you're finished with Print Preview, click the Close button to return to the previous document view mode.

Printing Options Explained

Print

You learned earlier that you can quickly print the entire document by clicking the Print button on the Print Preview or Standard toolbar. For more control over printing, you must use the Print dialog box, which is shown in Figure 9.7. You can, for example, print only part of the document, print multiple copies, and so on.

FIGURE 9.7

The Print dialog box is used to set various advanced printing options.

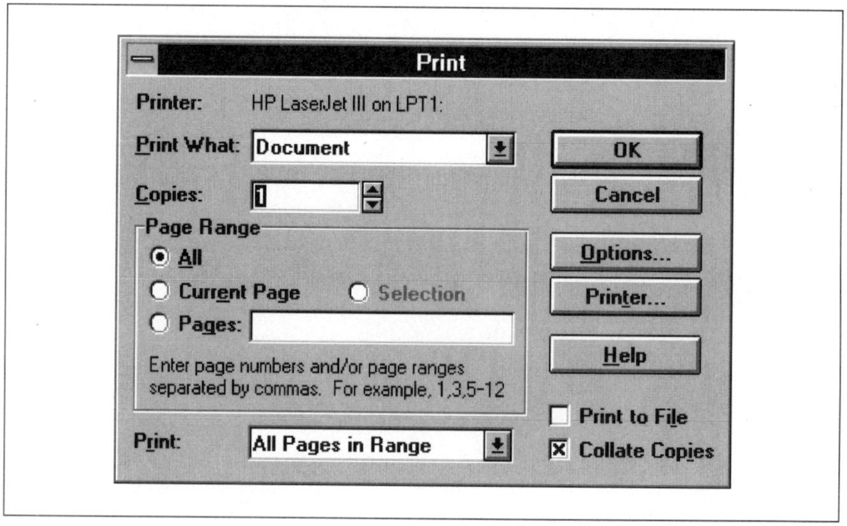

To specify print options in Word:

1. Choose <u>F</u>ile ➤ <u>P</u>rint to display the Print dialog box.

2. To tell Word what to print, choose from these options:

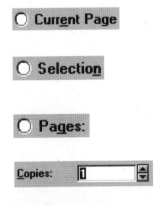

- To print only the current page, select the Current Page option.

- To print only selected text, select the Selection option (this option is available only if there is text selected in the document).

- To print a range of pages, select the Pages option and enter the page numbers in the box (as explained below).

- To print multiple copies of the document, enter the number of copies in the Copies box, or click the up and down arrows to change the value.

3. Click the OK button to start printing with the selected options.

When specifying a range of pages to print, you separate start and stop pages with a hyphen and individual pages with commas. Here are some examples:

To print this...	Type this in the pages box...
Page 8	8
Pages 1-5	1–5
Pages 3,6, and 7	3, 6, 7
Pages 3–5, page 6, and pages 7–10	3-5,6,7-10

Paper Source

You learned in Chapter 6 that you can specify different page sizes. Many printers have a single paper tray and also offer the option of manual feed for envelopes, letterhead, and the like. Fancier printers may have two or more paper trays and an envelope feeder. The Paper Source setting controls where your printer obtains paper when printing your document. The exact paper source options that are available to you depend on the printer that is installed.

You can change the paper source for the entire document, for selected text, or from the position of the insertion point onward. Here's how:

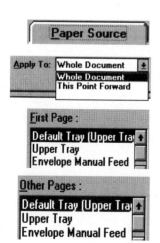

1. If you're changing the paper source for the entire document, the insertion point can be anywhere. Otherwise, select the text to be affected or move the insertion point to the location at which you want the changes to take effect.

2. Choose File ➤ Page Setup to display the Page Setup dialog box. If necessary, click the Paper Source tab to display the paper source options, as shown in Figure 9.8.

3. In the Apply To list specify the portion of the document that the new settings are to affect.

4. In the First Page list select the paper source for the first page of the document or section.

5. In the Other Pages list select the paper source for the remainder of the document or section.

6. Click the OK button or press ↵.

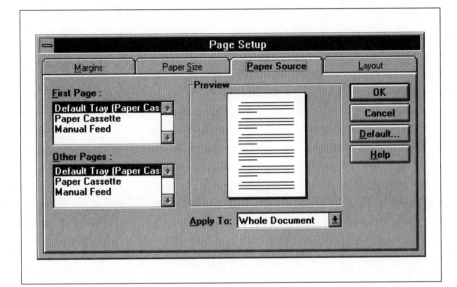

FIGURE 9.8

You can set Paper Source options in the Page Setup dialog box.

When you specify a different paper source for a portion of the document, Word inserts a section break at each location where the paper source changes.

NOTE

Please see your printer manual for information on manual feed techniques.

3

EXCEL

Getting Started
with Excel

WHERE MICROSOFT WORD is a word processor that lets you create and edit documents, Excel is a "number processor." In this chapter you will learn how to use Excel to manipulate and display data. You learned the first step, how to start Excel, in Chapter 1. I'll start by briefly describing what Excel is and how you can use it. Then we'll take a look at the Excel screen and learn how to enter data; move around; save, close, and open files; and exit the program.

What Is Excel?

Excel is a *spreadsheet* program that is designed to work with numbers. A spreadsheet is analogous to an accountant's ledger book, with pages that are ruled into rows and columns. You can write numbers, text, and other information in the book. Excel provides *electronic* "pages" on which you can enter just about any kind of data you can imagine—sales figures, population statistics, manufacturing quotas, etc. In Excel, each individual "page" is called a *sheet*, and the entire "book" is called a *workbook*.

Excel is much more than an electronic ledger book, however. The two main features that makes it so useful are:

- You can create formulas that perform calculations based on data in the workbook. If the data changes, the results of the formulas are updated automatically.

- You can quickly create graphs of your data. The graphs are automatically updated to reflect changes in the data.

Figure 10.1 shows an example of a small Excel workbook that includes data and a graph.

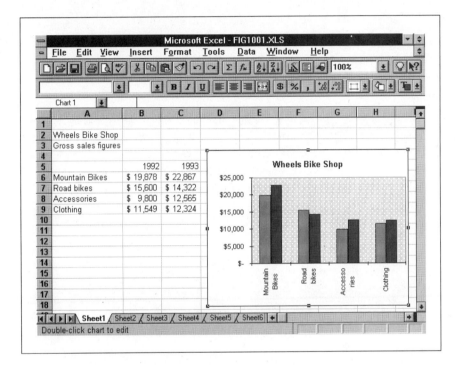

An Excel workbook is designed for manipulating and graphing numerical data.

Parts of the Excel Screen

When you start Excel you'll see the screen that is shown in Figure 10.2. This figure identifies the most important parts of the Excel screen. I'll explain the use of these components as needed throughout the book. For now it's important to be able to *recognize* these parts of the screen.

- The *title bar* displays the name of the current workbook, or file.

- The *menu bar* is used to access menus from which you select Excel's various commands.

FIGURE 10.2

You need to recognize these parts of the Excel screen.

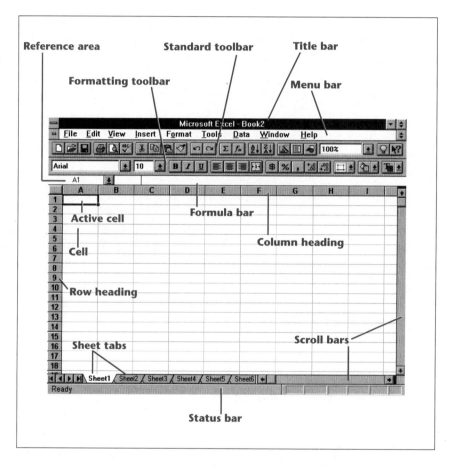

- The *Standard toolbar* displays buttons that you can click with the mouse to perform commonly needed tasks.

- The *Formatting toolbar* displays buttons and lists that you use to change the appearance of your data.

- The *reference area* displays various information about the current workbook cell.

- The *formula bar* is used to enter and edit data.

- *Cells* are where you place data and formulas.

- The *active cell* is indicated by a black outline.

- The *row heading* and *column heading* help to identify cells.

- The *sheet tabs* identify individual sheets, and can be used to move between them.

- The *status bar* displays information about the status of Excel and your system.

- The *scroll bars* are used to move around using the mouse.

Cell Addresses and Workbook Structure

The basic unit of data storage in Excel is the *cell*. Each cell can hold a number, a label, or a formula. Each individual cell is identified by the column and row in which it is located. There are 256 columns in each sheet, identified by letters. Yes, I know there are only 26 letters in the alphabet! After the first 26 columns (A–Z), double letters are used: the 27th through 52nd columns are BA through BZ, the next 26 are CA through CZ, and so on up to the rightmost column IV. Rows are identified by numbers from 1 to 16384.

Each cell is also located on a specific sheet. When you start Excel it has 16 sheets, named *sheet1* through *sheet16*. You can add additional sheets up to a maximum of 255.

A *workbook* consists of one or more sheets saved together in the same disk file. In some cases you may find that a single sheet is all you need. Other times, the ability to use multiple sheets—the third dimension, if you will—can greatly simplify the task of organizing and working with your data.

Moving around in Excel

When you're working in Excel, the active cell is where you will enter, edit, and format data. The active cell is indicated by the *cell selector*, a black rectangle outlining the cell. Obviously you need a way to move the cell selector to different cells! You can move around with either the keyboard or the mouse.

Each sheet has its own cell selector. Moving the cell selector in one sheet does not affect the selector in other sheets.

Moving with the Mouse

With the mouse, move the cell selector to any visible cell by clicking on it. Move to another sheet by clicking on its tab. To move to a cell that is

not visible, use the scroll bars to bring the cell into view, and then click on the cell. You learned how to use scroll bars in Chapter 2; here's a brief refresher:

- To move up or down one row click the up or down scroll arrow.

- To move up or down one screen click between the scroll box and the up or down scroll arrow.

- To move up or down a variable amount drag the scroll box up or down on the scroll bar.

The horizontal scroll bar operates in the same manner.

Moving with the Keyboard

Here's how to move the cell selector with the keyboard:

To move	Press
Up or down one cell	↑ or ↓
Left or right one cell	← or →
Up or down one screen	PgUp or PgDn
Left or right one screen	Alt+PgUp or Alt+PgDn
To column A in the current row	Home
To cell A1 in the current sheet	Ctrl+Home
To the next or previous sheet	Ctrl+PgDn or Ctrl+PgUp

When a sheet contains data, you can use the End key for some particularly useful moves:

To move	**Press**
In any direction to the first data-containing cell that is next to an empty cell	End followed by an arrow key
To the last cell in the sheet that contains data	End, Home

Using Go To

If you know exactly where you're going, you can use the Go To command. This technique is particularly useful if your destination is far away—for example, if you wish to move from cell A1 to cell BX1266.

1. Select Edit ➤ Go To or press F5.

2. Excel displays the Go To dialog box, shown in Figure 10.3. Select a cell reference from the list, or enter it in the Reference text box.

3. Click the OK button.

OK

> ### NOTE
>
> In step 2 above, you can also enter a name that you have assigned to a specific location, or range, in the workbook. You'll learn about assigning names to ranges in Chapter 11.

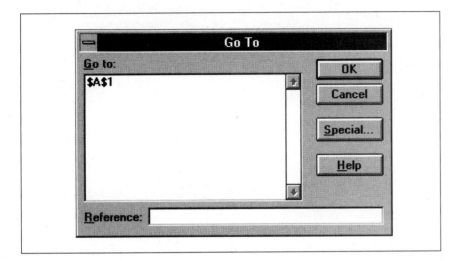

FIGURE 10.3

You can use the Go To dialog box to move quickly to any location in your workbook.

Types of Data

As I mentioned earlier, each cell in an Excel workbook can hold an item of data. There are several different types of data that you can use.

Numbers

A number is a value with which Excel can perform calculations. A number can contain the following characters:

- The digits 0–9
- A leading + or – sign

- A leading $
- A trailing %
- Parentheses
- A decimal point (period)
- Commas as thousands separators (e.g., 1,000,000)

A negative number can be entered with a leading minus sign or enclosed in parentheses. The way that numbers are displayed is controlled by the cell format, which is covered in Chapter 12.

Dates

When you enter a date in one of several formats, Excel recognizes it as a date and stores it as a special *date serial number*. A date serial number represents the number of days since January 1, 1900. For example, September 1, 1994 has the serial number 34578. The use of date serial numbers makes possible certain types of calculations, such as determining the number of days between two dates. The permitted date formats are shown here:

Format	Example
MM/DD/YY	6/1/94 or 06/01/1994
MMM-YY	Jun-94 (1st day of the month)
DD-MMM-YY	01-Jun-94
DD-MMM	01-Jun (current year assumed)

You'll learn how to control the way dates are displayed in Chapter 12.

Time

Like dates, times are stored as special serial numbers. The 24-hour day is represented by decimal values between 0 and 1. For example, 12:00 noon is 0.5, and 3:30 PM is 0.65. Excel recognizes the following formats as times:

Format	Example
HH:MM	12:45
HH:MM:SS	12:45:30
HH:MM AM/PM	12:45 AM
HH:MM:SS AM/PM	12:45:30 PM

Text

Text is anything that Excel does not treat as a number, date, or time. You can enter just about anything as text—names, addresses, etc. When you enter data into a cell that do not meet the format criteria for a date or time or contain characters not allowed in a number, Excel treats the data as a text entry. Here are some examples of entries that would be treated as text:

Entry	Reason
12 Oak Street	Contains non-number characters
John Smith	Contains non-number characters
10,00	Comma in wrong position
10:00AM	No space before "AM"
%8	% sign in wrong position

When you enter text that is longer than the width of the cell, the entire entry is displayed only if the cell(s) to the immediate right are empty. If the cell(s) to the right contain data, only part of the text entry is displayed (although the entire entry remains stored in the cell).

Formulas

A fifth kind of cell entry is a *formula*. Formulas are an important part of Excel. For example, the formula A5+A6 adds the numbers in cells A5 and A6 and displays the result. I'll cover formulas in detail in Chapter 13.

Entering Data

Now that you understand the different kinds of data that Excel can work with, we can get to the fun part—entering data into your workbook. The process is actually quite simple. When you enter data into a cell, it replaces any data that was there originally. Here's what to do:

1. Move the cell selector to the desired cell.

2. Start typing the entry. As you type, the data will appear in the cell and in the reference line. If you make an error, press Backspace to erase it, and then retype the entry.

3. To confirm the entry, click the Enter button on the formula bar, press ↵, or move the cell selector to another cell.

4. To cancel your entry, click the Cancel button on the formula bar or press Esc. If you cancel your entry, any data that was originally in the cell remains unchanged.

Entering Numbers or Dates as Text

There may be times when you want Excel to treat a number or a date as a label. For example, if you are using ZIP codes, entering them as labels rather than as numbers will enable printing and displaying the leading 0 in ZIP codes below 10000.

To enter as text data that Excel would normally treat as a number or date, precede it with ' (apostrophe). For example, for the ZIP code 01876 you would type

'01876

and then press ↵. The apostrophe is a *label prefix character* that instructs Excel to treat the data in the cell as text. You'll learn more about label prefix characters in Chapter 12.

> ### N O T E
>
> **To have all number entries in a range of workbook cells auto- matically treated as text (without entering the apostrophe), you can format the cells with the Text format before entering the data. See Chapter 12 for more information on cell formats.**

Saving Your Workbook

Save

You need to save your workbook in a disk file to have it available the next time you use Excel. To save a workbook, click the Save button on the Standard toolbar, or press Ctrl+S. One of two things will happen:

- If you have saved the workbook before, and it already has a name, Excel will save the file and return you to the workbook.

- If you haven't saved the workbook before, Excel will display the Save As dialog box, which is shown in Figure 10.4.

You can assign a name to the workbook that is one to eight characters long. The name must start with a letter, and can contain letters, num- bers, and the underscore character. Excel automatically adds a period and the extension XLS to the file name.

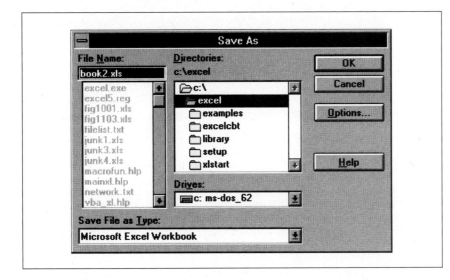

FIGURE 10.4

You use the Save As dialog box when saving a workbook for the first time.

Try to use descriptive names for your workbooks, even though creativity can be difficult when you're limited to a maximum of eight characters! Here are some examples:

Workbook contents	File name
1994 budget	BUDG_94
Sales projections for 1994	SALES_94
Capital costs	CAP_COST

Once the Save As dialog box is displayed, here's how you assign a name to your workbook:

1. Type the file name into the File Name box. The highlighted text that is displayed there will be replaced by what you type. If the

File **N**ame:

File Name box is not highlighted, press Alt+N before typing in the name.

2. Click the OK button or press ↵.

When you save a workbook for the first time, Excel may display the Summary Information dialog box. See the next section for details.

> ### N O T E
>
> It's a good idea to save a workbook at regular intervals— say every ten minutes—as you work on it, and whenever you take a break from your computer as well.

Entering Summary Information

Excel provides the option of saving a variety of summary information with each workbook. This information includes a workbook title, the subject, author, keywords, and comments. It can be very useful if you work on a large number of workbooks, or if you share workbooks with your co-workers.

You can display and edit the summary information at any time by selecting File ➤ Summary Info. Excel will display the Summary Information dialog box, shown in Figure 10.5.

Enter the desired information in the fields of the dialog box, and then click the OK button.

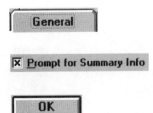

FIGURE 10.5

The Summary Info dialog box is used to record a variety of useful information about the workbook.

You can also specify that Excel display the Summary Info dialog box automatically when you save a new workbook for the first time:

1. Select Tools ➤ Options. Excel displays the Options dialog box.

2. Click the General tab, if necessary, to display the General section of the dialog box (shown in Figure 10.6).

3. Click the Prompt For Summary Info option to turn it on or off, as desired.

4. Click the OK button.

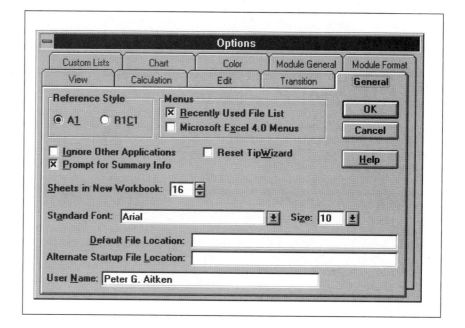

Closing a Workbook

When you have finished working on a workbook, and have saved it, you may want to *close* it and then continue working on another workbook. Closing a workbook removes it from the screen. To close a workbook, double-click the document control box at the left end of the menu bar.

If you haven't changed the workbook since you last saved it, it will be closed immediately. Otherwise Excel displays a dialog box asking if you want to save the changes to the workbook:

- Click the Yes button to save the changes, and then close the workbook.

- Click the No button to close the workbook without saving the changes. You will lose any changes that you made to the workbook since the last time you saved it.

- Click the Cancel button to return to the workbook without closing it.

Opening a Workbook

If you want to work on an existing workbook—one that you saved previously—you must *open* it. When you open a workbook, Excel reads it from disk and displays it ready for editing. To open a workbook, click the Open button on the Standard toolbar or press Ctrl+O.

Open

Excel will display the Open dialog box, shown in Figure 10.7. The components of the Open dialog box are as follows:

- The *File Name box* displays the name of the workbook to be opened.

- The *file list* displays the names of all the Excel workbooks in the current directory.

- The *Directories list* displays the names of the current directory at the top, and other directories in the box.

- The *Drives box* displays the letter and label of the current disk drive.

Follow these steps to open a workbook file:

1. Click the Open button on the Standard toolbar or press Ctrl+O to display the Open dialog box.

Open

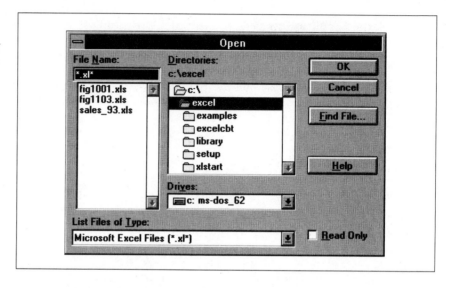

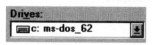

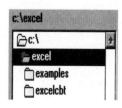

2. Highlight the desired file name in the file list, or type it into the File Name box.

3. Click the OK button or press ↵.

What if the workbook you want to open isn't listed? It's probably been saved to a different drive or directory. Here's what to do:

- To list files on a different disk, open the Drives box and select the desired drive.

- To list files in a different directory, double-click the directory name in the Directories list.

Starting a New Workbook

When you start Excel it displays a new, empty workbook on screen, ready for you to start entering data. There may also be times when you want to start a new workbook while you're working, for example, after closing another workbook. To do so, simply click the New button on the Standard toolbar.

New

Exiting Excel

When you're done using Excel, you should exit the program. You must exit Excel before exiting Windows or turning your computer off. To exit Excel, double-click the application control menu box (at the left end of the title bar) or press Alt+F4.

If you have not changed the workbook since you last saved it, Excel will exit immediately. Otherwise Excel displays a dialog box asking if you want to save the changes to the workbook:

- Click the Yes button to save the changes and then exit.

- Click the No button to exit without saving the changes. You will lose any changes that you made to the workbook since the last time you saved it.

- Click the Cancel button to return to the workbook without exiting or saving.

CHAPTER ELEVEN

Making Changes

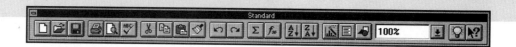

ONCE YOU HAVE started a workbook, it seems inevitable that you'll need to make changes to it. Excel provides a great deal of flexibility in changing your workbook. You can change the structure of the workbook or the data within it. This chapter shows you how, including the basics of working with ranges.

Editing Cell Data

To change the data in a cell, you must first move the cell selector to the cell. If the changes are major your best choice will be to replace old data by entering new data. For minor changes, however, you can use Excel's edit mode:

1. Press F2. Excel enters Edit mode, as indicated at the left end of the status bar. The Ready indicator changes to read "Edit" when you're in Edit mode. You can also double-click on the cell to be edited, or move the cell selector to the cell, click in the formula bar, and edit there. Excel displays a blinking vertical line in the cell. This is the *editing cursor*, and it tells you where your editing actions will take effect.

2. Type in new data and edit the cell data as desired (see below).

3. Now you can accept or cancel the changes:

 To accept the changes, click the Enter button on the formula bar or press ↵.

 To cancel the changes, click the Cancel button on the formula bar or press Esc.

While in Edit mode you can click anywhere in the cell to move the editing cursor to that location. You can also use the following keystrokes:

To do this...	Press this...
Move the cursor left or right one character	← or →
Move to the beginning or end of the cell	Home or End
Delete the character to the left of the cursor	Backspace
Delete the character to the right of the cursor	Del
Enter new data	Type the characters

Working with Ranges

The concept of a *range* is important to many of the things you'll do in Excel. A range is any rectangular block of cells, from a single cell to thousands of cells or an entire workbook. The only restriction is that a range be rectangular in shape. A range is referred to by its two *anchor cells*, the cells at the upper-left and lower-right corners. For example, the range starting at cell B2 and extending to cell F9 is referred to as B2:F9.

The advantage of ranges is that they permit Excel to treat a group of cells as a unit. Many of Excel's commands operate on ranges. For example, when changing cell format you can change the format of a single cell or of an entire range containing many cells. First, however, you must tell Excel which cells are in the range—this process is called *selecting*.

Selecting Data

The default selection is the single cell that the cell selector is on. To specify multiple cells, you must select the range.

As with most tasks in Excel, you can use either the mouse or the keyboard to select a range of data. To select with the mouse, simply point at one corner of the range and drag to the other corner. As you drag, the selected cells are highlighted. Release the mouse button, and the range remains highlighted on the screen.

To select a range with the keyboard:

1. Move the cell selector to the cell at one corner of the range.

2. Press and hold down the Shift key.

3. Use the arrow keys to move the cell selector to the opposite corner of the range.

4. Release the Shift key.

> **NOTE**
>
> **As you are selecting cells using either the mouse or keyboard, the reference bar displays the number of rows and columns currently highlighted. For example, 7R x 3C indicates that the selection currently covers 7 rows and 3 columns.**

Once you have selected a range, many commands you enter will affect every cell in that range. If you change your mind and want to cancel the selection without issuing a command, press Shift+Backspace.

Selection Shortcuts

Excel provides a few shortcuts for selecting certain parts of the workbook:

- To select an entire row, click the row heading or press Shift+Spacebar.

- To select an entire column, click the column heading or press Ctrl+Spacebar.

- To select the entire sheet, click the Select All button (the plain gray rectangle at the intersection of the column letters and row numbers) or press Ctrl+A.

Assigning Range Names

One of Excel's most powerful features is its ability to assign names to worksheet ranges. Once a range has been assigned a name, you can refer to the range by its name in formulas and when using the Go To command. This greatly simplifies many workbook tasks. It's a lot easier to remember that your sales figures are in the range named SALES than it is to remember they are in the range C5:D20. A range name can refer to anything from a single cell to an entire workbook.

Range names can be up to 255 characters long. They can contain letters, numbers, underscores (_), backslashes, (\), periods (.), and question marks (?). The first character of a range name must be a letter, the underscore character, or a backslash. Spaces are not allowed. Excel does not differentiate between uppercase and lowercase letters.

To create a new named range, change an existing named range, or delete a named range:

1. Select the range of cells.

2. Select Insert ➤ Name ➤ Define or press Ctrl+F3. Word displays the Define Name dialog box, shown in Figure 11.1.

The Names In Workbook list displays names of preexisting named ranges. The box at the top of the list may contain a suggested range name if the selected range of cells has a text label in the top or the left-most cell.

FIGURE 11.1

You use the Define Name dialog box to assign a name to a range of workbook cells.

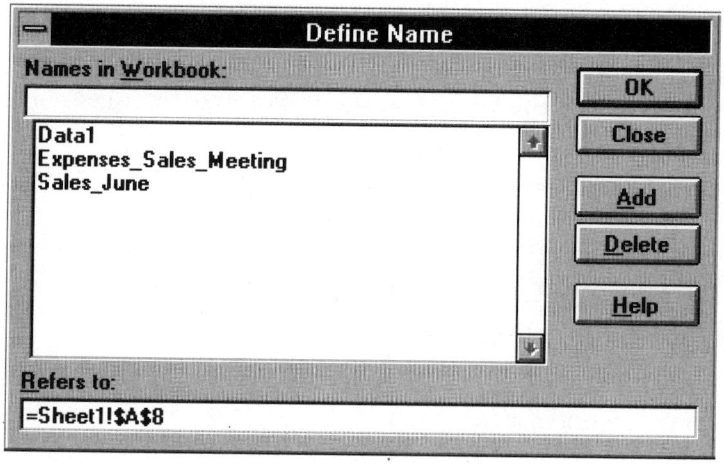

Define Name

Names in Workbook:

Data1
Expenses_Sales_Meeting
Sales_June

OK
Close
Add
Delete
Help

Refers to:
=Sheet1!$A$8

3. Take one of the following actions:

To assign a new name to the selected range, type the name in the box (or accept the suggested name) and then click the Add button.

To assign an existing name to the selected range, highlight the existing range name in the list and then click the Add button.

To delete an existing range name highlight the range name in the list and then click the Delete button.

4. When you are finished, click the OK button.

Here's a shortcut for assigning a name to a range:

1. Select the range of cells.

2. Click the Name Box at the left end of the formula bar.

3. Type in the range name.

4. Press ↵.

> ## N O T E
>
> **If the cell selector is on a cell that has been assigned a range name, or if you have selected a range that has been assigned a range name, the Name Box will display the range name instead of the cell address.**

Moving to Named Ranges

You can quickly move to and select any named range in the workbook:

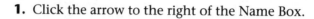

1. Click the arrow to the right of the Name Box.

2. Click the name of the desired range.

Shortcut Menus

When you click a workbook selection with the right mouse button, Excel displays a *shortcut menu* that contains commands that are often applied to cell selections. Figure 11.2 shows the shortcut menu displayed for a selection. The commands on the shortcut menu provide an alternative way of performing various actions. In all cases you can use the toolbar or the regular menus to perform the same commands. You'll learn how to apply the shortcut menu commands as needed throughout the book.

Moving and Copying Data

When you are working with Excel you will often find that you need to move or copy data to another part of the workbook.

1. Select the range of data to be moved or copied. Remember, a selection can be a single cell.

Copy   Cut

2. To copy the selected data, click the Copy button on the Standard toolbar or press Ctrl+C. To move the data, click the Cut button on the Standard toolbar or press Ctrl+X. As an alternative, display the selection's shortcut menu and select Cut or Copy.

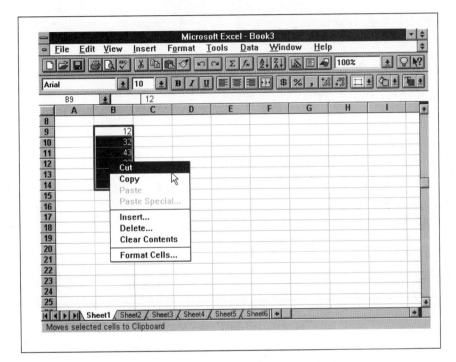

FIGURE 11.2

Display the shortcut menu by right-clicking a selection of cells.

3. Move the cell selector to the destination cell. If moving or copying a multiple cell range, move the cell selector to the upper-left corner of the destination range.

4. Click the Paste button on the Standard toolbar or press Ctrl+V. You can also display the cell's shortcut menu and select Paste.

Paste

Drag-and-Drop Shortcuts

Mouse users may prefer to use the drag-and-drop method for copying and moving data. It is particularly useful for single cells or relatively small selections. To move data:

1. Select the range to be moved.

2. Point to the border of the selection. The mouse cursor changes from a cross to an arrow.

3. Press the mouse button and drag. As the mouse cursor moves, an outline moves with it to indicate the size of the selection.

4. When the outline is over the cells to receive the data, release the mouse button.

To copy data, follow the same steps but press and hold down the Ctrl key before you start dragging. A small plus sign is displayed with the mouse cursor to indicate that you are copying data rather than moving it.

Deleting Data

To delete data from one or more cells, select the cells and then press Del. Mouse users can display the shortcut menu and select Clear Contents.

Undo

Being human, we all make mistakes. And being a good program, Excel provides a way for us to recover from at least some of our errors. The Undo command reverses most workbook actions, such as deleting data, moving or copying a range, and changing cell format. While not all actions can be undone, the mistakes you're most likely to make can be. You must issue the Undo command immediately after making the mistake, because it can undo only your most recent action.

To undo your last workbook change, click the Undo button on the Standard toolbar, press Ctrl+Z, or select Edit ➤ Undo. If your last action cannot be undone, the Undo command on the menu will be grayed, and Excel will beep if you click the Undo button or press Ctrl+Z.

Undo

If you change your mind you can "undo the undo"—in other words, redo the action that you just undid. To redo an action, click the Redo button on the Standard toolbar, or select Edit ➤ Redo.

Redo

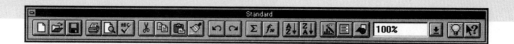

Inserting and Deleting Rows and Columns

Once a workbook has a modest amount of data in it, you may find the need to rearrange things a bit. You may want to insert new rows or columns, or delete existing ones. The ability to add and delete rows and columns means that you don't have to plan your entire workbook from the very beginning, but rather can modify it as you go along.

Inserting Rows and Columns

To insert a single row or column:

1. Move the cell selector to the location for the new row or column. For example, to insert a new column between existing columns B and C, position the cell selector in column B.

2. Right-click the column letter or row number to display the shortcut menu.

3. Click Insert.

To insert multiple rows or columns:

1. Select a range of cells that spans the number of rows or columns to insert. For example, to insert three new rows numbered 3 to 5, you would select any range that spans the existing rows 3 through 5.

2. Select Insert ➤ Rows or Insert ➤ Columns.

Inserting new rows or columns never causes Excel to delete data in existing rows or columns. Existing columns are moved to the right, or existing rows are moved down, to make room. For example, if you insert a new column B, the original column B will become column C, the original column C will become column D, and so on. The only exception is if there is data in the last row or column of the sheet, in which case the Insert command will not be allowed.

Deleting Rows and Columns

You can delete one or more rows or columns from your sheet. When you do so, columns to the right of the deleted column(s) move over, or rows below the deleted row(s) move up, to fill in. When you delete a row or column, the data is deleted as well. To delete a single row or column:

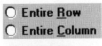

1. Right-click the heading of the row or column to be deleted to display the shortcut menu.

2. Select Delete.

To delete two or more adjacent rows or columns:

1. Select a range that spans the rows or columns to be deleted.

2. Select Edit ➤ Delete. Excel displays the Delete dialog box, which is shown in Figure 11.3.

3. Select either the Entire Row or Entire Column option.

4. Click the OK button.

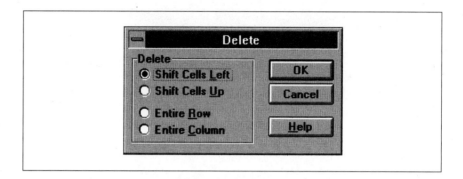

FIGURE 11.3

The Delete dialog box can be used to delete entire rows and columns or individual cells.

N O T E

When you are working in a multiple-sheet workbook, deleting or adding rows and columns affects only the current sheet.

Changing Column Width and Row Height

An Excel workbook starts out with a default column width and row height. Column width, which is measured in characters, is approximately 9. This means that a default column is wide enough to display 9 characters in the standard font. You can change the width of columns to any value between 0 and 255 characters.

Row height is measured in points, with 1 point equal to $1/72$ of an inch. The default row height setting is 12.75 points. Excel will automatically increase the height of a row to fit the largest font in that row (you'll learn about changing fonts in Chapter 12). You can also change row height manually.

Changing Column Width

The quickest way to change the width of a single column is with the mouse.

1. Point at the border to the right of the heading (letter) of the column. The mouse pointer will change to a vertical line with left- and right-pointing arrows.

2. Drag the column to the desired width and release the mouse button.

If you want to specify an exact numerical width for a column, follow these steps:

1. Right-click the column heading to display its shortcut menu.

2. Select Column Width. Excel displays the Column Width dialog box, shown in Figure 11.4.

3. Enter the desired column width, in characters, in the Column Width box.

4. Click the OK button.

You can also change the width of more than one column at the same time.

1. Select a range that spans the columns whose width you want to change.

2. Select Format ➤ Column ➤ Width. Excel displays the Column Width dialog box, shown in Figure 11.4.

FIGURE 11.4

You can specify an exact column width in the Column Width dialog box.

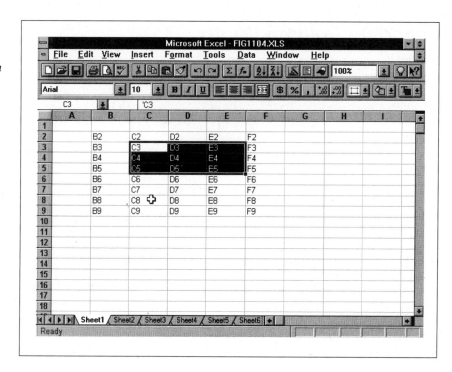

3. Enter the desired column width, in characters, in the Column Width box.

4. Click the OK button.

TIP

To set the width of *all* columns in the sheet, select the entire worksheet by clicking the Select All button in step 1 above.

Using AutoFit Column Width

A really useful feature is Excel's ability to automatically set a column width to display the widest data in the column. Here's how to do it:

1. Select a range that spans the columns to be autofit. For a single column, move the cell selector to any cell in the column.

2. Select F<u>o</u>rmat ➤ <u>C</u>olumn ➤ <u>A</u>utofit Selection.

> To quickly autofit a single column, double-click the border to the right of its column heading.

If you autofit a column and then change its data, the width will not automatically change to fit the new data. You must issue the F<u>o</u>rmat ➤ <u>C</u>olumn ➤ <u>A</u>utofit Selection command again.

Setting the Default Column Width

You can change the default column width for a sheet. The new default width will be applied to all columns in that sheet whose width has not been customized.

1. Select F<u>o</u>rmat ➤ <u>C</u>olumn ➤ <u>S</u>tandard Width. Excel displays the Standard Width dialog box, shown in Figure 11.5.

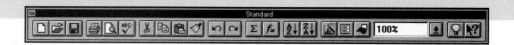

FIGURE 11.5

The Standard Width dialog box is used to set the sheet's default column width.

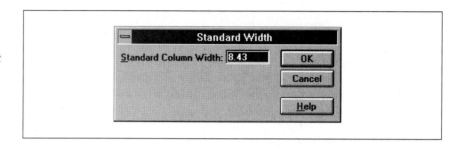

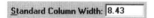

2. Enter the new standard column width in the Standard Column Width box.

3. Click the OK button.

Changing Row Height

You can change the height of a single row in the same way you change column width:

1. Point at the border below the heading (letter) of the row. The mouse pointer will change to a horizontal line with up- and down-pointing arrows.

2. Drag the row to the desired height and release the mouse button.

If you want to specify an exact numerical height for a row, follow these steps:

1. Right-click the row heading to display its shortcut menu.

2. Select Row Height. Excel displays the Row Height dialog box, shown in Figure 11.6.

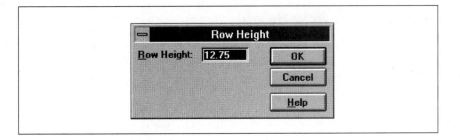

FIGURE 11.6

You can specify an exact row height in the Row Height dialog box.

3. Enter the desired row height, in points, in the Row Height box.

4. Click the OK button.

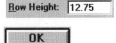

You can also change the height of more than one row at the same time.

1. Select a range that spans the rows whose height you want to change.

2. Select For̲mat ➤ R̲ow ➤ He̲ight. Excel displays the Row Height dialog box, shown above in Figure 11.6.

3. Enter the desired row height, in points, in the Row Height box.

4. Click the OK button.

T I P

To set the height of all rows in the sheet, select the entire sheet by clicking the Select All button in step 1 above.

Using AutoFit Row Height

Remember that Excel's default setting for row height is AutoFit, where the row height is adjusted to match the largest font in the row. If you have manually changed the height of one or more rows, you can return them to AutoFit as follows:

1. Select a range that spans the rows to be set to AutoFit. For a single row, move the cell selector to any cell in the row.

2. Select Format ➤ Row ➤ AutoFit.

T I P

To quickly set a single row to AutoFit, double-click the bottom border of its row heading.

Using Cell Notes

Excel's Note feature can help you remember certain points about the data with which you are working. You can attach a text note to any cell without actually including that note *in* the cell. Here's how:

1. Move the cell selector to the cell.

2. Select Insert ➤ Note or press Shift+F2. Excel displays the Cell Note dialog box, shown in Figure 11.7.

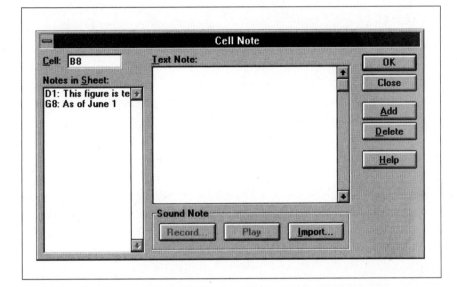

FIGURE 11.7

The Cell Note dialog box lets you attach text notes to cells in your workbook.

3. Type the note in the Text Note box. If the cell already has a note attached to it, the note will be displayed here. You can use the standard editing keys while entering text in this box.

4. When you are finished, click the OK button.

Cells that have a note attached are displayed with a small red dot in the upper-right corner. To display or edit a cell's note, move the cell selector to the cell and select Insert ➤ Note or press Shift+F2. Chapter 15 shows you how to print cell notes.

CHAPTER TWELVE

Formatting
Workbook Data

AS YOU ENTER and edit information in your workbook, you'll often want to change the appearance, or format, of the data. With Excel's formatting commands you can do more than create a more attractive workbook—you can also improve its clarity and impact. Any formatting changes you make are reflected in printed output as well as on-screen.

Number Format

Number format controls the way that number data is displayed. Clearly, different display formats are appropriate for different kinds of data. Financial figures should be displayed with a currency symbol, interest rates with a percent sign, and so on. Excel provides an extensive variety of number format options. Number formats apply to dates and times as well, since, as you may recall from Chapter 10, dates and times are stored as special serial numbers.

The default number format for all workbook cells is General. General format displays numbers without currency symbols or commas, and with as many decimal places as required. The only exceptions are if you enter a date or time in one of the accepted formats (as explained in Chapter 10), or a number with a leading currency symbol or trailing percent sign. In these cases Excel automatically assigns the appropriate format (Date, Time, Currency, or Percent) to the cell.

Changing Number Format

To change the number format of one or more cells:

1. Select the cell(s) to be changed.

2. Select Format ➤ Cells or press Ctrl+1. You can also right-click the selection and then select Format Cells from the shortcut menu.

3. Excel displays the Format Cells dialog box. Click the Number tab if necessary to display the number format section, as shown in Figure 12.1.

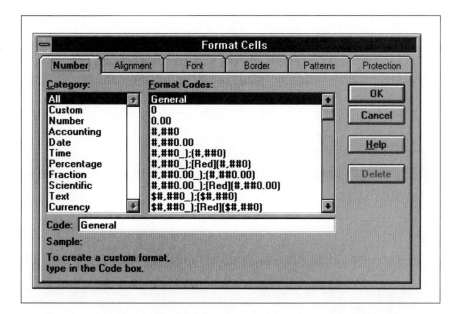

FIGURE 12.1

You use the Number section of the Format Cells dialog box to change number display format.

4. In the Category list, select a format category. In the Format Codes list, select the specific format desired. The Sample section of the dialog box shows what your data will look like with the currently selected format codes.

5. Click the OK button or press ↵.

> ## N O T E
>
> The Sample section of the Cell Format dialog box uses the number in the selected cell, or in the top-left corner of the selected range. If this cell is empty, no sample will be displayed.

You should remember that number format has no effect on the display of cells that contain text or are empty. You can, therefore, assign a number format to a range of cells and it will affect only those cells that contain numbers. If a number is later placed in a previously numberless cell, however, it will display with the format that was assigned earlier.

Number Format Shortcuts

Some of Excel's most commonly used number formats have been assigned to buttons on the Formatting toolbar. There are also buttons for changing decimal display. Finally, there are some keyboard shortcuts for applying formats.

With the mouse, select the cell(s) to be formatted, and then:

Currency

- To apply Currency format, click the Currency button on the Formatting toolbar.

Percent

- To apply Percent format, click the Percent button on the Formatting toolbar.

Comma

- To apply Comma format, click the Comma button on the Formatting toolbar.

- To increase the number of digits displayed to the right of the decimal point, click the Increase Decimal button on the Formatting toolbar.

- To decrease the number of digits displayed to the right of the decimal point, click the Decrease Decimal button on the Formatting toolbar.

Increase Decimal

Decrease Decimal

N O T E

If you try to change the decimal display on cells that have a format in which decimals are not used, Excel beeps.

The keyboard formatting shortcuts are as follows:

To apply	Press
General number format	Ctrl+Shift+~
Currency format with two decimal places	Ctrl+Shift+$
Percentage format with no decimal places	Ctrl+Shift+%
Exponential number format with two decimal places	Ctrl+Shift+^
Date format with day, month, and year	Ctrl+Shift+#
Time format with the hour and minute, and A.M. or P.M.	Ctrl+Shift+@
Two-decimal–place format with commas	Ctrl+Shift+!

Data Alignment and Orientation

Excel's default is to display text entries left-aligned in the cell, and to display number entries right-aligned. This arrangement is referred to as General alignment. You can modify the alignment of cell data, and can also change its display orientation.

Changing Data Alignment

Left Align

Center

Right Align

Data can be displayed left-aligned, right-aligned, or centered in the cell. For example, a table of data that includes numbers and column headings may be easier to read if both the headings and numbers are center-aligned. To change data alignment:

1. Select the cell(s) to be changed.

2. On the Formatting toolbar, click either the Left Align, Center, or Right Align button.

When the cell selector is on a cell that has its alignment set to Left, Center, or Right, the corresponding button on the Standard toolbar will appear depressed. To reset the cell to general alignment, toggle the button off.

N O T E

Alignment is relevant only when the data is narrower than the cell it's in. Otherwise the data fills the cell and the alignment setting has no effect on the way the data is displayed.

Wrapping Text in a Cell

For text data that is wider than the cell it's in, Excel's default is to display the label on one line. If the cells to the right are empty the entire label is displayed. Otherwise, it is truncated. You can also *wrap* text that is wider than its cell. Wrapped text automatically extends down two or more lines. Figure 12.2 shows a comparison between wrapped and normal text.

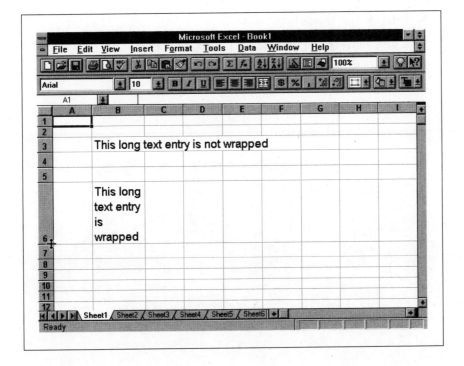

FIGURE 12.2

The Wrap text option can be used to split long text entries over two or more lines.

To enable text wrapping:

1. Select the cell(s) in which you want to enable wrapping.

2. Choose Format ➤ Cells or press Ctrl+1. You can also right-click the selection and select Format Cells from the shortcut menu.

3. Excel displays the Format Cells dialog box. Click the Alignment tab, if necessary, to display the alignment options, shown in Figure 12.3.

4. Turn on the Wrap Text option.

5. If you want the lines of text justified at the right and left edges of the cell, turn on the Justify option. Otherwise, lines of text will be left-justified.

6. Click the OK button or press ↵.

FIGURE 12.3

You set data alignment options in the Format Cells dialog box.

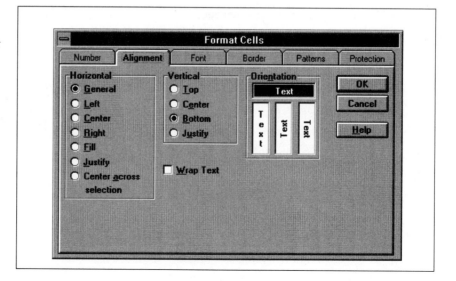

Using Fonts

Excel gives you complete control over the size and appearance of the fonts used to display and print your data. Using fonts in Excel is very similar to using fonts in Word. You can not only select the font and font size, but also apply underline, boldface, and italic formats. Fonts apply to both number and text data. To change the fonts in your worksheet:

1. Select the cell(s) whose font you want to change.

2. To change the font, pull down the font list on the Formatting toolbar and select the desired font.

3. To change the font size, pull down the font size list on the Formatting toolbar and select the desired point size.

4. To change the font appearance, click the Bold, Italic, and/or Underline button(s) on the Formatting toolbar.

Borders

You can use borders to help you format and organize a worksheet. Borders can separate headings from data, call attention to summary cells, and make the worksheet easier to read.

To apply borders to worksheet cells:

1. Select the cell(s) to which you want to apply borders.

2. Click the arrow next to the Borders button on the Formatting toolbar. Excel displays a palette of the available border selections.

3. On the Borders palette, click the desired border style.

Borders

Borders

Note that the Borders button displays the border style that you selected last. To apply that border style to the selected cells, simply click the Border button—there's no need to display the Borders palette.

Colors and Patterns

Since most computers these days are equipped with color displays, you can make good use of Excel's color capabilities to improve the appearance of your worksheets.

N O T E

You can print in color only if you have a color-capable printer. But even if you are limited to a black-and-white printer, you can still use color for your screen display.

Changing Font Color

Font Color

To change the color of the font used to display data:

1. Select the cell(s) whose font color you want to change.

2. Click the arrow next to the Font Color button on the Formatting toolbar. Excel displays a color palette.

3. Click the desired color.

Font Color

The Font Color button displays the color that you selected most recently. To apply that color to the selected cells, simply click the Font Color button.

Changing Background Color

To change the background color of cells:

1. Select the cell(s) whose background color you want to change.

2. Click the arrow next to the Color button on the Formatting toolbar. Excel displays a color palette.

3. Click the desired color.

The Color button displays the background color that you applied most recently. To apply that color to the background of selected cells, simply click the Color button on the Formatting toolbar.

Color

Color

Using Patterns

In addition to changing the color of your cell backgrounds, you can apply a variety of patterns, such as diagonal lines, cross-hatches, and stippling. The pattern you select will be combined with the cell's background color. To select a background pattern:

1. Select the cell(s) to be modified.

2. Choose Format ➤ Cells or press Ctrl+1. You can also right-click the selection and choose Format Cells from the shortcut menu.

3. Excel displays the Format Cells dialog box. If necessary, click the Patterns tab to display the Patterns section of the dialog box, shown in Figure 12.4.

FIGURE 12.4

You can select the color and pattern for cell backgrounds in the Format Cells dialog box.

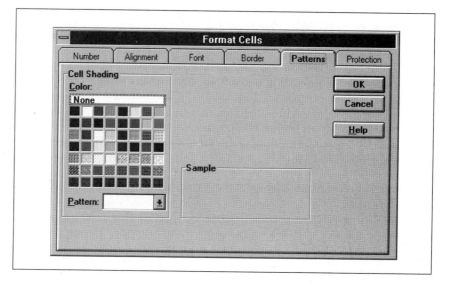

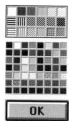

4. Pull down the Pattern list and select the desired pattern. Select the plain white pattern to remove an existing pattern.

5. To change backgound color, click the desired color in the Color palette.

6. Click the OK button or press ↵.

Using AutoFormat

When your worksheet data is organized in tables, the AutoFormat command can greatly simplify the task of formatting. AutoFormat provides

a variety of predefined table formats, including font, number format, borders, and shading. With a few keystrokes or mouse clicks you can apply a predefined format to a table in your worksheet. You can use a predefined table format as-is, or apply it and later modify it to suit your specific needs.

1. Select the range of cells to be formatted. Or, to format an existing table, place the cell selector in any cell in the table. In this context a table is defined as a range of cells surrounded on all four sides by blank cells (or the edge of the worksheet).

2. Select Format ➤ AutoFormat. Excel displays the AutoFormat dialog box, shown in Figure 12.5

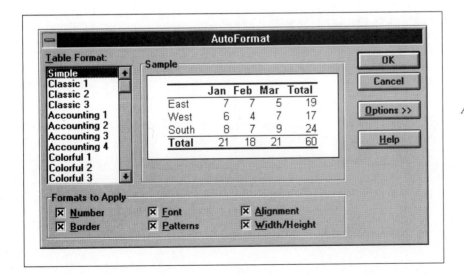

FIGURE 12.5

You can apply predefined table formats to worksheet data using the AutoFormat dialog box.

3. Scroll through the Table Format list. The Sample box shows the appearance of the highlighted format.

Options >>

4. To apply only part of the predefined format, click the Options button to display the Formats To Apply section of the dialog box (shown displayed in the figure). Turn options on or off to control which aspects of the predefined format will be used. The Sample box shows you the effect of your selections.

OK

5. Click the OK button or press ↵.

Once a predefined format has been applied to the worksheet, you can modify it as desired.

Working with Styles

A *style* is a defined set of cell formats that has been saved under an as-signed name. A style can include all aspects of cell formatting—font, color, number format, alignment, borders, patterns, and protection. Ex-cel comes with several predefined styles, and you can also create your own. If you use a particular combination of cell formatting frequently, you can define it as a style to save time. Also, if you later modify the style definition, all cells that have that style assigned will automatically change to reflect the new formatting. The default is for all cells to be as-signed the Normal style. Note that when you change a cell's format, such as its font or number format, your changes are applied on top of the formats defined by the cell's style.

Defining a Style

To define a new style:

1. Move the cell selector to a cell that has the formatting you want in the new style.

2. Select Format ➤ Style. Excel displays the Style dialog box, shown in Figure 12.6.

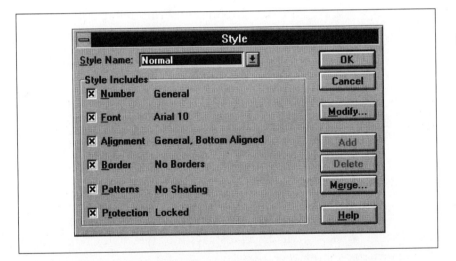

3. The Style Name box displays the name of the style currently assigned to the cell. Type in the name you want to use for the new style.

4. Click the OK button. The new style will be assigned to the selected cell and added to the style list.

Modifying a Style

You can modify an existing style at any time. Any modifications that you make will immediately be reflected in all workbook cells that have that style assigned. To modify a style:

1. Select Format ➤ Style. Excel will display the Style dialog box with the style name displayed.

2. Click the Modify button. Excel will display the Format Cells dialog box. Use the various components of this dialog box to modify formatting as desired.

3. When you are done making changes in the Format Cells dialog box, click the OK button. You will return to the Style dialog box.

4. Click the OK button or press ↵.

Applying a Style

To apply a style to workbook cells:

1. Select the cell(s) to which you want to apply the style.

2. Select Format ➤ Style. Excel displays the Style dialog box, shown above in Figure 12.6.

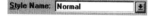

3. Pull down the Style Name list and highlight the desired style name.

4. In the Style Includes section, select options to specify the components of the style formatting that you want applied. For example, leave the Number option on to have the style's number

format applied to the cell. Turn the Number option off to have the cell keep its original number format. To apply all components of the style leave all options turned on.

5. Click the OK button or press ↵.

The Format Painter

The Format Painter simplifies the task of copying formatting from one region of the workbook to another. Here's how it works:

1. Move the cell selector to a cell that has the formatting you want to copy.

2. To copy the formats to a single destination, click the Format Painter button on the Formatting toolbar. To copy the formats to more than one destination, double-click the Format Painter button. The mouse cursor will display as a cross with a small paintbrush symbol.

Format Painter

3. Click the destination cell, or drag over the destination range.

4. If you double-clicked the Format Painter button in step 2, repeat step 3 as many times as needed to paint the format to all the desired destinations. Then, toggle the Format Painter button off to terminate painting.

CHAPTER THIRTEEN

Formulas
and Functions

BEING ABLE TO put numbers and labels in your workbooks is just the beginning with Excel. You'll start to see the real power of this program when you begin to use formulas. A *formula* performs calculations on numerical data in the workbook. The calculations can be as simple as adding up a column of numbers, or as complex as calculating depreciation on a fleet of oil tankers. This chapter shows you how to use formulas, both ones you create yourself and the ones that are built into Excel.

Creating a Formula

A formula has to specify two things—what data is to be used, and what operation is to be performed. Let's look at a simple example. Enter the following into a workbook cell:

=5+4

Once you confirm the entry you'll see that the cell displays 9. Congratulations! You've just written your first formula. Look now at the parts of the formula. The 5 and 4 are the data, of course. The + between the 4 and 5 is an *operator* telling Excel what to do with the data—in this case, add them together. The leading = tells Excel that the cell contains a formula.

Formula Data

In the example above, the formula data consisted of numbers entered directly into the formula. Such numbers are called *constants*.

Formulas can also operate on data already in the workbook, and in fact this is the way you'll use them most often. Let's rewrite the above

formula. Place the value **5** in cell A1, and the value **4** in cell A2. Then in cell A3 enter the following formula:

=A1+A2

In this case the formula contains two cell addresses, called *references*, that specify the location of the data to be used. The formula will again evaluate to 9. If you now change the value in cell A1 to 10, the formula display immediately changes to 14, because when you change workbook data, formulas based on the data are automatically updated. The A1 and A2 references tell the formula to use the data in those cells. If you don't specify a sheet in a reference the current sheet is assumed. You can also reference cells in other sheets in a formula. For example, to display in a cell in Sheet1 the sum of cells A1 and A2 from Sheet2 you would type:

=Sheet2!A1+Sheet2!A2

The third way to specify data is by using names that you have assigned to workbook cells. If, for example, you had used the Insert ➤ Name ➤ Define command (as covered in Chapter 11) to assign the names Data1 and Data2 to cells A1 and A2, you could write the formula as follows:

=Data1+Data2

NOTE

The simplest type of formula consists of only a single cell reference, as in =A2. You can use formulas like this to "copy" data from one cell to other cells.

Operators

Operators are symbols that instruct Excel how to perform calculations in a formula. Excel's operators fall into three categories: Arithmetic, Logical, and Text.

Arithmetic Operators

Excel has six arithmetic operators that you can use in formulas. They are explained below. I have used constants in the examples, but remember that you can use cell addresses or assigned names as well.

Operator	Action	Example	Result
+	Addition	=4+5	9
-	Subtraction	=10-4	6
/	Division	=20/4	5
*	Multiplication	=2*6	12
%	Percent	15%	0.15
^	Exponentiation	4^2	16

The first four operators in this table are probably familiar to most readers, but the last two may not be. The Percent operator must be placed after a number, and has the effect of dividing the number by 100 to express the percent value as a decimal. The Exponentiation operator raises a number to a power. For example, 4^2 is the same as 4*4, 3^4 is the same as 3*3*3*3, and so on.

Logical Operators

There are also six *logical* operators that are used to perform comparisons between values. For example, you can ask whether two values are equal to each other. The result of a formula that uses a logical operator is either TRUE or FALSE depending on the comparison being performed.

Operator	Comparison	Example	Result
=	Equal to	=5=6	FALSE
>	Greater than	=5>6	FALSE
<	Less than	=5<6	TRUE
>=	Greater than or equal to	=5>=6	FALSE
<=	Less than or equal to	=5<=6	TRUE
<>	Not equal to	=5<>6	TRUE

In the workbook a logical formula's result is displayed as either TRUE or FALSE. Mathematically, however, the result is treated as either 0 (FALSE) or 1 (TRUE). Here's an illustration. Enter the formula

    =5<6

in cell A1. When you confirm the entry it will display TRUE since 5 is indeed less than 6. Now in cell A2 enter the formula

    =2+A1

You'll see it displays as 3. The TRUE result of the formula in cell A1 is treated as the value 1. If you now edit the formula in cell A1 to read

    =5>6

you'll see that cell A1 displays as FALSE and cell A2 displays as 2.

Text Operator

There is a single text operator that operates on worksheet labels. This operator, &, joins two labels together. For example, if cell A1 contains the label Pushbutton and cell A2 contains the label Guide, then the formula

    =A1&A2

will evaluate to PushbuttonGuide. Note that if one or both cells contain a value, the operator treats them as text. Thus, if cells A1 and A2 contain the values 3 and 4 respectively, then

    =A1&A2

evaluates to the value 34. If, however, cell A1 contains the value 3 and cell A2 contains the label Data, then the formula evaluates to the label 3Data.

Operator Precedence

A formula that contains more than one operator can be confusing. Here's an example. The formula

    =5+2*3

could be evaluated two ways. If the + operation is performed first, the formula becomes

    =7*3

and evaluates to 21. If, however, the multiplication is performed first, the formula becomes

    =5+6

and evaluates to 11. Which is correct?

The answer is provided by Excel's *operator precedence*. Each operator has a precedence level that controls when it is performed in relation to other operators. Excel's operators are listed in order of decreasing precedence in this table.

Operator(s)	Action
-	Negation (as in -4)
%	Percent
^	Exponentiation
* and /	Multiplication and division
+ and -	Addition and subtraction
= > < >= <= <>	Comparison

Operators with the same precedence, such as * and /, are performed in left-to-right order in a formula. Given these precedence levels we can see that in the formula

    =5+2*3

the multiplication, having a higher precedence, will be performed first and the result will be 11.

Using Parentheses in Formulas

What can you do if you want to use a different operator precedence from Excel's default operator precedence? In the formula =5+2*3, for example, you might want the addition to be performed first. You can use parentheses to control the order of evaluation.

When a formula contains parentheses, anything inside parentheses is evaluated first regardless of operator precedence. Thus, if you write

=(5+2)*3

the 5+2 will be performed first because of the parentheses and the formula will evaluate to 21. When using parentheses in a formula, keep these points in mind:

- Parentheses must always be paired. There must be a left parenthesis for each right parenthesis.

- Parentheses can be nested, as in =5*(4+2^(2+1)). Evaluation always starts with the inner set of parentheses and works its way outward. Thus, the 2+1 would be performed first in this example.

- You can use parentheses in a formula even when they are not needed to modify evaluation order. This is particularly useful with long and complex formulas, when judicious use of parentheses can improve clarity.

If you attempt to enter a formula that contains unmatched parentheses, Excel displays a dialog box with the "Parentheses do not Match" message. Click the OK button to return to the cell to edit and correct the mistake.

Entering Formulas

You enter a formula into a cell like other workbook information, simply by typing it in. As you type, your entry appears in the current cell as well as on the formula bar.

When the formula is complete you complete the entry by clicking the Enter button on the formula bar, by pressing ↵, or by moving the cell selector to another cell. You can cancel your entry by clicking the Cancel button or by pressing Esc.

> **N O T E**
>
> **When you enter a right parenthesis in a formula, Excel briefly emphasizes the matching left parenthesis in the formula display in the cell (not in the formula bar). This ensures you that the formula contains a matching left parenthesis for every right parenthesis.**

In many formulas that you create, you will be using references or names to refer to data located in specific workbook cells. You can type a reference or a name directly into a formula, but there are some special Excel features that can make things easier.

Entering References in Formulas

The easiest way to enter a reference in a formula is with Point mode. You literally point to the cell or cells that you want to reference, and Excel automatically enters their address in the formula. You can point using either the mouse or the keyboard. With the mouse:

1. Enter the formula up to the point at which you need the reference.

2. Move the mouse pointer to the cell that you want to reference in the formula. If it's not in view, you can use the scroll bars or sheet tabs to bring it into view.

3. To reference a single cell, click it. To reference a range of cells, drag over them.

4. After you click or drag, the reference address is entered in the formula and the cell or range is surrounded by an animated border. The mode indicator on the Status bar displays Point.

5. If you made an error, repeat step 3 to specify the correct reference.

6. Continue typing in the formula.

If you prefer using the keyboard:

1. Enter the formula up to the point at which you need the reference.

2. Use the movement keys to move the dotted outline to the cell that you want to reference.

3. To reference that one cell, go to step 4. To reference a range, press and hold down the Shift key and use the movement keys to expand the dotted outline to cover the range.

4. Continue typing in the formula.

A concrete example may help you to understand this process. Let's use Point mode to enter a formula in cell A5 that adds the numbers in cells A1 and A2 and divides the sum by 2.

1. Move the cell selector to cell A5.

2. Type =(.

3. Press ↑ four times to move the dotted outline to cell A1. You'll see that the formula now reads =(A1.

4. Type +.

5. Press ↑ three times to move the dotted outline to cell A2. The
   formula now reads =(A1+A2.

6. Type)/2.

7. Click the Enter button or press ↵.

Entering Names in Formulas

If you have assigned names to cells in your workbook, you can use
them to refer to cells in formulas. As I have mentioned, you can always
just type in an assigned name. There's an easier way, however, that
saves time and reduces the chance of errors.

1. Enter the formula up to the point at which you need to enter
   a name.

2. Press F3 to display the Paste Name dialog box, which is shown
   in Figure 13.1.

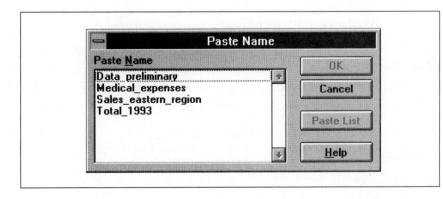

FIGURE 13.1

*You can use the Paste
Name dialog box to
quickly and accurately
insert a name in a
formula.*

3. Highlight the desired name in the list.

OK

4. Click the OK button or press ↵. The selected name is entered in the formula.

5. Continue typing in the formula.

N O T E

If the Paste Name dialog box is not displayed when you press F3, the workbook contains no assigned range names.

Using Functions

A *function* is a formula that is built into Excel. There is a wide variety of functions available to perform many commonly needed calculations. A function can be used by itself in a cell, or as part of a formula. Functions can save a great deal of time and effort. Instead of having to figure out the formula yourself, all you need to do is enter the function name and specify which data it is to operate on.

Each function has two parts: a *name*, which specifies the calculation performed, and *arguments* that specify which data to use (a few functions take no argument). Here's an example. If you wanted to add all the values in cells A1 through A10, you could type:

=A1+A2+A3+A4+A5+A6+A7+A8+A9+A10

or you could use the SUM() function as shown here:

=SUM(A1:A10)

SUM is the function name, and the range reference in the parentheses is the argument. This function takes only one argument, but others take more than one. When more than one argument is required, they must be separated by commas. An argument can be a constant, a reference, a range name, or even another function.

Excel provides a large number of functions, way too many to cover in this book. For full reference information please refer to the Excel Help system:

1. In Ready mode, press F1 to display the Help Table Of Contents screen.

2. Select Reference Information.

3. Select Worksheet Functions. Help displays the screen shown in Figure 13.2.

4. Select the topic of interest. For example, to see a list of categories of functions, select Worksheet Functions Listed By Category.

Entering Functions

A function and its arguments can be typed directly into a cell formula. As described earlier in the chapter you can use Point mode to enter cell references as function arguments, and you can also press F3 to display the Paste Name dialog box to insert a range name. However, it is usually easier, particularly when you are not all that familiar with the functions and their arguments, to use the Function Wizard.

FIGURE 13.2

You can obtain different kinds of information about Excel's functions from this Help screen.

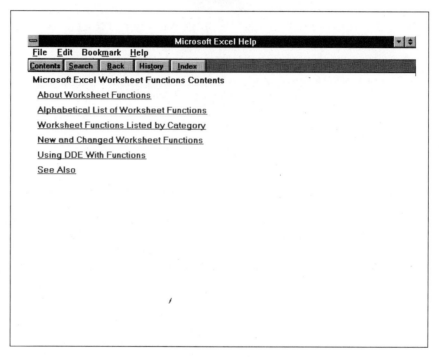

The Function Wizard

The Function Wizard guides you through the steps of selecting a function and entering its arguments. Here's how to use it:

1. Start entering the formula (for example, type **=**). At the point at which you need to enter the function, stop.

2. Click the Function Wizard button. There's one on the Standard toolbar as well as one on the formula bar. Excel displays the Function Wizard dialog box, shown in Figure 13.3.

Function Wizard

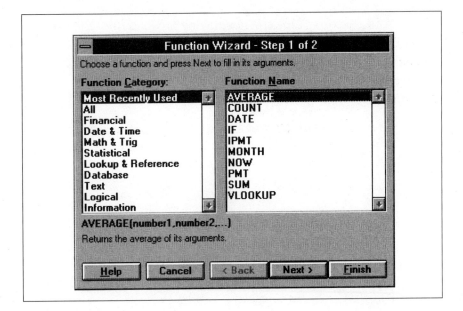

FIGURE 13.3

The Function Wizard walks you through the steps of entering a function and its arguments.

3. In the Function category list, click the category of functions from which you want to select. Select Most Recently Used for a list of the functions you have used recently.

4. In the Function name list, click the name of the desired function. Below the list Excel displays a brief description of the highlighted function.

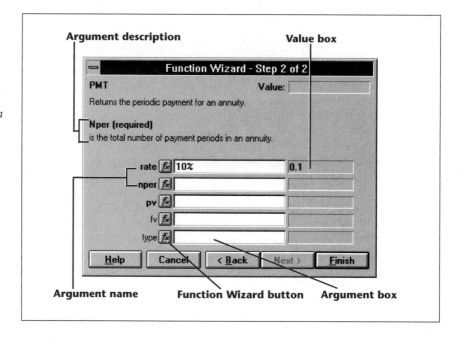

Next >

5. Click the Next button. The next dialog box describes the function further, and if the function requires arguments, it presents one or more boxes in which you specify each argument. Figure 13.4 shows the dialog box for the PMT() function, as well as some important parts of the dialog box:

- The argument description explains the argument whose box is currently active (as indicated by the vertical cursor). Click or press Tab or Shift+Tab to move between boxes.

- The name of each argument.

FIGURE 13.4

The second Function Wizard dialog box prompts you for the arguments required by the selected function, in this case PMT().

- The Function Wizard button lets you use the Function Wizard to enter a function as an argument.

- The argument box lets you enter a constant or a reference as an argument.

- The value box displays the current value of the selected argument (if one has been entered).

6. To enter an argument, activate the corresponding box and then do one of the following:

- Type in a constant, cell reference, function, or range name.

- Use Point mode to specify a cell reference.

- Press F3 and select a range name from the Paste Name dialog box.

- Click the Function Wizard button and enter a function.

7. While working in this dialog box, click the Help button to view detailed Help information about the selected function.

8. Once all the arguments have been entered, click the Finish button. The function and its arguments will be entered in the workbook cell.

The AutoSum Tool

One of the most commonly used functions is SUM(), which calculates the sum of a range of values. In many cases, the SUM() function is entered in the cell just below the column of values, or to the right of the

row of values, to be summed. Excel's AutoSum tool simplifies the task of summing columns or rows of values:

AutoSum

1. Move the cell selector to the cell in which you want the sum. It is ideal, although not required, if this cell is just below the column or to the right of the row to be summed.

2. Click the AutoSum button on the Standard toolbar. Excel enters the SUM() function with an argument consisting of the range of cells above or to the left of the cell; the range itself is marked by an animated border. If there is no such range, the SUM() function is entered without an argument.

3. If the range suggested by Excel is correct, press ↵. If it is not, use Point mode to specify the correct range (or type it in), and then press ↵.

Copying and Moving Formulas

You can use the Copy and Cut commands to copy or move formulas to a new location in the workbook (these commands were covered in Chapter 11). There's no difference in the procedures for copying or moving data or formulas—you can copy or move a range that contains just data, just formulas, or a combination of both.

Because formulas usually contain cell references, however, there are some special considerations involved. First, you need to know the distinction between relative and absolute cell references.

Absolute and Relative References

The default type of cell reference used by Excel in formulas is *relative*. This means that the address in a formula refers to a location relative to the cell containing the formula. Let's look at an example.

If you want to display the sum of cells A1:A5, you will enter the formula **SUM(A1:A5)**, say in cell A6. The A1:A5 is a relative reference with the meaning "the 5 cells immediately above this cell." If you now copy the formula from cell A6 to cell B6, you will find that the reference in the copied formula has changed to B1:B5. Note, however, that the relative meaning of the reference has stayed the same: the five cells immediately above this cell.

Excel's adjustment of relative cell addresses can be used to your advantage. Let's say you have ten columns of numbers, in A1:A10, B1:B10, and so on up to J1:J10. You want to display the sum of each column immediately below it. Rather than entering the appropriate formula for each cell individually, you can enter it once, below the first column, and then copy it to the cells below the other nine columns. Because of the relative cell reference, each formula will be adjusted to correctly sum the column of numbers above it.

There are times, however, when you do not want a cell reference to be relative. Rather, you want it to refer to the same exact workbook location no matter where it's copied to. For this you need an *absolute* cell reference. To create an absolute cell reference you place a dollar sign before the column letter and the row number in the reference: $A$1:$A$5. An absolute cell reference will remain unchanged in any copy or move operation.

You can also create *mixed* cell references, where the column is absolute and the row is relative, or vice versa. To create a mixed cell reference,

place a dollar sign in the appropriate location. With a mixed reference only the relative part is adjusted when the formula is copied or moved. We have, therefore, a total of four different types of cell references. They are given, with an example of the changes when copied, in this table.

Type	Example	If copied from A6 to B11
Relative	A1:A5	B6:B10
Absolute	$A$1:$A$5	$A$1:$A$5
Mixed	$A1:$A5	$A6:$A10
Mixed	A$1:A$5	B$1:B$5

It's important to remember that relative cell references are adjusted only when a formula is copied. If you use the Cut command to move a formula, its cell references remain unchanged.

Moving Data That Is Referenced in Formulas

If you move data that is referenced in a formula, the formula reference is automatically modified to refer to the same data in its new location. This is done whether the reference is relative or absolute. For instance, say that you had the formula SUM(A1:A5) in the workbook. If the data in A1:A5 were moved to G6:G10, the formula would change to SUM(G6:G10).

Note that this adjustment occurs only if you move the entire data range that the formula references. If you move only part of it—cells A2:A4 in the above example, for instance—the formula's reference is not adjusted.

Recalculation of Formulas

Excel's default setting is to calculate all formulas each time the workbook changes, thus ensuring that all displayed results are always up to date and accurate. In most small- to medium-sized workbooks, the recalculation takes place so quickly that you don't even notice the delay.

If you're working on a large workbook that contains many formulas, however, the time lag for recalculation may become noticeable—and annoying! You can solve the problem by setting Excel's recalculation mode to manual. In this mode the workbook's formulas are recalculated only when you specify, by pressing F9. You need to calculate the workbook only at times when you wish the values of formulas to accurately reflect changed or new data.

To set workbook calculation mode:

1. Select Tools ➤ Options.

2. Excel displays the Options dialog box. If necessary, click the Calculation tab to display the calculation options, shown in Figure 13.5.

3. Select the Manual option to enable manual calculation. If the Recalculate Before Save option is on, the workbook will be recalculated each time you save it to disk.

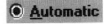

4. Select the Automatic option to return to automatic calculation.

5. Click the OK button or press ↵.

FIGURE 13.5

You use the Calculation tab in the Options dialog box to set the workbook's calculation mode.

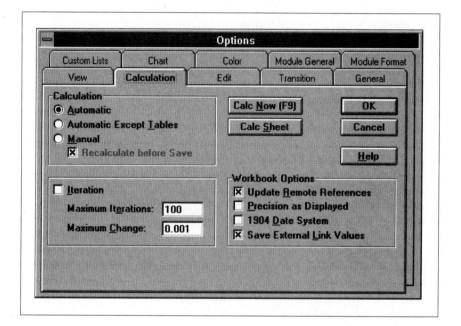

N O T E

If a workbook is set to manual calculation, the status bar displays the Calculate indicator on the status bar when the workbook needs to be recalculated—that is, when data that is used in a formula has changed.

Displaying Formulas in the Workbook

When a cell contains a formula, Excel normally displays the result of the formula in the cell. You will see the formula itself in the formula bar when the cell selector is on the cell, but this permits you to view only a single formula at a time. When you are developing or debugging a workbook you may find it useful to have the entire workbook display formulas instead of results in all cells. To toggle the workbook between formula display and result display, press Ctrl+' (left single quotation mark, to the left of the 1 key on your keyboard).

Formula Errors

A variety of problems can prevent Excel from calculating a formula. When problems occur a message is displayed in the cell indicating the nature of the error.

Message	Meaning
#DIV/0!	The formula attempts to divide by 0.
#N/A	The formula refers to a value that is not available.
#NAME?	The formula uses an undefined range name.
#NULL!	There is an error in a range specification.
#NUM!	The formula uses a number incorrectly, such as using a negative number as an argument to a function that required a positive argument.

Message	Meaning
#REF!	Cells to which the formula refers were deleted or pasted over.
#VALUE!	The formula uses an incorrect argument or operand, as in specifying a label argument to a function when a value argument is required.
#####	The result of the formula is too wide to display in the cell.

CHAPTER FOURTEEN

Creating Charts of
Your Data

F A PICTURE is worth a thousand words, then a chart may be worth a thousand numbers! There's no doubt that charts are very effective tools for illustrating numerical data. It's often the case that trends or conclusions that are obvious in a chart could not be detected at all by simply viewing the columns of numbers. In this chapter I will show you how to create and enhance Excel charts.

Chart Basics

A chart is a visual representation of data in your workbook. Numerical values from cells are shown as points, bars, lines, or other shapes depending on the chart type. In most chart types, labels from the workbook are used to group the data points into data series. Each data series on the chart is distinguished by the color, pattern, or shape of the elements used to show it. If you change the workbook data, the chart is automatically updated to reflect the change.

Parts of a Chart

In order to discuss charts, we first need to cover some terminology. Figure 14.1 shows an Excel chart with its parts labeled.

Data Organization

The relationship between data series in the workbook and the elements of a chart is illustrated in Figure 14.2.

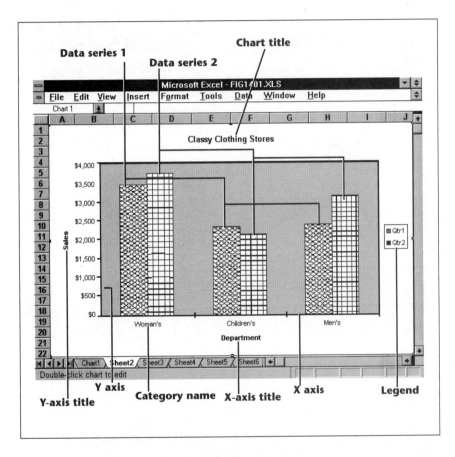

FIGURE 14.1

You need to know the names of the various chart components.

You can see that each individual value, or cell, is represented as a single data point in the chart. Likewise, you can see that each data series is contained in adjacent cells in the sheet. In this example, there are two data series. The first, whose values are in cells C4:C6, is represented by the bars with the diagonal pattern. The second series, in cells D4:D6, is

FIGURE 14.2

Each data series in the workbook is represented by an element on the chart.

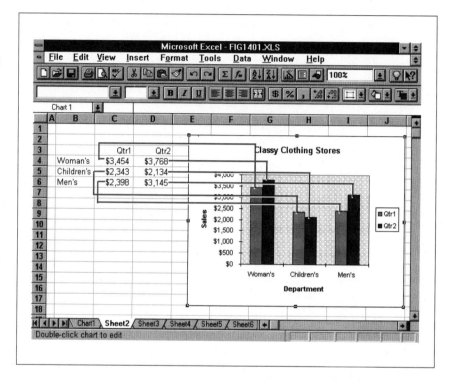

represented by the bars with the check pattern. The rows in the sheet represent different categories of data.

In this chart I have placed each data series in its own column and used rows to represent categories. You can also use rows for the data series and columns for the categories. Note also that all of the chart's data is contained in adjacent rows and columns. This is the way that most chart data is organized, but it is also possible to create a chart from data scattered in different areas of the workbook. In this chapter, however, I will limit discussion to situations in which the data to be charted is all together in one area.

Embedded Charts vs. Chart Sheets

When you create a chart you have two display options. An *embedded* chart is displayed as an object on a sheet. This display option is a good choice for reports because it enables you to place a chart next to its data. A *chart sheet* is a separate sheet that contains nothing but a chart. This option is best when you want to display each chart by itself. You'll learn both methods in this chapter.

Types of Charts

When you create a chart in Excel you can select from several different types of charts. Most of the chart types are available in several different varieties. You choose a chart type on the basis of its visual appearance and the data being plotted. Certain types of charts are more suitable for displaying certain kinds of data. Fortunately, Excel makes it easy to switch a chart from one type to another, so you can define a chart and then change your mind. And you can continue to experiment until you have found the best chart type for a particular set of data.

Before getting into the details of creating a chart, let's take a look at the various chart types available and the kinds of data for which they are best suited. Following the descriptions are samples of the chart types that are used most often.

- Column and bar charts (see Figure 14.3) display each data point as a vertical or horizontal bar. The length of the bar represents the value of the data point. Column and bar charts are well suited for showing the differences between categories.

FIGURE 14.3

A bar or column chart is a good choice for showing the differences between categories.

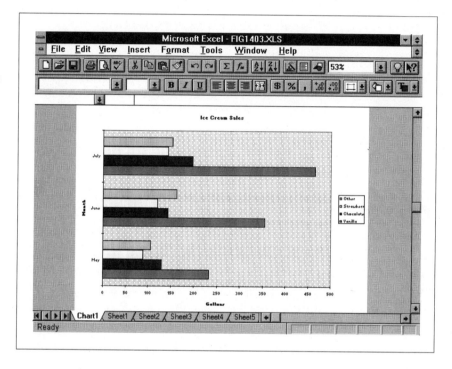

- Line charts (see Figure 14.4) represent each data point with a symbol; symbols in each data series are connected by a line. Line charts are ideal for showing changes over time.

- Area charts are a variant of line charts in which the data series are "stacked" on top of one another with the space between the lines filled with a color or pattern. You can use area charts to illustrate the contribution of different groups to the total.

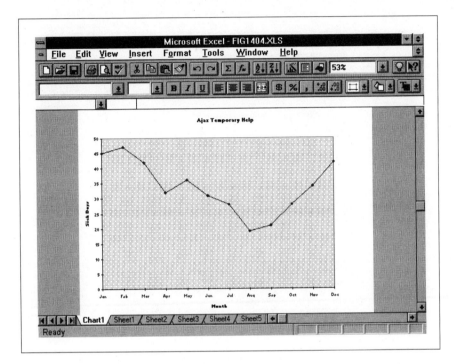

FIGURE 14.4

A line chart can be used to show changes occurring over time.

- Combination charts combine a line chart with a column or bar chart. One or more data series are plotted as lines, and the others are plotted as bars or columns.

- XY charts (see Figure 14.5), also called scatter charts, plot series of values against other series of values. In this chart type the X axis represents numerical values rather than categories, as in other chart types. Use XY charts to show the relationship between two sets of numerical measurements.

FIGURE 14.5

An XY or scatter chart is intended to illustrate the relationship between two sets of numerical measurements.

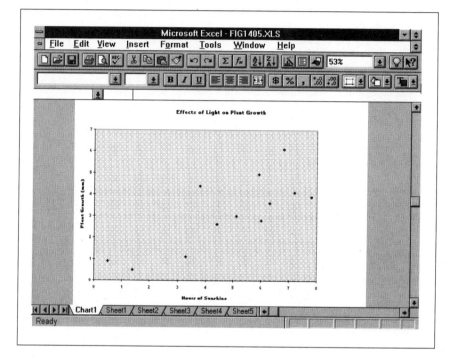

- Pie charts (see Figure 14.6) plot a single series of data as a circle, or "pie." Each individual data point is represented by a wedge of the pie, with the wedge size proportional to the data point's value. Use a pie chart to show the contribution of each individual value to the overall total. A doughnut chart is a variant of a pie chart.

- Radar charts plot data points as symbols surrounding a central point. Each data point's value is represented by the symbol's distance from the center.

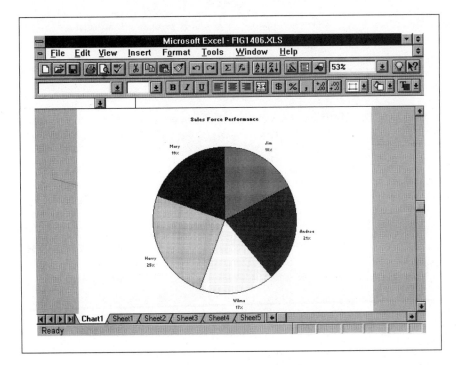

FIGURE 14.6

You can use a pie chart to show the contribution of each individual data point to the overall total.

- 3-D charts are variants of basic chart types that have a three-dimensional perspective.

Creating an Embedded Chart

The first step in creating a chart is to organize the data series that you want to plot in adjacent rows or columns of the workbook. Since this is

almost always the way the data is organized anyway, you will usually not have to take any special steps to do this. Then:

ChartWizard

1. Select the range containing the chart data. You can omit this step and select the data range later, if you prefer.

2. Click the ChartWizard button on the Standard toolbar. The mouse pointer changes to crosshairs with a small chart symbol.

3. Drag over the range in the workbook where you want to place the chart. When you release the mouse button, Excel displays the ChartWizard—Step 1 Of 5 dialog box, shown in Figure 14.7.

N O T E

You can place a chart over workbook data. It will hide, but not erase, the data. Move the chart to see the data again.

FIGURE 14.7

The first ChartWizard dialog box is used to specify the range containing the data to be charted.

4. If you selected a data range in step 1, it will be indicated in the Range box. If you did not specify a range in step 1 you must do so now, either by using Point mode or by typing in a range reference.

5. Click the Next button to display the next ChartWizard dialog box, which is shown in Figure 14.8.

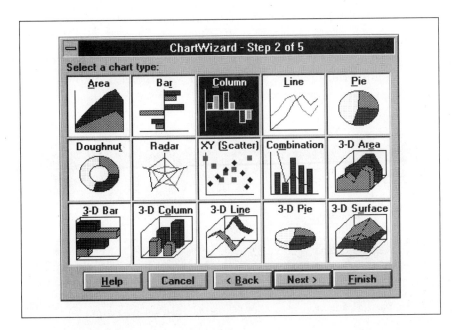

FIGURE 14.8

The second ChartWizard dialog box lets you select the chart type.

6. Click the type of chart desired.

7. Now, or at any time while using the ChartWizard, you can:

- Click the Back button to return to the previous dialog box to modify.

Cancel

Finish

- Click the Cancel button to cancel creation of the chart.

- Click the Finish button to create the chart with the settings specified so far.

Next >

8. Click the Next button to display the next ChartWizard dialog box, which lets you select the desired format for the chart type you selected previously. Click the desired chart format, and then click the Next button.

9. In the next ChartWizard dialog box, shown in Figure 14.9, you specify certain chart options. The exact options offered will depend on your previous selections, so your screen may not appear exactly as in the figure.

FIGURE 14.9

You use this ChartWizard dialog box to set a variety of chart options.

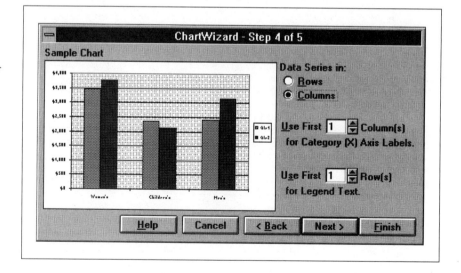

10. Under Data Series In, select the Rows or Columns option depending on whether your data series are oriented in rows or columns.

11. The next two options determine how the first row and column (depending on your choice in step 10) are used: for X data (XY chart), chart title (pie and doughnut charts), axis labels, or legend text. If you specify 0 the first row or column is plotted as a data series. As you make selections the appearance of the final chart is shown in the Sample Chart box.

12. Click the Next button to go on to the final ChartWizard dialog box, which is shown in Figure 14.10. As before, the exact appearance of this dialog box will depend on your previous selections, so your screen may look different.

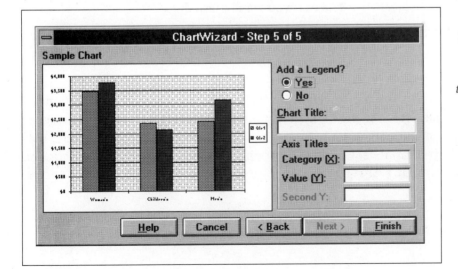

FIGURE 14.10

The final ChartWizard dialog box lets you specify the legend and the chart and axis titles.

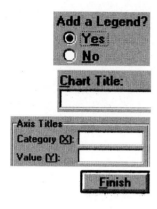

13. Under Add A Legend click Yes or No to specify whether the chart will display a legend.

14. If you want the chart to have a title, enter it in the Chart Title box.

15. In the Axis Titles section, enter the text of the X- and Y-axis titles.

16. Click the Finish button to complete the chart and display it in the workbook.

Creating a Chart Sheet

The procedures for creating a chart sheet are almost identical to those for creating an embedded chart.

1. Select the data that you want charted.

2. Choose Insert ➤ Chart ➤ As New Sheet. Excel displays the ChartWizard. Use the ChartWizard as described above for creating an embedded chart.

When you create a chart sheet, the new sheet is placed to the immediate left of the sheet containing the chart's data. Chart sheets are assigned default names in the form Chart1, Chart2, and so on. Remember that you can rename a sheet by double-clicking its name tab or by choosing Format ➤ Sheet ➤ Rename.

N O T E

To quickly create a chart sheet using the default settings, select the data and then press F11. Excel will display the ChartWizard only if it needs additional information. Otherwise it will create a column chart with a legend.

Modifying a Chart

Depending on the type of modifications you want to make, you must either activate or select the chart.

- To select an embedded chart, click anywhere on the chart. An embedded chart displays a thin black border with small boxes, called *handles*, on the corners and edges.

- To activate an embedded chart, double-click it. An activated chart displays a thick gray border with handles.

- To deactivate or deselect an embedded chart, click anywhere on the sheet outside the chart.

- To activate a chart sheet, click the sheet tab.

Certain chart operations are simplified by use of the Chart toolbar. To display this toolbar, choose <u>V</u>iew ➤ <u>T</u>oolbars. In the resulting dialog box click the Chart option, and then click the OK button.

OK

Moving, Resizing, or Deleting a Chart

To move, resize, or delete an embedded chart, select it. Then, to move the chart:

Cut

Paste

1. Click the Cut button on the Standard toolbar.

2. Move the cell selector to the cell in which you want to place the top-left corner of the chart.

3. Click the Paste button on the Standard toolbar.

N O T E

To quickly move a chart a short distance, point anywhere in the chart and drag it to the new location.

To resize the selected chart:

1. Point to one of the chart's handles. The mouse cursor changes to a two-headed arrow.

2. Drag the handle. As you drag, a dotted outline is displayed to show the new chart size.

3. At the desired size, release the mouse button.

To delete the selected chart, press Del.

> **NOTE**
>
> You cannot select a chart sheet. Moving and resizing are meaningless operations for a chart sheet. To delete a chart sheet, activate it, select Edit ➤ Delete Sheet, and then click the OK button.

Modifying Your Chart

When a chart is activated you can modify it. To do so, you must first select the element that you want to modify. A selected item is marked with one or more handles; in addition, its name is displayed at the left end of the formula bar. Figure 14.11 shows an activated chart in which the legend is selected.

- To select an item with the mouse, click on it.

- To select with the keyboard, use the arrow keys to cycle the selection from item to item.

- To undo the selection of an item, press Esc.

Chart Elements You Can Select

The elements that you can select in a chart depend to some extent on the type and format of the specific chart. You can select gridlines, for example, only if the chart has gridlines. If you are unsure of what elements can be selected on one of your charts, activate the chart and then use ← and → to cycle the selection among the various elements.

FIGURE 14.11

When you select an element in an activated chart, that element is displayed with handles and its name is displayed in the formula bar.

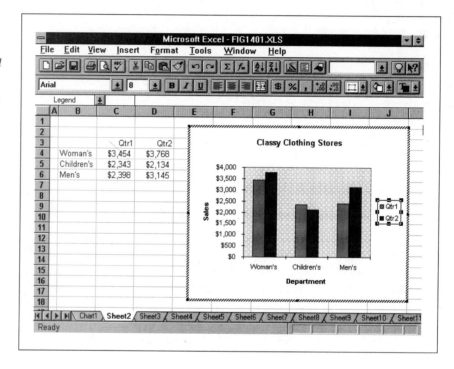

Here are some of the elements you will probably need to select as you work:

- Each individual data series. For example, in a bar chart all bars associated with a particular data series.

- An individual data marker. For example, a single bar in a bar chart.

- The X or Y axis.

- The chart title or an axis title.

- The legend. Note that you can select the legend as a unit, or select individual parts of the legend.

Modifying Chart Elements

The type of modifications that you can apply to a chart element depends to a large degree on the nature of the element. With a title, for example, you can modify its font, alignment, and background color. You can modify the line style of gridlines, but modifying the font of a gridline makes no sense!

Because of the many different types of chart elements and the variety of aspects that can be modified, it is not practical to provide details of every single modification you can make. Rather, I will explain the basic procedures and let you figure out the details as you need them. The dialog boxes that you use to make changes are generally clear and self-explanatory, so you should not have any problem. Remember, you can always use the Undo command to reverse a change you made.

1. Activate the chart.

2. Select the element that you want to modify.

3. Press Ctrl+1 or choose F*o*rmat ➤ S*e*lected... to display the dialog box for the selected element. The exact wording of the S*e*lected... command will depend on the specific element you have selected.

4. In the dialog box, make the necessary entries and selections. Click dialog box tabs, if needed, to display different sections of the dialog box.

5. When done, click the OK button or press ↵. The dialog box will close and the changes that you specified will be shown in the chart.

OK

NOTE

To quickly display the Format dialog box for a specific chart element, double-click the element.

Changing Chart Type

After you create a chart, you can quickly change its type at any time, so you can try out different chart types to see which one you like best. You can change the type of the entire chart (i.e., all data series) or of selected data series. By changing selected data series you can create a single chart that combines two or more chart types. For example, Figure 14.12 shows a chart in which one data series is plotted as the column type and the other is plotted as the line type. Combination charts such as this one can be quite effective for illustrating certain types of data.

To change the chart type:

1. Activate the chart. If you want to change the type of a single data series, select the series.

2. Select Format ➤ Chart Type. Excel displays the Chart Type dialog box, shown in Figure 14.13. The chart's primary type is highlighted in the dialog box.

3. In the Apply To section of the dialog box, select the part of the chart to be changed:

   Selected Series

   - **Selected Series:** Change the type of the selected data series. This option is available only if you selected a data series in step 1.

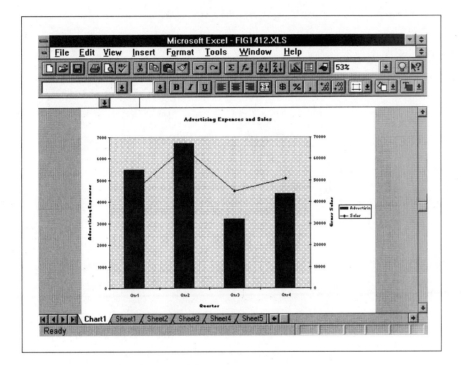

FIGURE 14.12

A chart can combine two or more different types, as in this case, which combines column and line types.

- **Group:** A group of one or more data series based on type. This option is available only if the chart contains two or more types of data series, such as line and column. You could, for example, change the line group to area type. Select the group in the list.

- **Entire Chart:** Change all data series in the chart.

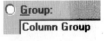

FIGURE 14.13

You use the Chart Type dialog box to change the type of an existing chart.

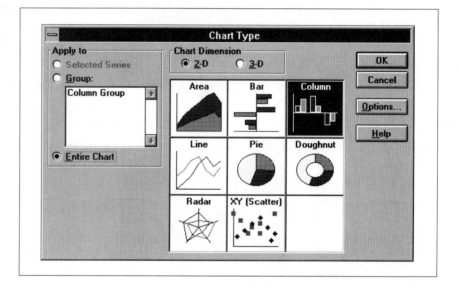

4. In the Chart Dimension section, click 2-D or 3-D to display the chart in two-dimensional or three-dimensional perspective.

5. Click the OK button or press ↵.

Chart
Type

> ### NOTE
>
> To quickly change the type of the entire chart, click the arrow next to the Chart Type button on the Chart toolbar. Excel will display a palette of chart type icons. Click the icon representing the desired chart type.

Adding and Deleting Chart Elements

To delete a chart element, simply activate the chart, select the element, and press Del.

To insert chart elements, use the Insert menu or buttons on the Chart toolbar. Not all items can be added to all chart types. You cannot, for example, add gridlines to a pie chart. If an item cannot be added to the current chart type, its command on the Insert menu will be grayed and if it has a button on the Chart toolbar, the button will not operate.

Adding Gridlines

Gridlines are vertical or horizontal lines that extend across a chart's plot area. X-axis gridlines are vertical, and Y-axis gridlines are horizontal. They can be displayed at major tick intervals, minor tick intervals, or both. Ticks are the short lines along an axis that mark intervals. To control the display of gridlines:

1. Choose Insert ➤ Gridlines. Excel displays the Gridlines dialog box, shown in Figure 14.14.

2. Select one or more gridline options, or turn options off to remove gridlines.

3. Click the OK button or press ↵

OK

FIGURE 14.14

The Gridlines dialog box lets you add gridlines to a chart.

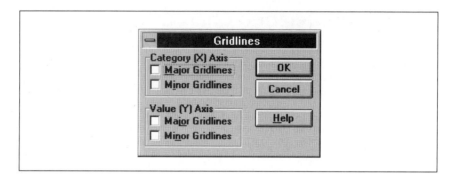

Adding a Legend

A legend is a key that identifies the various data series in a graph by color, pattern, or line style.

Legend

To add a legend to a chart, click the Legend button on the Chart toolbar or select Insert ➤ Legend.

Changing Legend Text   The text entries in a legend are normally taken automatically from sheet labels at the top of the columns, or at the left of the rows, containing the data series values. You can use labels from other workbook cells if you prefer, or type in totally new text.

1. In the activated chart, double-click the data series whose legend text you want to change. Excel displays the Format Data Series dialog box.

2. If necessary, click the Name And Values tab to display the Name And Values section of the dialog box, shown in Figure 14.15.

Name and Values

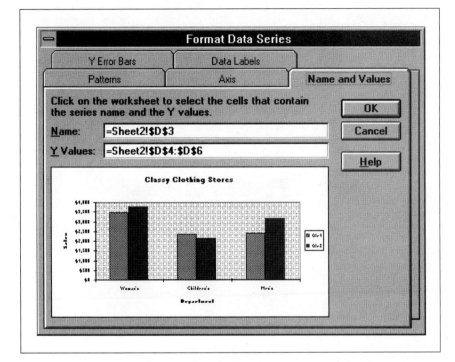

FIGURE 14.15

*In the Names And
Values section of the
Format Data Series
dialog box you can
change the chart's
legend text.*

3. The Name box gives the cell reference of the current legend text
label.

- To use a label from a different cell, type its reference in the
  name box. Or, you can click the Name box, click anywhere
  in the sheet, and then click the cell containing the label
  that you want to use. Its reference will be entered in the
  Name box.

- To use other text, type it into the Name box.

4. Click the OK button or press ↵.

Adding Titles

All types of charts can have a main title, which by default is displayed centered at the top of the chart. A chart with axes can also have an X-axis title and a Y-axis title. To add and modify titles:

1. Select Insert ➤ Titles. Excel displays the Titles dialog box, shown in Figure 14.16.

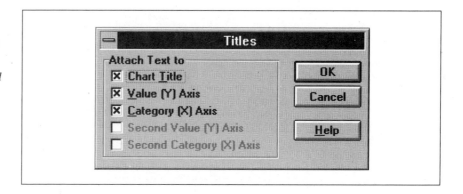

2. Click the options corresponding to the titles you want in the chart.

3. Click the OK button or press ↵.

When you first add titles to a chart, Excel adds the standard text "Title" for the chart title, "Y" for the Y- axis title, and "X" for the X-axis title. To edit a chart title:

1. Click the title once to select it.

2. Click it again to enter editing mode. A blinking vertical cursor will be displayed in the title text at the point at which you clicked.

3. Edit the text using the usual text-editing methods.

4. Click outside the title to terminate editing.

> **NOTE**
>
> In steps 1 and 2 above you do *not* want to double-click the title. Doing so will bring up the Format Chart Title dialog box. Rather, you want to single-click the title twice.

Using AutoFormat

Instead of manually formatting the various chart elements yourself, you may want to use a Chart AutoFormat. An AutoFormat is a predefined set of chart formatting that can be applied to any chart. Each AutoFormat is based on a specific chart type. It can also include specifications for various other chart elements, including subtype, legend, gridlines, data labels, colors, and patterns. Excel provides a selection of predefined Auto-Formats. You can also create your own AutoFormat definitions.

Applying an AutoFormat

To apply an AutoFormat to a chart:

1. Activate the chart that you want to format.

2. Select Format ➤ AutoFormat. Excel displays the AutoFormat dialog box, shown in Figure 14.17.

FIGURE 14.17

The AutoFormat dialog box lets you apply predefined formatting to your charts.

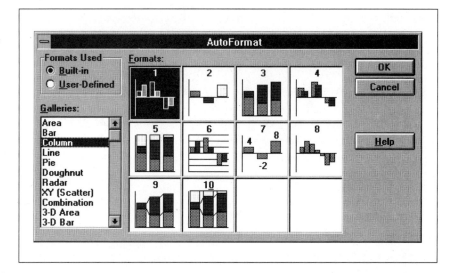

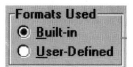

3. In the Formats Used section, select the Built-In option to choose from Excel's built-in AutoFormats, or select the User-Defined option to select from user-defined AutoFormats.

4. If you selected Built-In, the Galleries list displays a list of chart types and the Formats box displays small sketches of the various formats available for the selected type. Click the desired format.

5. If you selected User-Defined, the Galleries list changes to the Formats list, displaying the available user-defined AutoFormats. Click the format you want. The Preview box displays the appearance of the format that is highlighted in the list.

6. Click the OK button or press ↵.

NOTE

After applying an AutoFormat you can click the Undo button on the Standard toolbar to clear the AutoFormat from the chart.

Undo

Creating a Custom AutoFormat

You can create your own AutoFormat definitions as follows.

1. Format a chart with the desired formatting. Be sure the chart is activated.

2. Select Format ➤ AutoFormat.

3. Select the User-defined option.

4. Click the Customize button. Excel displays the User-Defined AutoFormats dialog box, shown in Figure 14.18.

5. Click the Add button. Excel displays the Add Custom Auto-Format dialog box. Enter a name and a description for the new AutoFormat in the boxes provided.

6. Click the OK button or press ↵ to return to the User-Defined AutoFormats dialog box. You'll see that the new format has been added to the Formats list.

7. Click the Close button or press ↵.

The User-Defined AutoFormats dialog box permits you to create your own AutoFormat definitions.

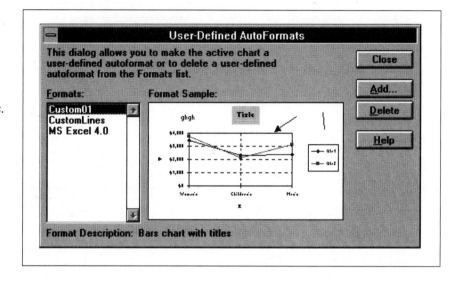

CHAPTER FIFTEEN

Printing Your Data and Charts

YOU WILL OFTEN need to print information from your Excel workbooks. Whether you need a quick copy of a single page or a full-length polished report, Excel can provide what you need. This chapter covers printing from Excel.

In order to print, you must, of course, have a printer connected to your computer. The printer must be turned on, loaded with paper, and "on-line."

Printing with the Default Settings

Excel has a variety of print settings that control the way your printed output is created. You'll see later in this chapter how to use these settings to fine-tune your print jobs. You can use the default print settings, however, which are fine for many printing tasks.

Printing an Entire Sheet

Print

To quickly print the entire current sheet (the one containing the cell selector), click the Print button on the Standard toolbar. Excel will print using the current print settings in the Page Setup dialog box. You'll learn how to modify these settings later in the chapter.

Controlling What's Printed

You are not limited to printing entire sheets. You can specify exactly what's printed, from a small range of cells to the entire workbook.

1. If you want to print a range of data, select the range. If you want to print two or more entire sheets, select them.

2. Select File ➤ Print or press Ctrl+P. Excel displays the Print dialog box, shown in Figure 15.1.

3. In the Print What section of the dialog box, choose an option as follows:

- Choose Selection to print the range of cells you selected in step 1.

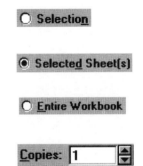

- Choose Selected Sheet(s) to print all data on the selected sheets.

- Choose the Entire Workbook option to print all sheets in the workbook.

4. To print more than one copy, enter the desired number in the Copies box or click the up and down arrows to increase or decrease the displayed value.

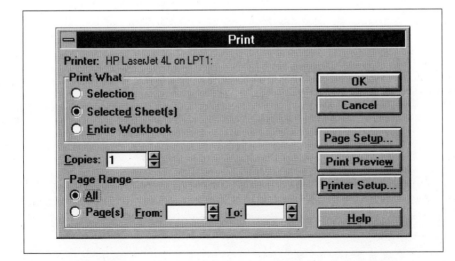

FIGURE 15.1

The Print dialog box lets you specify exactly what part of your workbook to print.

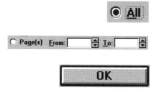

5. To print all pages in the report, select the All option. To print a specified range of pages, select the Pages option and then enter the starting and ending page numbers in the From and To boxes.

6. Click the OK button or press ↵ to start printing.

Printing Charts

There is no special trick to printing charts. When you print a workbook range, any embedded charts in the range will be printed along with the data, just like you see it on your screen. To print a chart sheet, simply display the sheet by clicking its tab, and then print the sheet.

Pages in Excel Printouts

When the data to be printed will not fit on a single page, Excel automatically splits it over two or more pages. In a single sheet, data is by default broken into pages first top-to-bottom and then left-to-right. You can change this setting so that the order is left-to-right followed by top-to-bottom by using the Page Setup dialog box, described in the next section. When printing several sheets, the entire top worksheet is printed first followed by the sheets below it in top-down order.

Changing the Page Setup

While the default print settings are fine in some circumstances, you'll often want to change them in order to get exactly the printed output you want. Excel's Page Setup options let you control a wide variety of

printing options, such as paper size, page margins, headers and footers, and the printing of cell notes.

All Page Setup options are controlled from the Page Setup dialog box. There are several ways to display this dialog box:

- Select <u>F</u>ile ➤ Page Set<u>u</u>p.

- Click the Page Setup button in the Print dialog box (remember, you display the Print dialog box by selecting <u>F</u>ile ➤ <u>P</u>rint or pressing Ctrl+P).

  Page Setup...

- Click the Page Setup button in the Print Preview window. You'll learn about using Print Preview later in the chapter.

  Page Setup...

In the sections that follow I will not be repeating the instructions for displaying the Page Setup dialog box. I'll assume you remember how to do it, and are starting with the dialog box displayed.

N O T E

If you use the <u>F</u>ile ➤ Page Set<u>u</u>p command to display the Page Setup dialog box, the box will display Print and Preview buttons that you can click to go to those parts of the program. If, however, you activated the Page Setup dialog box from the Print dialog box or the Preview window, these buttons will not be displayed.

Setting Paper Options

The paper options you can set include the print orientation, paper size, and the print quality. To set paper options:

1. Display the Page Setup dialog box.

2. If necessary, click the Page tab to display the page option section of the dialog box, shown in Figure 15.2.

3. In the Orientation section, select one of the following options:

- Select Landscape to print with the workbook rows parallel to the long edge of the paper. Landscape mode lets you get as many columns as possible on a page.

FIGURE 15.2

The Page section of the Page Setup dialog box lets you specify paper size and print orientation.

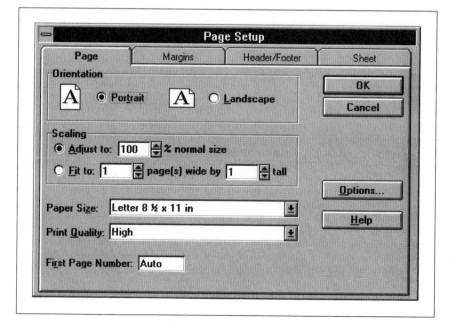

- Select Portrait mode to print with worksheet rows parallel to the short edge of the paper.

4. To specify the size of paper being used, pull down the Paper Size list and select the desired page size. Be sure that your printer is loaded with the correct paper size before printing!

5. To set print quality, pull down the Print Quality list and select one of the choices presented. This option is not available for all printers. Select a low resolution, such as 150 dpi (dots per inch), for draft quality printing that is relatively fast and saves toner. Select a high resolution, such as 300 dpi, for highest quality output.

6. Click the Print button to display the Print dialog box, or click the OK button to return to the workbook.

Using Headers, Footers, and Page Numbers

Excel can include a header and/or a footer on printed pages. The default header is the name of the sheet (the same name as is displayed on the sheet tab), and the default footer is the page number. You can create your own header and footer as follows:

1. In the Page Setup dialog box, click the Header/Footer tab to display the Header/Footer section of the dialog box, shown in Figure 15.3.

2. To select one of the built-in headers or footers, click the arrow at the end of the Header or Footer box and select from the list. The built-in headers and footers are constructed using the name and company name that were entered when Office was installed.

Standard

FIGURE 15.3

The Header/Footer dialog box lets you customize the header and footer printed on each page.

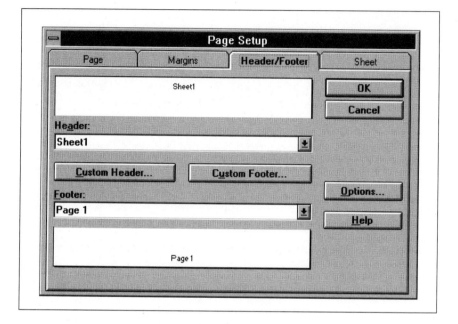

Select (none) from the list to remove an existing header or footer. The Preview section of the dialog box shows you the final printed appearance of the header and footer.

3. To create a customized header, click the Customize Header button to display the Header dialog box, shown in Figure 15.4. The three boxes let you position elements of the header left-aligned, centered, or right-aligned on the page.

4. To enter text in a header section, click the corresponding box and use the usual editing and text entry methods.

5. To apply character formatting, select the text and click the Font button to display the Font dialog box.

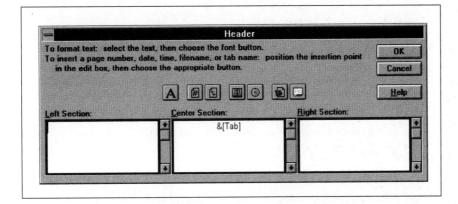

FIGURE 15.4

You create a customized header in the Header dialog box.

6. To insert special header codes, click the corresponding button. The codes display as codes in the Header dialog box but as their results in the Page Setup preview (and when printed, of course). The buttons are as follows:

Button	Displays	Code
	Page number	&[Page]
	Total pages in report	&[Pages]
	Current date	&[Date]
	Current time	$[Time]

Button	Displays	Code
	Workbook file name	&[File]
	Sheet name	&[Tab]

7. When finished, click the OK button to return to the Page Setup dialog box.

8. To customize the footer, click the Customize Footer button and repeat the above steps 4 through 7 to specify the footer text.

9. When the previews in the Page Setup dialog box show the header and footer as you want them, click the Print button to display the Print dialog box, or click the OK button to return to the workbook.

NOTE

In a header or footer, an ampersand (&) signals the start of a special code. To actually display an ampersand you must enter two ampersands (&&).

Sheet Printing Options

When printing sheet data (as opposed to a chart sheet) Excel provides several options that control the output. To change sheet printing options:

1. Click the Sheet tab to display the sheet options in the Page Setup dialog box, shown in Figure 15.5.

FIGURE 15.5

You use this section of the Page Setup dialog box to set sheet printing options.

2. Click the Print Area box and then drag through the sheet to specify the range to be printed. Enter a Print Area range only if you will print the same range of the sheet each time it is printed. If you will print a different range each time, it's easier to select the range each time before you issue the Print command.

3. In the Print Titles section, specify rows and/or columns to print as titles on each page of the report. By repeating row or column titles on each page you can identify data that stretches over two or more pages. Click the Columns To Repeat... or Rows To Repeat... box and then drag in the workbook over a range spanning the rows or columns to repeat.

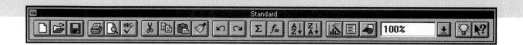

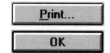

4. In the Page Order section, click Down, Then Across or Across, Then Down to specify the order in which Excel prints the pages of a multiple page report.

5. In the Print section select from among the following options:

- Select the Gridlines option to include the vertical and horizontal lines between the cells in the printout.

- Select the Notes option to print any cell notes that are present in the print range on a separate sheet.

- Select the Draft Quality option for faster printing. With Draft Quality enabled, gridline printing is suppressed and fewer graphics are printed.

- Select the Black And White option if you are using a black and white printer and want to print items formatted with colors as black and white rather than as shades of gray.

- Select the Row And Column headings option to include the row numbers and column letters in the printout.

6. When you are done setting options, click the Print button to display the Print dialog box, or click the OK button to save the settings and return to your workbook.

Scaling Output Size

Excel gives you a good deal of control over the size of the final printed output. The "normal" size is referred to as 100% scaling, and produces output that is approximately the same size as that seen on the screen. You can enlarge or reduce the printing size, and can also tell Excel to fit the output on a specified number of pages.

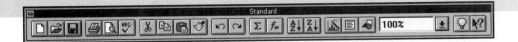

1. In the Page Setup dialog box click the Page tab to display the Page options. This dialog box was shown earlier in Figure 15.2.

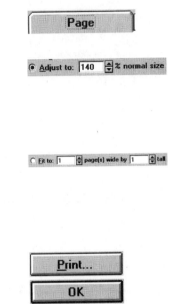

2. To change scaling manually, enter a new scaling value in the Scaling box, or click the up and down arrows to change the displayed value. You can specify scaling in the range of 10-400 percent. 10 percent gives one-tenth normal size, while 400 percent gives four times normal size.

3. To fit the output to a specified number of pages, click the Fit To option to enter the maximum number of pages in the boxes. The report will be scaled to fit in the specified number of pages while maintaining its relative proportions. It may print on fewer pages than specified.

4. When done, click the Print button to display the Print dialog box, or click the OK button to save the settings and return to your workbook.

Setting the Margins

Margins are the blank areas between your printed data and the edge of the page. You can control the size of all four margin in your printouts, and can also specify the spacing between headers and footers and the page edges.

1. In the Page Setup dialog box, click the Margins tab to display the Margin options, shown in Figure 15.6.

2. To change the left, right, top, or bottom margin, enter the desired margin value (in inches) in the corresponding box, or click the up and down arrows to change the value already entered there.

FIGURE 15.6

You use the Page Setup dialog box to control the size of page margins.

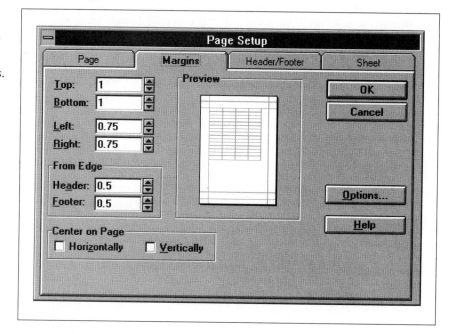

3. To change the distance between the header or footer and the page edge, enter the desired value in the corresponding box, or click the up and down arrows.

4. As you work, the Preview box shows you the dimension you are changing by darkening the corresponding line. It does *not*, however, show you the actual position of the margins.

5. To center the printed area either vertically or horizontally on the page, click the Horizontally and/or Vertically option in the Center On Page section. These options have an effect only if the printed area is shorter or narrower than the page size between the margins.

6. When done, click the Print button to display the Print dialog box, or click the OK button to save the settings and return to your workbook.

Chart Sheet Options

There are some special options that control the printing of chart sheets. These options are available only if the current sheet is a chart sheet when the Page Setup dialog box is displayed.

1. In the Page Setup dialog box, click the Chart tab to display the Chart options, shown in Figure 15.7.

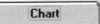

FIGURE 15.7

There are several options available to control the printing of chart sheets.

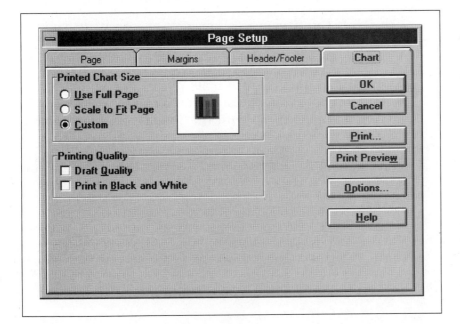

2. To control the final printed size of the chart, select one of the following options:

- **Use Full Page:** expands the chart to fill the entire page. The relative height or width of the chart may be changed with this option.

- **Scale to Fit Page:** prints the largest chart size that will fit on the page without changing the relative width or height of the chart.

- **Custom:** scales the chart as it appears on-screen. You can then scale the chart in the sheet to modify the final printed size.

3. Under Printing Quality, select from the following options:

- **Draft Quality:** increases memory efficiency when using a plotter for output. Use this option if you receive "low memory" messages during printing.

- **Print in Black and White:** When using a black and white printer, this option causes colored data series to print as different patterns. The default is for colors to print as shades of gray.

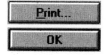

4. When the desired options are selected, click the Print button to display the Print dialog box, or click the OK button to save the settings and return to your workbook.

Using Print Preview

The Print Preview feature lets you see what your printouts will look like without actually printing them. Proper use of Print Preview can save you a great deal of time and paper. You can display the Print Preview screen in several ways:

- Click the Print Preview button on the Standard toolbar.
- Select File ➤ Print Preview.
- Click the Print Preview button in the Page Setup Dialog box.

Print Preview

The Print Preview screen is shown in Figure 15.8 with a page of an Excel report displayed.

In the Print Preview window, when the mouse cursor is over the page it is displayed as a small magnifying glass. Click anywhere on the page to magnify the view of that area, and then click again to return to Whole Page view. You can also take the following actions:

- Click the Next or Previous button to preview the next or previous page in a multiple page report. These buttons are grayed if there is no next or previous page.

- Click the Zoom button to enlarge the display. Click it again to return to Full Page view.

- Click the Print button to display the Print dialog box, from which you can print the report.

- Click the Setup button to display the Page Setup dialog box. When you close the Page Setup dialog box you will return to the Print Preview screen.

FIGURE 15.8

The Print Preview screen shows you what your printout will look like, and also lets you set page margins and column widths visually.

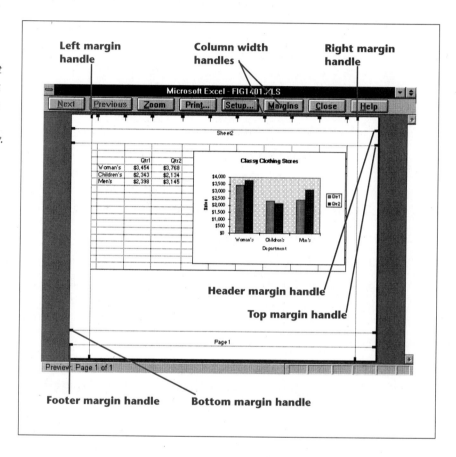

Margins

- Click the Margins button to display margin lines on the preview (as shown in Figure 15.8). Each margin line has a small handle at either end. Point to the handle and drag to change the margin. The handles along the top of the page represent the column boundaries. Point to a handle and drag to change column width. Click the Margin button again to hide the margin lines.

- Click the Close button to close Print Preview and return to your workbook.

Inserting Page Breaks

A *page break* is the location at which Excel starts printing on a new page. There are both horizontal page breaks, which separate the last row on one page from the first row on the next, and vertical page breaks, which separate columns. Normally, Excel positions page breaks automatically on the basis of the paper and margin size, print scaling, and other factors. You can, however, insert page breaks manually to obtain exact control over which data prints on which pages. To set a manual page break:

1. Move the cell selector to the location for the page break:

- To insert both vertical and horizontal page breaks, select the cell that you want to place at the top-left of the new page.

- To insert a vertical page break, select the column that you want to place on the left edge of the new page.

- To insert a horizontal page break, select the row that you want at the top of the new page.

2. Select Insert ➤ Page Break.

PART FOUR

POWERPOINT

CHAPTER SIXTEEN

Getting Started
with PowerPoint

POWERPOINT is the presentation graphics component of Microsoft Office. You use PowerPoint to create *presentations*, collections of pictures and text that, as the name implies, you present to other people. You learned how to start PowerPoint in Chapter 1. In this chapter you will learn what PowerPoint does, the parts of its screen, and how to begin, open, and save a presentation.

What Is PowerPoint?

PowerPoint is designed to help you effectively communicate information to others. Whether you're talking about a new advertising campaign, the design of a modern intensive care unit, or the details of a new health insurance plan, you need to communicate your information in a clear, concise, and interesting manner. PowerPoint helps you to both create and organize the materials in your presentation.

The Parts of a Presentation

You may use a variety of elements in each PowerPoint presentation, depending on your needs.

- A *slide* is a visual image that can contain text, graphics, charts—just about anything you can imagine! A slide may be displayed on paper, as an overhead transparency, on the computer screen, or as an actual slide that you project.

- *Audience handouts* provide printed copies of your slides along with supporting text.

- *Speaker's notes* provide small images of your slides along with your notes, to serve as a speaking aid for you while you deliver the presentation.

- *Outline pages* provide an outline of the entire presentation, without graphics.

When you create a PowerPoint presentation, all parts of it are stored in a single presentation file.

Starting a Presentation

When you start PowerPoint, the PowerPoint startup dialog box, shown in Figure 16.1, will be displayed. If the startup dialog box is not displayed when you start PowerPoint, you can display it by clicking the New button. You can also click the New button while working in Power-Point to start a *new* presentation.

New

1. Select one of the options in the dialog box:

   - Select AutoContent Wizard if you would like to start by working on the organization and content of your presentation.

   - Select Pick A Look Wizard if you want to start by working on the appearance of your presentation.

   - Select Template if you want to start by selecting a template that specifies certain aspects of your presentation, such as color schemes and fonts.

○ **AutoContent Wizard**

○ **Pick a Look Wizard**

○ **Template**

FIGURE 16.1

The PowerPoint startup dialog box lets you select how you will start a new presentation.

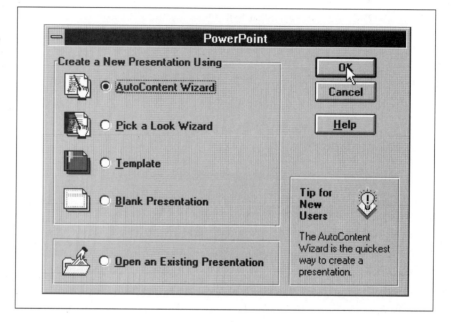

NOTE

The *template* defines the overall look and feel of a presentation. In effect, a template consists of a presentation's four masters (slide, handout, notes, and outline, described later in this chapter and in chapter 18) and its color scheme. The *color scheme* determines the colors used for the various elements of your presentation. A color scheme is a set of eight colors for different parts of the slides, handouts, etc.

- Select Blank Presentation if you want to create a presentation "from scratch" using all of PowerPoint's default settings for color, font, and so on.

- Select Open An Existing Presentation if you want to continue to work on an existing presentation.

2. Click the OK button or press ↵.

What happens next depends on the option you selected in the dialog box. More details are provided later in this chapter.

If you click the Cancel button in this dialog box, you are returned to the main PowerPoint screen.

The PowerPoint Screen

Figure 16.2 shows the PowerPoint screen with its most important components labeled. This screen shows a slide displayed, which you won't see if you've just started PowerPoint and selected Cancel from the initial dialog box.

NOTE

Shortcut menus are provided for many PowerPoint objects, such as a slide title or a box in an organizational chart. Shortcut menus provide quick access to certain PowerPoint commands. To display an object's shortcut menu, point to it with the mouse and click the right button. Each object's shortcut menu contains only those commands that are relevant to that object.

FIGURE 16.2

The main PowerPoint screen contains a variety of components you use in creating presentations.

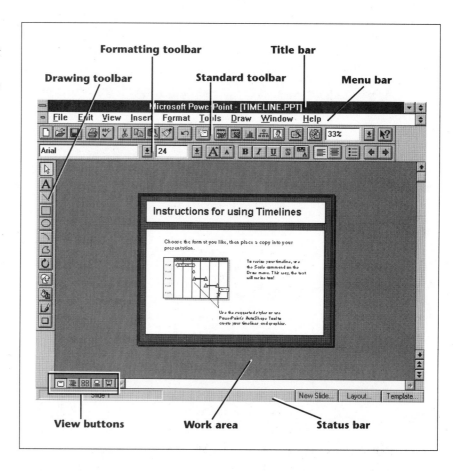

Cue Cards

Cue Cards are a nifty feature that can help you through many Power-Point procedures. PowerPoint may pop up a Cue Card when it thinks you need one. You can also display Cue Cards as needed. Cue Cards remain

on-screen as you work, and display step-by-step instructions for performing common tasks. To use Cue Cards, select <u>H</u>elp ➤ C<u>u</u>e Cards. PowerPoint displays the Cue Card menu, shown in Figure 16.3.

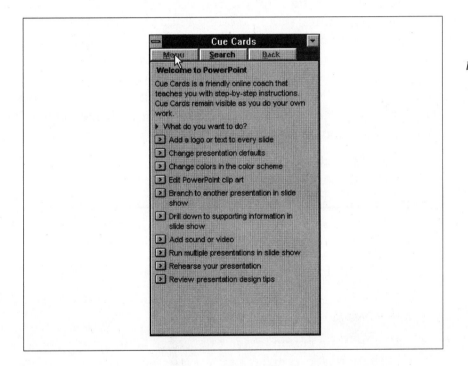

FIGURE 16.3

The Cue Card menu lets you select the Cue Card topic that you want to view.

While a Cue Card is displayed, you can work in PowerPoint as usual. You can also move the Cue Card by dragging its title bar, search for other Cue Cards using the Search button, click the Back or Next button to display other Cue Cards, or click the Menu button to go to the main Cue Card menu. To close the Cue Card, double-click its control box.

Starting a Presentation with the AutoContent Wizard

The AutoContent Wizard helps you organize your ideas when you start a new presentation. You start by creating a title slide, and then select from several common presentation categories, such as Selling a Product, Recommending a Strategy, or Communicating Bad News. The Wizard's prompts help you to create a presentation outline based on the presentation category you selected and the specific details of your presentation. When the Wizard is finished, you can work with the outline to complete the presentation.

To use the AutoContent Wizard, select the AutoContent Wizard option in the PowerPoint dialog box, and then click the OK button.

The Wizard has a series of four dialog boxes, each of which prompts you for specific choices or information about your presentation. In each dialog box you control the Wizard with the following four buttons:

- Click the Next button to go to the next Wizard dialog box.

- Click the Back button to return to the previous Wizard dialog box, where you can change your entries.

- Click the Finish button to create the presentation outline based on the information entered so far.

- Click the Cancel button to abort the Wizard without creating a presentation outline.

Here's a description of the various AutoContent Wizard dialog boxes:

1. The first dialog box introduces the Wizard.

2. The second dialog box prompts you for title-slide information, such as the title of your presentation and your name.

3. The third dialog box asks you to select from six general presentation types. When you click an option, the preview on the left shows the general structure of the selected presentation.

4. The final dialog box in the AutoContent Wizard summarizes some of the additional changes you can make once the Wizard is complete.

When the AutoContent Wizard is finished your screen will display the outline of your presentation in Outline view (one of PowerPoint's five screen views, which I'll describe soon). A Cue Card will be displayed as well. You should next save the presentation to disk, and can then continue working on it. The next step may be to design the appearance of the presentation. You can do this with the Pick A Look Wizard, described next.

Starting a Presentation with the Pick a Look Wizard

The Pick A Look Wizard assists you in designing the overall appearance of your presentation. The exact number of dialog boxes you'll see depends on the options you select. Use the Next, Back, Finish, and Cancel buttons to move through the Wizard. Remember that any presentation settings you make with the Wizard can always be changed.

Here's a guide to the various steps in this Wizard:

1. To use the Pick A Look Wizard on a new document, select it from the PowerPoint startup dialog box or click the New button. To run the Pick A Look Wizard for an existing presentation, select Format ➤ Pick a Look Wizard. You will see an introductory dialog box.

2. In the second dialog box you select the type of output for the presentation: black-and-white overheads, color overheads, screen show, or 35mm slides.

3. In the third dialog box, you select a template for the presentation. This dialog box is shown in Figure 16.4. A *template* defines the basic appearance, such as background and design elements, of your slides.

FIGURE 16.4

You select a template for your presentation in step 3 of the Pick a Look Wizard.

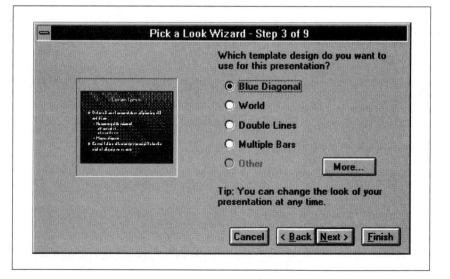

4. To select a template, click one of the four template options offered; the preview in the left part of the dialog box shows the
appearance of the selected template. If you don't want to use
one of these four templates, click the More button. PowerPoint
will display the Presentation Template dialog box. Use this dialog box to select the template for your presentation, as described
in "Starting a Presentation with a Template." When done, click
the Apply button to return to the Pick A Look Wizard.

5. The fourth Pick A Look Wizard dialog box asks you which printing options you want to use.

6. The final Pick A Look Wizard steps let you specify certain information that will be displayed on each output page. You'll see between one and four dialog boxes, one for each of the printing
options that you selected in the previous step (slides, audience
handouts, etc.).

7. The final Pick A Look Wizard step is an informational dialog
box requiring no input from you.

Remember that you can run the Pick A Look Wizard at any time, not
just when you are starting a presentation. The various options and settings controlled by the Wizard can also be set individually with program commands, as you'll learn in the following chapters.

Starting a Presentation
with a Template

The third way to start a presentation is to specify a template. A *template*
is a definition of the color scheme of a presentation and its format—the

appearance and location of text. PowerPoint comes with over 100 professionally designed templates. You can also use any existing presentation as a template for a new presentation. A template can be assigned at any point during the creation of the presentation, and does not prevent you from making changes to the format and color of individual slides in the presentation. You select templates in the Presentation Template dialog box, shown in Figure 16.5.

This dialog box is displayed if you select the Template option in the PowerPoint startup dialog box.

You assign a template to your presentation using the Presentation Template dialog box.

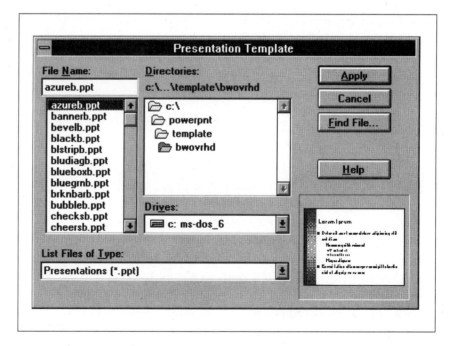

You can also display this dialog box at any time by clicking the Template button on the status bar. To select a template from this dialog box:

Template...

1. Click the desired template name in the File Name list. The preview section on the right side of the dialog box shows you the appearance of the selected template.

2. To select a template on a different drive, pull down the Drives list and select the desired drive.

3. To select a template in a different directory, double-click the new directory in the Directories list.

4. Click the Apply button.

Apply

If you apply a template to a presentation that already has a template applied, then the old template is replaced by the new one. You cannot reverse the act of applying a template. If the old template is a custom one that you may want to use again, be sure to save at least one slide from the presentation before applying the new template.

Starting a Presentation from Scratch

If you select the Blank Presentation option, there will be no predefined template or outline, and you will be using the default Slide Master. The *Slide Master* defines certain elements that will appear on every slide in the presentation. The Slide Master controls the format of the title and text on all slides, and can also include background items that you want displayed on each slide (for example, your company logo). If you change the Slide Master all slides in the presentation are automatically

changed. You can add or delete elements from individual slides to have them depart from the Slide Master. In addition to the Slide Master, a presentation can also use masters for the audience handouts, speaker notes, and outline. These will be explained in Chapter 18. You can add a template or another Slide Master later, of course, or define your own. You start out, however, by creating your first slide.

When starting a blank presentation, PowerPoint's default setup is to display the New Slide dialog box, shown in Figure 16.6. In this dialog box you select a *layout,* sometimes called an *AutoLayout,* for the slide. A layout specifies the placement of individual items on a slide. For example, one slide's layout may include a title at the top and a chart below, while another slide's layout may include a bulleted list and an organizational chart. Layouts are applied to individual slides.

FIGURE 16.6

You create a new slide by selecting an AutoLayout in the New Slide dialog box.

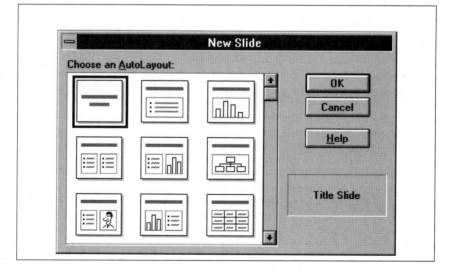

Use of this dialog box is explained fully in Chapter 17, in the section titled "Creating a New Slide." Depending on PowerPoint option settings, however, this dialog box may not be displayed when you create a new slide. Instead, PowerPoint will create a new slide based on the default AutoLayout and display the slide for editing. This too is covered in Chapter 17.

To control whether PowerPoint displays the New Slide dialog box when creating a new slide:

1. Select Tools ➤ Options to display the Options dialog box.

2. In the General section of the dialog box, click the Show New Slide Dialog option to toggle display of the New Slide dialog box on or off.

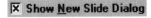

3. Click the OK button or press ↵.

PowerPoint's Five Views

PowerPoint provides five different ways of looking at your presentation. Each view is appropriate for certain tasks. Switch between views by using the View buttons at the bottom-left edge of the screen, or with the corresponding command on the View menu.

Slide View

Slide view, illustrated in Figure 16.7, shows the single current slide on-screen, permitting you to edit and modify it.

FIGURE 16.7

In Slide view you can work on the contents and appearance of a single slide.

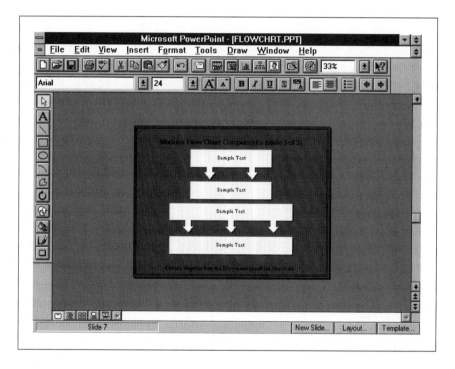

To switch to Slide view, click the Slide View button or select <u>V</u>iew ➤ <u>S</u>lides. In Slide view you can take the following actions:

- To view the next or previous slide in the presentation, click the Next Slide or Previous Slide button (below the vertical scroll bar) or press PgUp or PgDn.

- To enlarge or reduce the display size of the slide, click the arrow on the Zoom control on the Standard toolbar and select a zoom factor.

- If the slide is enlarged so that only part of it displays on-screen, use the vertical and horizontal scroll bars to scroll the view to different parts of the slide.

Outline View

Outline view (see Figure 16.8) displays only the titles and other text on your slides in an outline format. You use Outline view to organize a presentation and work on its content.

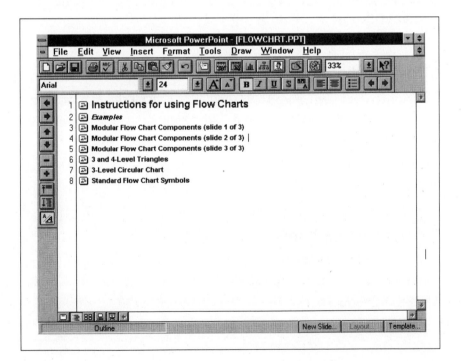

FIGURE 16.8

In Outline view only the titles and text of your slides are displayed.

To switch to Outline view, click the Outline View button or select <u>V</u>iew ➤ <u>O</u>utline. There are some special buttons you can use to control the display in Outline view:

- Click the Show Titles button to display only slide titles in the outline.

- Click the Show All button to display slide text as well as titles in the outline.

- Click the Show Formatting button to toggle between displaying the outline text fully formatted (as on the slides) or as plain, un-formatted text.

Slide Sorter View

Slide Sorter view (see Figure 16.9) shows you several slides on screen at once, in miniature. You use Slide Sorter view to change the order of slides, add transitions, and set timings for on-screen presentations.

To switch to Slide Sorter view, click the Slide Sorter View button or select <u>V</u>iew ➤ Sli<u>d</u>e Sorter.

Notes Pages View

Notes Pages view (shown in Figure 16.10) displays the speaker's note page for each slide. Each page corresponds to a single slide. In Notes Pages view you create and edit speaker's notes for your presentation.

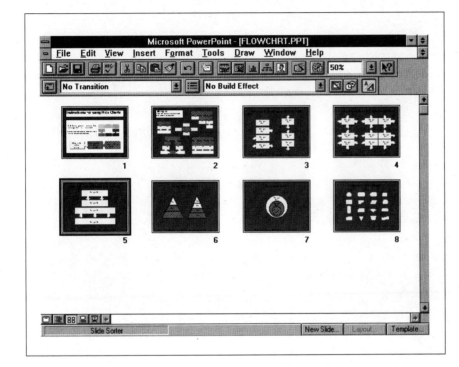

FIGURE 16.9

Slide Sorter view lets you view several slides at once.

To switch to Notes Pages view, click the Notes Pages View button or select <u>V</u>iew ➤ <u>N</u>otes Pages. While in Notes Pages view you can enlarge or reduce the display using the Zoom button on the Standard toolbar and navigate using the Next Slide button (or PgDn), the Previous Slide button (or PgUp), and the scroll bars.

FIGURE 16.10

You use Notes Pages view to create and edit speaker's notes for a presentation.

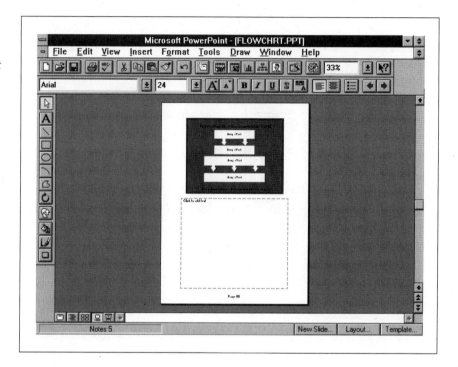

Slide Show

Slide Show (see Figure 16.11) displays your slides one at a time, full-screen, as an on-screen presentation. You use Slide Show to view the effects of the transitions and timing that you set in Slide Sorter view, and to present the presentation electronically to an audience.

To switch to Slide Show click the Slide Show button or select View ➤ Slide Show. To cancel Slide Show, press Esc.

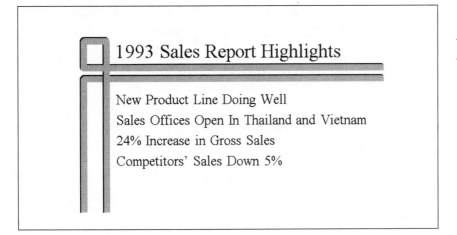

FIGURE 16.11

In Slide Show slides are presented one at a time at full-screen size.

Saving a Presentation

As you work, it's a good idea to save the presentation regularly, so you won't lose much work in the event of a power outage or other problem. You must save the presentation before exiting PowerPoint.

When you start a new presentation, PowerPoint assigns it a name in the form Presentation1, Presentation2, and so on. When you save it you must assign a different name up to eight characters long (PowerPoint will add a .PPT extension). Once a presentation has been named, the name is displayed in the title bar. To save a presentation:

1. Click the Save button on the Standard toolbar or select File ➤ Save.

Save

2. If you have previously saved and named the presentation, the current version is saved and you are returned to the work screen. If the presentation has not yet been named, PowerPoint displays the Save As dialog box, which is covered in Chapter 2.

Opening a Presentation

Open

To open a presentation that was previously saved to disk, click the Open button on the Standard toolbar or select File ➤ Open. PowerPoint displays the Open dialog box, which is covered in Chapter 2.

The Undo Command

As with Word and Excel, PowerPoint has an Undo command that reverses your most recent action. Undo can recover from most Powerpoint actions, such as deleting a slide, changing formatting, or adding text.

Undo

To undo your most recent action, click the Undo button on the Standard toolbar, or select Edit ➤ Undo.

Note that PowerPoint's Undo command is limited to undoing only the most recent action. Note also that, unlike in Word, there is no Redo command.

CHAPTER SEVENTEEN

Working with Slides

SLIDES ARE THE backbone of any presentation. They are the primary tool that you use to get your ideas and information across. Most of the time you spend working in PowerPoint will be devoted to creating and modifying slides.

Slides, Objects, and Placeholders

When you first create a new slide it will have one or more *placeholders* on it. A placeholder is a box, initially empty, into which you can place something—text or a chart, for example. Figure 17.1 shows a new slide

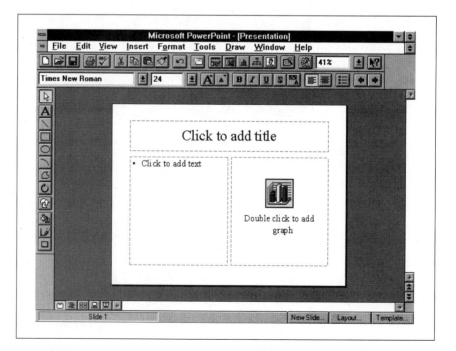

with placeholders. Some placeholders are specialized to hold a particular type of item—clip art, for example, or text. There is also a generic "object" placeholder that can hold any type of object. An *object* is any item (text, clip art, a chart, etc.) on a slide. In other words, anything that you put in a placeholder is an object, as is an empty placeholder itself.

Selecting a Slide

Most of the operations covered in this chapter are performed in Slide view, which shows a single slide at a time on-screen.

To find the slide you want while in Slide view, click on the Next Slide or Previous Slide button (below the vertical scroll bar), or use the PgUp and PgDn keys, to move between slides.

If, however, your presentation has a lot of slides, click on the Slide Sorter View button to the left of the horizontal scroll bar to switch to Slide Sorter view, and select the desired slide by clicking it. Return to Slide view by clicking on the Slide View button to the left of the horizontal scroll bar. You can also select a slide by clicking its title in Outline view.

Creating a New Slide

When you create a new slide, it is placed immediately after the current slide in the presentation. If you're starting a new presentation, it will be the first slide. You can insert a new slide from any of PowerPoint's views except Slide Show.

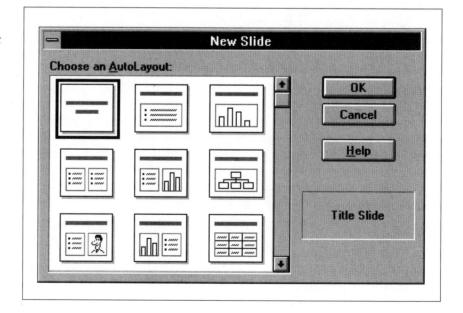

1. Click on the New Slide button on the status bar or select Insert ➤ New Slide. PowerPoint displays the New Slide dialog box, shown in Figure 17.2.

2. Click the AutoLayout sketch that you want; if necessary, use the scroll bar to scroll through the display of AutoLayouts. If you're not sure which one to select, don't worry—you can always change the AutoLayout later.

3. Click on the OK button or press ↵. PowerPoint displays a blank slide with the placeholders specified by the selected AutoLayout. Figure 17.1 shows an example.

FIGURE 17.2

You specify the layout of a new slide in the New Slide dialog box.

Once you have created a slide, you can add objects by filling in the placeholders. These procedures are explained later in the chapter. You can add objects immediately after creating the slide, or create additional slides and come back to them later.

Changing a Slide's Layout

You can change a slide's layout at any time. If a slide already has some objects on it, you will not lose any of them by changing layout. Rather, new placeholders will be added to the slide. You can then resize the slide's text and graphics boxes to accommodate the new layout.

To change a slide's layout, display the slide in Slide view. Then:

1. Click on the Layout button on the status bar or select F_ormat ➤ Slide Lay_out. PowerPoint displays the Slide Layout dialog box.

2. Click on the AutoLayout sketch that you want applied to the slide.

3. Click on the OK button or press ↵. The new layout will be applied to the slide.

Adding Text to Placeholders

Most new slides contain one or more placeholders for text. They are initially identified by a descriptive label such as "Click to add title" or "Click to add text." A text placeholder that is not a title placeholder can contain text at five different levels, which differ in indentation, bullets, and style.

To add text to a text placeholder, just click in the placeholder and type. While typing you can control text layout as follows:

Left Align

Center

Promote   Demote

- Press ↵ to end one paragraph and start another.
- Click on the Left Align button on the Formatting toolbar to left-align the current paragraph in the placeholder.
- Click on the Center button on the Formatting toolbar to center the current paragraph in the placeholder.
- Click on the Promote or Demote button on the Formatting toolbar to promote or demote non-title text one level.
- Use the arrow keys or point and click to move the insertion point.
- Press Del or Backspace to delete single characters.

When you're done, click outside the text placeholder. To change text formatting, see the section titled "Formatting Text."

Using the Text Tool

The Text Tool lets you place text anywhere on a slide. You could, for example, add a caption below a chart using the Text Tool. To add text with the Text Tool:

Text Tool

1. Click on the Text Tool button on the Drawing toolbar.

2. For non-wrapping text, with each paragraph on a single line that's as long as needed, click on the slide at the location at which you want the text to start. For text that automatically

wraps to a new line once it reaches a certain width, point to the slide and drag a box of the desired width.

3. Type the text.

Using Text from Word or Excel

You can quickly copy text from either a Word document or an Excel workbook for use in a PowerPoint slide.

1. While entering text in a placeholder or with the Text Tool, position the insertion point where you want to copy the text.

2. Switch to Word or Excel by clicking the Word or Excel button on either the Office Manager or the Microsoft toolbar.

Word   Excel

3. In Word, select the text to be copied. In Excel, select the cell(s) containing the text.

4. Click on the Copy button on the Word or Excel Standard toolbar.

Copy

5. Switch back to PowerPoint by clicking on the PowerPoint button on the Office Manager or the Microsoft toolbar.

PowerPoint

6. Click on the Paste button on the Standard toolbar. The copied text is inserted at the location of the insertion point.

Paste

NOTE

If you copy more than one cell of text from Excel into your PowerPoint presentation, then columns will be separated by tabs and each row will be placed in its own paragraph.

Selecting Text

You must select text before performing many of PowerPoint's text formatting and editing actions. Selecting text in PowerPoint is much like selecting text in a Word document. Refer to "Selecting Text" in Chapter 3 for more information. Once you have selected text you can proceed to the formatting or editing steps. If you change your mind, you can deselect the text.

Formatting Text

Text, whether typed in a text placeholder or with the Text Tool, can be formatted in a variety of ways. Text in a placeholder is by default formatted as specified in the presentation's Slide Master. If you modify text formatting using the techniques presented in this section, the new formats are applied in addition to whatever formats the Slide Master contains.

To format existing text, select the text and then issue the formatting command(s). To format new text, move the insertion point to the location for the text and then issue the formatting command(s).

**Increase
Font Size**

**Decrease
Font Size**

- To increase the font size, click on the Increase Font Size button on the Formatting toolbar.

- To decrease the font size, click on the Decrease Font Size button on the Formatting toolbar.

- To set a specific font size, pull down the Font Size list on the Formatting toolbar and select the desired size.

- To change font, pull down the Font list on the Formatting toolbar and select the desired font.

- To apply or remove boldface, underline, or italic format, click on the corresponding button on the Formatting toolbar.

- To apply or remove a shadow, click on the Text Shadow button on the Formatting toolbar.

- To change text color, click on the Text Color button on the Formatting toolbar and select a color from the palette that is displayed.

Bold   Underline Italic

Text Shadow

Text Color

NOTE

Text that has already been entered onto a slide can be edited. Editing techniques are covered in Chapter 3.

Adding Visuals to Slides

A *visual* is anything you place on a slide that is not text. Visuals include items you draw yourself using PowerPoint's tools, clip art imported from disk files, and pictures created in other applications, such as Excel.

Drawing AutoShape Objects

Most of PowerPoint's drawing objects are *AutoShapes*. AutoShapes are a special PowerPoint tool that you can use to draw shapes such as arrows, speech balloons, stars, and cubes. AutoShapes have several characteristics

that make them much more useful than the standard drawing tools you may be used to:

- An AutoShape can be quickly changed into any other AutoShape— a rectangle to an arrow, for example—without altering its size, color, or other attributes.

- Many AutoShapes have an adjustment handle that lets you alter the proportions of the shape.

- Text can be added to any AutoShape.

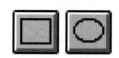

Rectangle   Ellipse

You activate AutoShape tools by clicking on toolbar buttons. Two of the AutoShape tool buttons, Rectangle and Ellipse, are located on the Drawing toolbar. The others, some two dozen in all, are located on the AutoShapes toolbar.

AutoShapes

To display the AutoShapes toolbar, click on the AutoShapes button on the Drawing toolbar.

To add an AutoShape to a slide:

1. Click on the desired AutoShape button on the Drawing or AutoShapes toolbar.

2. Point to the slide and drag. As you do, an outline expands to show the size and location of the object.

3. Release the mouse button.

To draw a *regular* shape, press and hold down the Shift key while drawing the AutoShape. A regular shape is one that can be inscribed in a square. For example, hold down the Shift key while drawing an ellipse and you'll get a circle.

To draw a shape from the center outward, rather than from one corner, press and hold down the Ctrl key while drawing. This technique is useful when you need to precisely position the center of an AutoShape object.

To draw a regular shape from the center outward, press and hold Shift+Ctrl while drawing.

Drawing Other Objects

A few of PowerPoint's drawing objects are not AutoShapes, and are therefore not quite as flexible.

- To draw a line (any straight line), click on the Line button on the Drawing toolbar and then drag from the start to the end of the line.

Line

- To draw an arc (a curved line segment), click on the Arc button on the Drawing toolbar and then drag on the slide.

Arc

- To draw a freeform object (any shape you draw freehand), click on the Freeform button on the Drawing toolbar and then drag on the slide, using the mouse pointer as you would a pencil.

Freeform

- To draw a polygon (a closed or open figure consisting of three or more points connected by straight lines):

  1. Click on the Freeform button on the Drawing toolbar.

  2. Click on the slide where you want to place the first vertex of the polygon (do not drag or you'll get a freeform!).

  3. Click at the location of the second vertex.

  4. Continue clicking until you have the shape you want.

Freeform

5. To close the polygon, click next to the first vertex. For an open polygon, double-click to place the last vertex.

Adding Clip Art

PowerPoint comes with over 1000 clip art images. You can insert a clip art image in a clip art placeholder or anywhere else on a slide.

Insert Clip Art

1. To insert clip art in a clip art placeholder, double-click the placeholder or click on the Insert Clip Art button on the Standard toolbar. PowerPoint displays the Microsoft ClipArt Gallery, shown in Figure 17.3.

FIGURE 17.3

You select clip art images from the Clip Art Gallery.

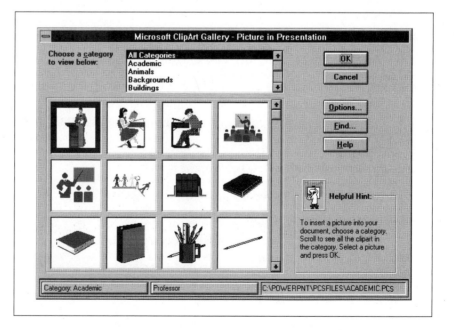

2. In the list at the top of the dialog box, select the category of clip art that you want to use.

3. Click on the image that you want to use. If necessary, use the vertical scroll bar to scroll through the available images. The bar at the bottom of the dialog box displays the category, name, and file name of the selected image.

4. Click on the OK button or press ↵.

Depending on what you did in step 1, the clip art image is inserted into the placeholder or in the center of the slide (not in any placeholder). In either case you can move and resize the clip art image as desired, using techniques described later in this chapter.

Adding an Organizational Chart

An *organizational chart* is a specialized diagram used for showing the organization of personnel in a company (see Figure 17.4).

You create an organizational chart using Microsoft Organizational Chart, a separate application that is provided as part of the PowerPoint package.

To add an organizational chart to a slide:

1. If the slide layout has a placeholder for an organizational chart, double-click the placeholder. If not, select Insert ➤ Object, select Microsoft Organizational Chart from the list, and then click on the OK button.

FIGURE 17.4

An organization chart shows the relationships between people in an organization.

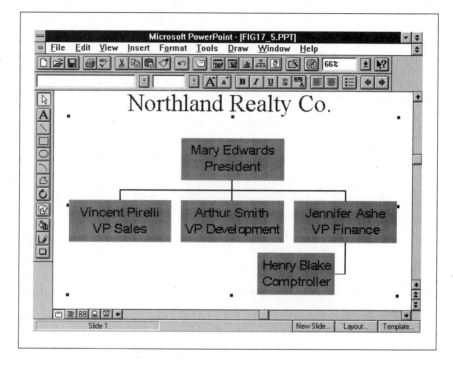

2. The organizational chart application starts, and is displayed in a window over the PowerPoint screen. A sample chart is displayed.

3. Use the features of the program to create your chart. Note that the title bar indicates that the chart is an object in the presentation you were working on.

4. When you're finished, select File ➤ Exit And Return To *Name* (where *name* is the name of your presentation).

5. A dialog box is displayed asking if you want to update the object in your presentation.

6. Click on the Yes button to return to PowerPoint, with the new organizational chart in place.

To modify an existing organizational chart, double-click the chart. The Organizational Chart application will start and display the chart for modification. When you're finished, follow steps 4 through 6 above to update the chart and return to PowerPoint.

Using the Organizational Chart Tools

Many of the procedures for using the Organizational Chart application are similar to those you've learned for the other Office applications. Use the Help system for more information.

Adding Special Text Effects

Use WordArt to create text with different shapes, orientations, textures, and shadows. WordArt is a separate application, just like Organizational Chart, and is used in much the same way. To start WordArt, select Insert ➤ Object, then select Microsoft WordArt and click on the OK button. To close WordArt and return to your slide, follow steps 4 through 6 above.

Creating a Graph

You can create a chart or graph in a PowerPoint presentation by using Microsoft Excel, and then inserting the chart on a slide. This method, which is better if the data to be charted already exists in an Excel workbook, is described in the next section. You can also use the Microsoft

Graph application to create a chart or graph. Use this method if you have a relatively small amount of data to graph, and it is not already in a workbook.

To insert a graph:

Insert Graph

1. Double-click a Graph placeholder or click on the Insert Graph button on the Standard toolbar. The Graph sample datasheet and graph (see Figure 17.5) appear.

FIGURE 17.5

When you insert a graph, a sample datasheet and graph are displayed.

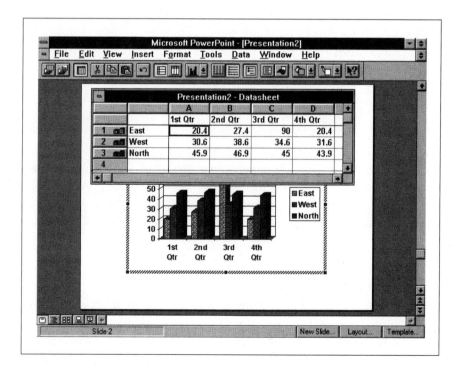

2. Click the datasheet window and start entering your data (and deleting the sample data). You enter and edit data using the same procedures as in an Excel workbook. Changes you make are immediately reflected in the graph. You can change the datasheet size or position by dragging its border or title bar.

3. Click the graph to hide the data sheet and view the graph. Click on the View Datasheet button to redisplay the datasheet.

4. Use the menus and toolbar to modify your graph. The procedures you use to modify and enhance a graph are very similar to those you learned for Excel charts earlier in this book. If you need more information, you can use the Microsoft Graph Help system.

Adding an Excel Chart

Charts that you create with Excel can be used in a PowerPoint presentation. This shortcut can be a great time-saver, because you create the chart only once. As an added bonus, you can *link* the PowerPoint chart to the original Excel chart so that changes in the latter are automatically reflected in your presentation.

To insert and optionally link an Excel chart:

1. To insert the chart in an object placeholder, select the placeholder by clicking it. Otherwise the chart will be inserted in the middle of the slide and you can move it to the desired position.

2. Start Excel by clicking on the Excel button on the Microsoft or Office Manager toolbar.

Excel

3. In Excel, open the desired workbook, if necessary. Select the desired chart by clicking it.

4. Click on the Copy button on Excel's Standard toolbar.

5. Switch back to PowerPoint by clicking on the PowerPoint button on the Microsoft or Office Manager toolbar.

6. Select Edit ➤ Paste Special. PowerPoint displays the Paste Special dialog box, shown in Figure 17.6.

Copy

PowerPoint

FIGURE 17.6

You use the Paste Special dialog box to insert an Excel chart into a PowerPoint slide.

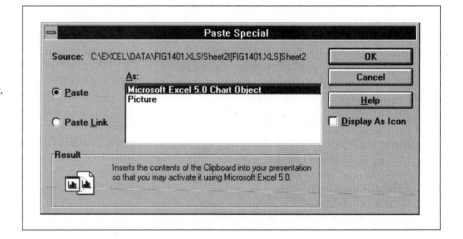

7. In the As list be sure that Microsoft Excel Chart Object is selected.

8. Select Paste to insert the chart without a link. It will *not* be updated in your presentation if the original Excel chart changes.

Select Paste Link to insert the chart with a link. Changes to the original chart will be reflected in your presentation.

9. Click on the OK button or press ↵.

○ Paste **L**ink

OK

Selecting and Grouping Objects

To modify slide objects you must first select them. You can also *group* two or more objects so that PowerPoint treats them as a single object, permitting you to make changes that apply to the entire group.

To select a single object, click on a visible part of the object. A selected object or group is displayed with handles at the corners and on the edges of its rectangular bounding box. To deselect an object, press Esc.

To select multiple objects, press and hold down the Shift key while clicking the objects. To deselect a single object, click it a second time while holding down the Shift key. To deselect all objects, release the Shift key and press Esc. You can select multiple contiguous objects by using the mouse to drag a selection rectangle around them. To select all objects on the slide, press Ctrl+A.

To group objects, select the objects to be grouped and then choose **D**raw ➤ **G**roup. When a group of objects is selected, handles are displayed on the boundary surrounding the entire group and *not* around each individual object. To ungroup objects, select the group and then choose **D**raw ➤ **U**ngroup.

NOTE

To select a text object, click on its border if it has one. If there's no border, click inside the object to activate Edit mode and then click on the thick border that is displayed.

To regroup objects, select one object that was in the group previously and then choose Draw ➤ Regroup. PowerPoint will recreate the group that the selected object was most recently in. If the object was never in a group this command will not be available.

Changing Object Size and Position

You can change the size and position of any object on a slide. You can also align objects with one another. You must first select the object(s) or group that you are working with.

- To move an object, point to the object (for a text object, point to its border) and drag the outline to the new position.

- To resize an object, point to one of its handles (the mouse pointer changes to a two-headed arrow) and drag the outline to the new size.

- To align objects, choose Draw ➤ Align and then select the desired alignment from the menu. The Align command is available only if two or more objects are selected.

Enhancing Objects

Every PowerPoint object has a set of attributes that define its border, fill, and shadow style. By modifying these settings you can improve the appearance of your slides.

To change border and fill settings:

1. Select the object(s) to be modified.

2. Select Format ➤ Colors and Lines. PowerPoint displays the Colors And Lines dialog box, shown in Figure 17.7.

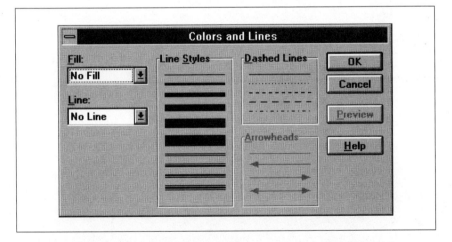

FIGURE 17.7

You change an object's border and fill attributes in the Colors And Lines dialog box.

3. To change the object's fill, pull down the Fill list and make a selection from the palette that is displayed. You can select a solid color or a shaded or patterns fill. Some selections on this list display other dialog boxes from which you select.

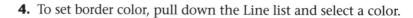

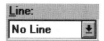

4. To set border color, pull down the Line list and select a color.

5. Select the border line style in the Line Styles and Dashed Lines sections of the dialog box.

6. If appropriate for the type of object selected, choose arrowhead placement in the Arrowheads section of the dialog box.

7. To see the effect of your selections without closing the dialog box, click on the Preview button. If the dialog box is covering the object, point to the title bar and drag it out of the way.

8. When finished, click on the OK button or press ↵.

To change an object's shadow:

1. Select the object(s).

2. Choose Format ➤ Shadow. PowerPoint displays the Shadow dialog box, shown in Figure 17.8.

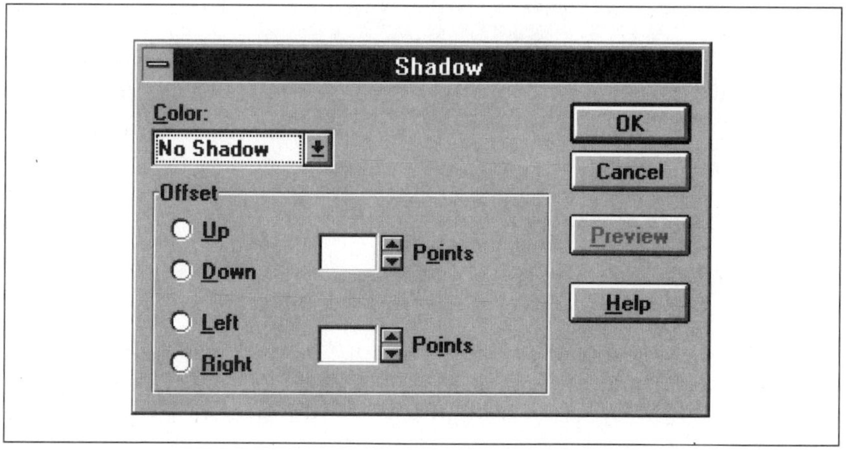

FIGURE 17.8

The Shadow dialog box lets you create shadows for objects.

3. Pull down the Color list and select a color or style for the shadow, or select No Shadow.

4. In the Offset section of the dialog box, select the direction and thickness of the shadow.

5. Click on the Preview button to see the effects of your choices without closing the dialog box.

6. When finished, click on the OK button or press ↵.

Editing Inserted Objects

Many of the objects that you use on PowerPoint slides are created with other applications and then inserted onto the slide. Examples include WordArt text, Microsoft Graph charts, and Excel charts. You can select these objects like any other objects and move, resize, and align them. In most cases you can change their border style, fill, and shadow too. To change their contents, however, you must double-click the object to activate the original application that created it. The object will be displayed with a thick, stippled border, and the original application's menu and toolbars will be displayed in place of PowerPoint's menu and toolbars. You use the application's commands and procedures to edit the object. When finished, click anywhere on the slide outside the object to return to PowerPoint.

Using the Slide Master

The Slide Master is the slide that defines the default format for the title and other text objects on all slides in the presentation. It also can hold

any items, such as clip art of your company's logo, that you want to appear on every slide in the presentation. You can modify the Slide Master at any time, and the changes will automatically be applied to every slide in the presentation.

To change the Slide Master:

1. Select View ➤ Master ➤ Slide Master. PowerPoint displays the Slide Master. The default Slide Master is shown in Figure 17.9.

FIGURE 17.9

Changes you make to the Slide Master are reflected in all slides in the presentation.

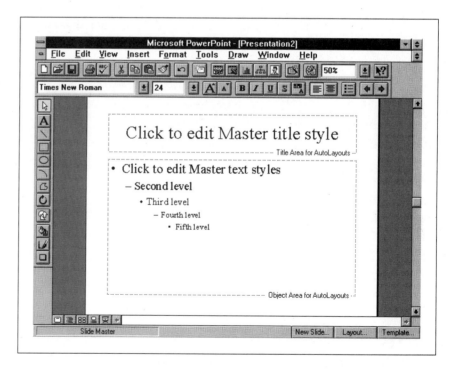

2. To change the format of slide-title text, click the Title Area For AutoLayouts box and apply the desired formatting to the text in the box.

3. To change the formatting of the five levels of text in text objects, click on the Object Area For AutoLayouts box and apply the desired formatting to each level.

4. To insert an object that will appear in the background of every slide, add the object to the Slide Master using the usual techniques.

5. When finished, click on the Slide View button (or one of the other view buttons) to close the Slide Master.

While you can edit the text on the Slide Master, such edits will have no effect on your presentation. The purpose of this text is only for you to apply formatting. Changes to the Slide Master affect only text that is in text placeholders—they do not affect text added to slides with the Text Tool.

N O T E

Text formatting that you apply to individual slides, such as changes in font, are not overridden by the Slide Master.

Modifying the Color Scheme

You can use color schemes to ensure that your color presentations are well balanced and professional-looking. In addition, changing the color scheme of a presentation automatically changes the colors of all the slides, making it a quick and easy task to experiment with different colors.

When you start a presentation it uses PowerPoint's default color scheme, or, if you based the presentation on a template, the color scheme of that template. You can change the color scheme used by the entire presentation or by selected slides.

1. Select Format ➤ Slide Color Scheme. PowerPoint displays the Slide Color Scheme dialog box, shown in Figure 17.10.

FIGURE 17.10

You use the Slide Color Scheme dialog box to modify the current color scheme or assign a new one.

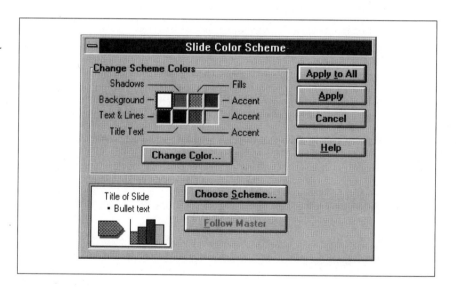

2. The Change Scheme Colors box displays the eight colors of the current scheme. To change an individual color in the scheme, select the sample by clicking it and then click on the Change Color button. A color palette dialog box is displayed.

3. Click the desired color, and then click on the OK button to return to the Slide Color Scheme dialog box.

4. To select a different scheme, click on the Choose Scheme button. PowerPoint displays the Choose Scheme dialog box, shown
in Figure 17.11.

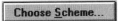

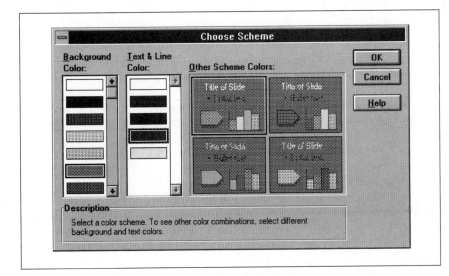

FIGURE 17.11

*You select a different
color scheme in the
Choose Scheme
dialog box.*

5. Select a background color in the Background Color list. An
assortment of coordinated colors for text and lines will be
displayed in the Text And Line Colors list.

6. Select a color in the Text And Line Colors list.

7. The Other Scheme Colors box shows samples of slides using
four color schemes based on the selected colors. Click the sample that has the appearance you want.

8. Click on the OK button or press ↵ to return to the Slide Color Scheme dialog box.

9. Click on the Apply button to apply the new color scheme to the current slide only. Click the Apply To All button to apply it to all slides in the presentation.

Changing Slide Order

You can change the order of the slides in your presentation at any time. To change slide order in Outline View:

1. Point to the slide icon next to the title of the slide to be moved.

2. Drag to the new position in the list.

To change slide order in Slide Sorter view:

1. Point to the slide to be moved.

2. Drag it to the new position.

CHAPTER EIGHTEEN

Enhancing Your Presentations

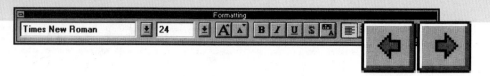

POWERPOINT provides several tools that you can use to enhance your presentation: speaker's notes, audience handouts, and outlines. You can also correct misspelled word with the Spelling Checker. This chapter shows you how to use these features to make your presentations the best they can be.

Creating Speaker's Notes

Whether you're an experienced public speaker or a nervous novice, speaker's notes can help to ensure that your presentation goes smoothly. Each slide in a presentation has a *notes page* associated with it. This page includes the slide itself as well as an area for you to enter your notes. You record salient points, important figures, and the like on notes pages, and then refer to them during the presentation. Figure 18.1 shows a notes page; in this example the notes area is empty.

To create a notes page for a given slide, or modify notes created earlier, make that slide current. Then:

1. Click on the Notes Pages View button at the lower-left edge of the screen. PowerPoint displays the notes page for the current slide, as shown in Figure 18.1.

2. Click the text box.

3. Type and edit text using the same techniques you learned in Chapter 17.

Promote   Demote

4. Promote and demote paragraphs by clicking on the Promote and Demote buttons on the Formatting toolbar. The text on a notes page has the same five levels of text as non-title text on a slide.

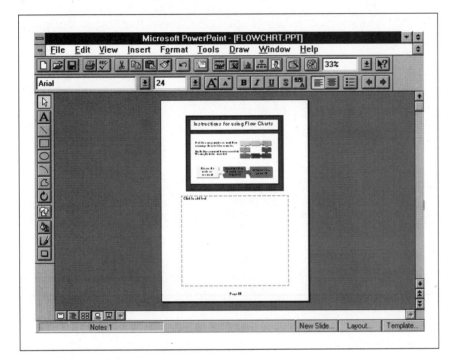

FIGURE 18.1

*A notes page includes
the slide as well as an
area for you to enter
your notes.*

5. Assign fonts and other formatting to the text using the same
techniques you learned in Chapter 17.

While working on a notes page you can use the zoom control to change
the size of the displayed page. You can control the appearance of all of the
notes pages using the Notes Master, described in the next section. You
can also take the following actions to format an individual page:

- Select the slide or the text placeholder, and then use the mouse
  to change its size or position.

- Add a border to the slide or the text box.

- Add clip art, charts, AutoShapes, text, and other objects using the same techniques you learned in Chapter 17.

The Notes Master

The formatting of each notes page is controlled by the *Notes Master*. The Notes Master functions in the same way as does the Slide Master that you learned about in Chapter 17.

To modify the Notes Master:

1. Select <u>V</u>iew ➤ <u>M</u>aster ➤ <u>N</u>otes Master. PowerPoint displays the Notes Master, shown in Figure 18.2.

2. Click in the text box and apply the desired formatting to the five levels of text displayed there. The text itself will not appear on your notes pages, but the formatting you specify will be applied to the corresponding text levels.

3. When done, click on the Notes Pages View button in the lower-left of the screen to close the Notes Master and display the notes page for the current slide.

Using Audience Handouts

Audience handouts can be a very useful feature of presentations. They permit members of the audience to take copies of some or all of your slides with them, and can also provide space for taking notes. Each handout sheet contains two, three, or six slides plus text, images, or other objects you have added. Other than the slides, the objects on

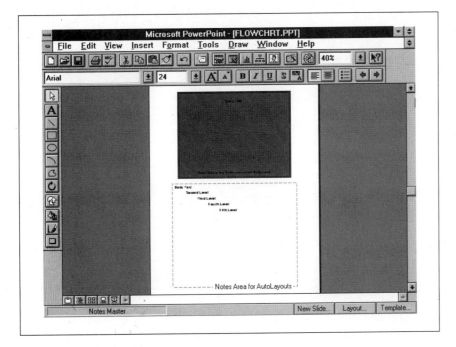

FIGURE 18.2

You specify the default notes page formatting on the Notes Master.

each handout page are identical for every page in the presentation. Items you might want to include on each handout page include your company's name, your name, the date, or blank lines to permit taking of handwritten notes.

The formatting and contents of audience handout pages is controlled by a *Handout Master*. If you want the handouts to include only copies of your slides, you do not need to modify the Handout Master. Otherwise, here's how to add items to the handouts:

1. Select <u>V</u>iew ➤ <u>M</u>aster ➤ <u>H</u>andout Master. PowerPoint displays the Handout Master, shown in Figure 18.3.

FIGURE 18.3

The Handout Master lets you add text and other items to your audience handouts.

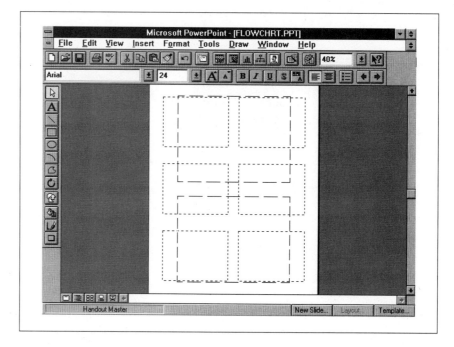

2. The boxes on the Handout Master represent where your slides will be printed. You specify the number of slides per page when you print the masters. The boxes are used as follows:

- When printing two slides per page the two large boxes are used.

- When printing three slides per page the three smaller boxes along the left edge of the page are used.

- When printing six slides per page all the smaller boxes are used.

3. Add text (using the Text Tool), lines, AutoShapes, clip art, and
so on to the page, using the same techniques you learned in
Chapter 16. These objects should be added outside the boundaries of the slide boxes that you will use.

4. To add the date, time, or page number, select Insert ➤ Date,
Insert ➤ Time, or Insert ➤ Page Number, and then drag the box
that appears in the middle of the page to the desired position
and size.

5. When you are done, click on one of the View buttons to close
the Handout Master.

Using an Outline

You learned in Chapter 16 that PowerPoint's Outline view displays your
presentation's text in the form of an outline.

Remember, to switch to Outline view click on the Outline View button
at the lower-left edge of the screen. In Outline view, the Drawing toolbar is replaced by the Outlining toolbar.

An outline has a maximum of six levels. The top level for each slide is
represented by the slide's title—text typed into an AutoLayout title area.

The other five levels are represented by the five levels of text in an Auto-Layout text area.

N O T E

Text added to a slide with the Text Tool does not appear in outlines.

Figure 18.4 shows a slide with a title and five levels of text. Figure 18.5 shows how this slide's text appears in Outline view.

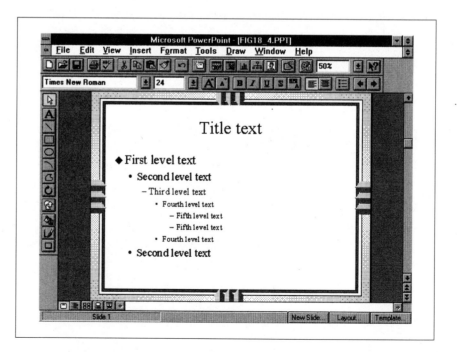

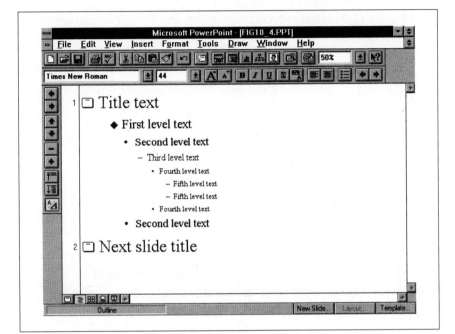

FIGURE 18.5

This is the Outline view of the slide in the previous figure showing how the text levels are displayed.

Outline view can be very useful when you are concentrating on the content and organization of your presentation rather than on its appearance. You can view the text content of many slides at once, see the relationship of one slide to the others, and see how the flow of ideas and topics progresses through the presentation. You can also format, edit, and rearrange text in Outline view. You position the insertion point in the outline by clicking with the mouse or using the arrow keys.

As you may have guessed, you must select text in an outline before you can format or edit it:

To select	Do this
Any text	Drag over the text or press Shift+arrow.
One word	Double-click the word.
One paragraph and its sublevels	Click to the left of the paragraph (mouse cursor is a four-headed arrow).
One entire slide	Click on the slide icon to the left of the slide's title text.
The entire outline	Press Ctrl+A.

You edit text using the regular editing procedures. To format text, select the text and then apply formatting using the techniques you learned in Chapter 16. Remember that formatting you apply to text is added to the formatting specified by the presentation's Slide Master.

Outline view is also well suited for rearranging your presentation. You can change the order of slides as well as rearrange the text on each slide or move text from one slide to another.

To move a slide:

1. Select the slide.

2. Click on the Move Up or Move Down button on the Outlining toolbar.

Move   Move
Up   Down

If you prefer to use the mouse:

1. Point to the slide icon to the left of the title text. The mouse cursor changes to a four-headed arrow.

2. Drag the slide up or down to the new position.

To move a text paragraph:

1. To move just a single paragraph, position the insertion point in the paragraph. To move the paragraph along with all of its subordinate paragraphs, select the paragraph.

2. Click on the Move Up or Move Down button on the Outlining toolbar.

You can move a paragraph and its subordinate paragraphs with the mouse:

Move Up   Move Down

1. Move the mouse pointer to the left of the paragraph. The mouse cursor changes to a four-headed arrow.

2. Drag the paragraph to its new position.

N O T E

You can drag a paragraph to a new position on the same slide or on a different slide.

To promote or demote a paragraph:

1. To promote/demote the paragraph and all of its subordinate paragraphs, select the paragraph. To promote/demote the paragraph alone, without affecting its subordinate paragraphs, position the insertion point in the paragraph.

Promote   Demote

2. Click on the Promote or Demote button on the Outlining or Formatting toolbar.

You cannot demote a fifth-level paragraph or a block of paragraphs that contains a fifth-level paragraph. If you promote a first-level paragraph it becomes the title of a new slide. If you demote title text it becomes first-level text and the slide's title will be blank.

Show Formatting

Outline view can display either formatted or unformatted text. You'll probably want to use unformatted text display when you're dealing with the presentation's content. Click on the Show Formatting button on the Outlining toolbar to toggle between formatted and unformatted text.

Sometimes you'll want all of the text on each slide to display in Outline view. At other times you may prefer for only the slide's title to be displayed. You can control the display mode for the entire outline or for individual slides:

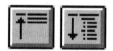

**Show   Show All
Titles**

To show only titles for the entire outline, click on the Show Titles button on the Outlining toolbar. To return to full text display, click on the Show All button.

**Collapse   Expand
Selection   Selection**

To display only the title for the current slide, click on the Collapse Selection button on the Outlining toolbar. To return the current slide to full text display, click on the Expand Selection button.

The Outline Master

PowerPoint's *Outline Master* lets you specify items, such as headers and footers, that will be printed on every page of your outline. The Outline Master does not control the formatting or appearance of the outline

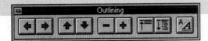

text itself—that is controlled by the Slide Master and by formatting you have applied to individual slides.

To modify the Outline Master:

1. Select <u>V</u>iew ➤ <u>M</u>aster ➤ <u>O</u>utline Master. The Outline Master is shown in Figure 18.6. The dotted box shows the area on the page in which the outline will be printed.

2. Add text (using the Text Tool), lines, AutoShapes, clip art, and so on to the Outline Master page, using the same techniques you learned in Chapter 16. These objects should be added outside the boundary of the outline.

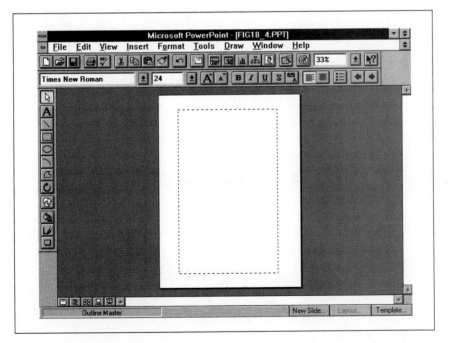

FIGURE 18.6

The Outline Master lets you specify items that will be printed on every page of the outline.

3. To add the date, time, or page number, select Insert ➤ Date, Insert ➤ Time, or Insert ➤ Page Number, and then drag the box that appears in the middle of the page to the desired position and size.

4. When you are done, click on one of the View buttons to close the Outline Master.

Checking Your Spelling

There are few things more embarrassing than displaying a slide with a misspelled word to a room full of your co-workers. PowerPoint's Spelling Checker can save you from such experiences. The Spelling Checker checks the entire presentation—slides, handouts, etc. To check spelling:

Spelling

1. Click the Spelling button on the Standard toolbar or press F7.

2. PowerPoint starts checking words in the presentation. If it finds a word that is not in its dictionary, it displays the Spelling dialog box, shown in Figure 18.7. The word in question is displayed in the Not In Dictionary box and is also highlighted in the presentation.

3. When this dialog box is displayed you can take the following actions:

   ■ Click the Ignore button to ignore only this occurrence of the word.

   ■ Click the Ignore All button to ignore this and all other occurrences of the word.

FIGURE 18.7

PowerPoint's Spelling Checker can find and correct misspelled words in your presentation.

- Click on the Change button to replace the word in question with the word in the Change To box. If necessary, select the proper replacement from the Suggestions list, or edit the word in the Change To box.

- Click on the Change All button to replace all occurrences of the word in the presentation with the word in the Change To box.

- Click on the Add button to add the word to the dictionary.

- Click on the Close button to end the spelling check.

N O T E

The Spelling Checker does not check the spelling of words in objects you have inserted from other applications, such as WordArt.

CHAPTER NINETEEN

Slide Shows and Printing

THE "BOTTOM LINE" with any presentation is when you show it to an audience. The show involves either printing the presentation or creating an electronic slide show for on-screen display. These are the topics of this chapter.

Slide Shows

A *slide show* is an on-screen show of your presentation. During a slide show only the slide is displayed on-screen—you will see nothing of the PowerPoint program itself. Delivering your presentation to the audience with a slide show offers a number of advantages over the more traditional methods of using photographic slides or overhead transparencies. You can run a slide show using PowerPoint's default settings. All of the slides will be shown, in order, with changes to the next slides triggered by a key press or mouse click. There will be no special transition between slides.

Assigning Slide Transitions and Slide Timings

A *transition* is a special visual effect when the slide show is changing from one slide to the next. Instead of one slide simply being replaced by the next instantaneously, there is a short transition period when the first slide "blends" into the second. PowerPoint offers a wide variety of interesting slide transitions. You can also control slide timing, specifying that the slide advance only with a mouse click or key press, or automatically after a specified number of seconds.

To add transitions and timing to your slide show:

1. Click the Slide Sorter View button in the lower-left corner of your screen.

2. Select the slide for which you're setting the transition.

3. Select <u>T</u>ools ➤ <u>T</u>ransition. PowerPoint displays the Transition dialog box, shown in Figure 19.1.

4. Pull down the Effect list and select the desired transition. The picture in the preview box shows the selected transition. Click the preview picture to see the transition again.

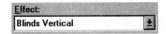

5. Select the speed of the transition in the Speed section of the dialog box. Speed options are not available for all effects.

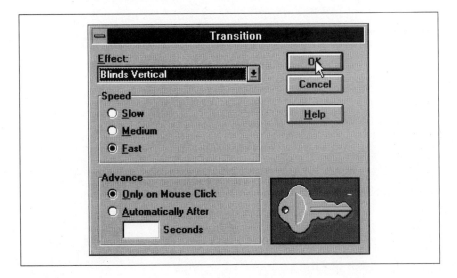

FIGURE 19.1

You set slide show transitions in the Transition dialog box.

Automatically After

OK

6. To have the slide advance automatically, select the Automatically After option and enter the desired delay in the box.

7. Click the OK button or press ↵.

In Slide Sorter view, a small Transition icon is displayed beneath each slide for which you've set a transition. Click on this icon to view the transition. If automatic advance is set, the time in seconds is also displayed beneath the slide.

TIP

Don't use too many different transitions in a slide show—it can be distracting.

Assigning Slide Timings during Rehearsal

If you're not sure how much time to assign to each slide, you can assign the timings while rehearsing the presentation. PowerPoint keeps track of how much time you spend on each slide and assigns that as the slide's display time. To assign times during rehearsal:

1. Select View ➤ Slide Show.

Rehearse New Timings

OK

2. In the Slide Show dialog box select the Rehearse New Timings option.

3. Click the OK button or press ↵. PowerPoint starts the slide show. A clock is displayed in the lower-left corner of the screen showing you how long each slide has been displayed.

4. Click the mouse button or press the spacebar to advance to the next slide.

5. At the end of the show PowerPoint asks if you want to save the recorded times. Click the Yes button to save the times for each slide or click the No button to discard the times.

Creating Build Slides

A *build slide* (sometimes called a progressive disclosure slide) contains a bulleted list in which the individual bulleted items appear one at a time. Use a build slide when you want to reveal the items in the list individually.

In a basic build slide the individual items simply appear in-place one at a time. You can specify special effects, such as having new items "fly" into the slide. You can also specify that as each new item is added, previous items are dimmed. To create a build slide:

1. Click the Slide Sorter View button in the lower-left corner of your screen to display your presentation in Slide Sorter view.

2. Click the desired slide.

3. Select Tools ➤ Build. PowerPoint displays the Build dialog box, shown in Figure 19.2.

4. For a basic build, select the Build Body Text option.

5. Select the Dim Previous Points option if you want previous paragraphs dimmed as each new one is added to the slide. Pull down the color list and select the color for previous points to be displayed in. Use a medium gray color to have points appear dimmed out.

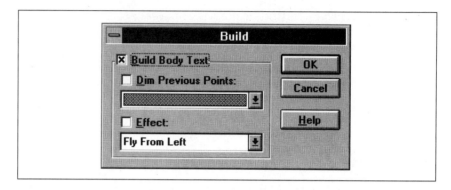

6. Select the Effect option, and select an effect from the list, to have new items appear on the slide in a special way.

7. Click the OK button or press ↵.

During a slide show, each "step" in a build slide must be triggered by pressing the mouse button or spacebar. In Slide Sorter view, each build slide has a small Build icon displayed below it.

Creating Hidden Slides

A hidden slide is not displayed during a presentation unless you specifically request it. Use hidden slides to show information that may not be necessary, depending on the questions asked by the audience. To create a hidden slide, or to unhide a slide:

1. Make the slide current. In Slide Sorter view you can select more than one slide to hide (hold down the Shift key and click each slide).

2. Select Tools ➤ Hide Slide.

In Slide Sorter view, hidden slides are indicated by a box with a diagonal line over their slide number.

During a slide show, the slide preceding a hidden slide displays the Hidden Slide icon in the lower-right corner of the screen. To display the hidden slide, click on this icon. Click elsewhere on the screen, or press the spacebar, to skip the hidden slide.

> ### N O T E
>
> **You cannot display hidden slides when using slide timings to automatically advance the slides.**

Running a Slide Show

To run a slide show:

1. Select <u>V</u>iew ➤ Slide Sho<u>w</u>. PowerPoint displays the Slide Show dialog box, shown in Figure 19.3.

2. To include all of the presentation's slides in the show, select All. To display only some of the slides, select From and enter the starting and ending slide numbers in the boxes.

3. In the Advance section of the dialog box specify how you want the slide advance to be controlled:

■ Select Manual Advance to change slides with a mouse click or spacebar.

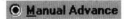

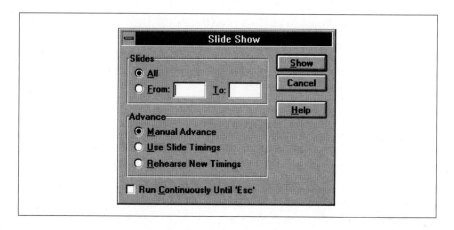

- Select Use Slide Timings to have slides advance automatically with the assigned timings. This option is not available if you have not assigned timings to slides in the presentation.

4. Select Run Continuously Until 'Esc' if you want the slide show to repeat itself continuously until the Esc key is pressed.

5. To start the show, click the OK button or press ↵.

Printing a Presentation

If you are not going to use an on-screen presentation, you'll have to print your slides. In any event you'll have to print your speaker's notes and audience handouts. You can print on any printer that is installed for Windows and connected to your computer, either directly or through a network.

Setting Up for Printing

Before printing you must specify certain setup information that controls the size and orientation of your printouts.

1. Select File ➤ Slide Setup. PowerPoint displays the Slide Setup dialog box, shown in Figure 19.4.

2. Pull down the Slides Sized For list and select the desired output format for slides:

- Select On-screen Show if you will be giving your presentation electronically and not printing the slides.

- Select 35mm Slides if you will be printing to a slide printer or on paper for later copying onto slides. This option creates output with the same height:width ratio as slides.

- Select Custom for any other size, and then enter the height and width measurements in the boxes.

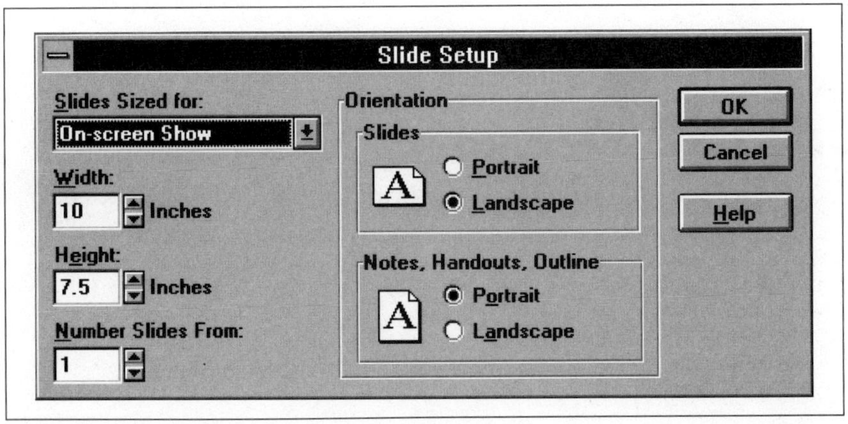

FIGURE 19.4

You control the setup for printing your presentation in the Slide Setup dialog box.

3. Select either Portrait orientation or Landscape orientation for slides and for notes, handouts, and outlines.

4. Click the OK button or press ⏎.

You can change the orientation and/or size of your slides at any time, and any existing slides will automatically be reformatted for the new settings.

Controlling Printing

To print all or part of a presentation:

1. Select File ➤ Print or press Ctrl+P. PowerPoint displays the Print dialog box, shown in Figure 19.5.

2. Pull down the Print What box and select the part of the presentation to be printed:

- Slides
- Notes Pages
- Handouts with two, three, or six slides per page
- Outline view

3. Enter the number of copies to print in the Copies box, or click the up and down arrows to change the displayed value.

4. In the Slide Range section specify the range of the presentation to print.

FIGURE 19.5

You control printing options in the Print dialog box.

5. Select other options as needed:

- **Print to File:** Sends output to a disk file that you can send to a service bureau for creating slides.

☐ Print to File

- **Print Hidden Slides:** Prints slides designated as hidden.

☐ Print Hidden Slides

- **Black & White:** Colored fills are printed as white and un-bordered objects are printed with a thin black frame.

☐ Black & White

- **Collate Copies:** Collates multiple copies at the expense of printing speed.

☒ Collate Copies

- **Scale to Fit Paper:** Slides are rescaled to exactly fit the specified paper size.

- **Pure Black & White:** All colored fills are printed as white, and all lines and text as black; outlines or borders are added to all filled objects, and pictures are printed in grayscale.

6. Click the OK button to start printing.

N O T E

If you are using a black and white printer to print a presentation that uses a lot of color, you will probably get best results if you select the Black & White or Pure Black & White option.

To quickly print the currently defined job, click on the Print button on the Standard toolbar.

Print

5

MAIL

CHAPTER TWENTY

Using
Microsoft Mail

MICROSOFT MAIL, hereafter called simply Mail, is the electronic mail component of Office. With Mail you can send messages and files to, and receive them from, other computer users who are also connected to the mail network. In this chapter you'll learn the basics of using Mail.

It's important to remember that you can use Mail only if your computer is connected to a network. A *network* is a system that connects computers to permit sharing of programs, files, and printers. Mail uses the network to send and receive its messages. Some of the details of running Mail are dependent on the way this network is set up. Certain problems you may encounter may be the fault of the network, and not the result of an error on your part. There is usually an individual in charge of keeping the network running smoothly—the network or system administrator. You should find out who your system administrator is in case you need his or her help.

Starting Mail and Signing In

To start Mail,

Mail

1. Click on the Mail icon on the Office Manager toolbar, or double click the Mail icon on the Program Manager screen. Mail starts and displays the Mail Sign In dialog box, shown in Figure 20.1.

2. Type the name assigned to you by your system administrator in the Name box.

3. Type your password in the Password box. As you type, the box displays asterisks to keep your password hidden.

OK

4. Click on the OK button or press ⏎.

FIGURE 20.1

*You use this dialog box
to sign into Mail.*

> **N O T E**
>
> The first time you sign onto Mail you will need to specify the name of your postoffice, the "location" on the network where your mail is delivered. Select your postoffice from the list that is displayed, and then go on to the remainder of the sign-on procedure. See your system administrator if you don't know your postoffice name.

When you sign onto Mail you'll see a screen like that shown in Figure 20.2. From here you can go on to read, create, and send messages. But let's first look at the parts of this screen.

The left part of the screen shows your *folders,* which hold your messages —both those you received and those you sent. (Your folder list will be different from the one shown in Figure 20.2). You can use multiple Mail folders to organize your messages by subject. You can have only one folder open at a time. The open folder will be indicated by an open folder icon next to the folder name. The contents of the open folder are displayed on the right side of the screen. One of the folders, called Inbox, holds messages you have received. This is the folder that is displayed in

Figure 20.2. To open a folder, double-click on its name or icon in the Folders list. The title bar displays the name of the open folder.

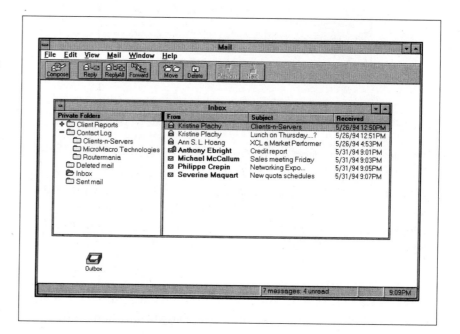

Reading Messages

To read a message, first be sure that your Inbox folder is open. Then:

1. In the message list, click the message you want to read.

2. Press ↲ or select File ➤ Open. The message is displayed, as shown in Figure 20.3. If the message is too long to fit in the

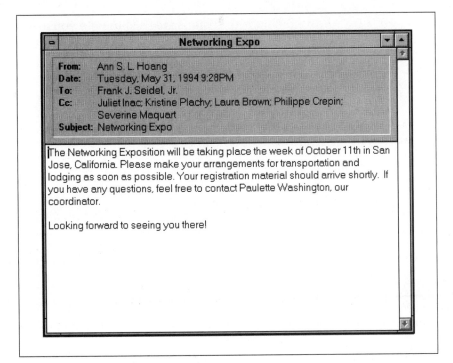

FIGURE 20.3

The message is displayed for reading.

window, you can use the scroll bar or PgUp and PgDn to display different parts of the message.

3. After reading the message, there are several actions you can take:

- To read the next message in the list, click on the Next button.

- To read the previous message in the list, click on the Previous button.

- To close the message, press Esc.

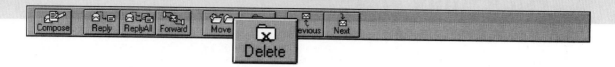

In the Inbox list, the following conventions are used to help you identify messages:

- Unread messages have closed envelope icons.

- Messages that you have read have open envelope icons.

- A high priority message has an exclamation point displayed next to its envelope icon.

- A low priority message has a downward-pointing arrow displayed next to its envelope icon.

- A normal priority message has no symbol displayed next to its icon.

- A message with an attachment has a paper clip displayed on its envelope icon.

You can also reply to messages you have received, forward them to other recipients, save them, or delete them. These topics are covered below.

Deleting Messages

After reading a message you can delete it if you're sure you won't need to refer to it again. You cannot delete an open message—you must close it first. Then, select it in the message list and click the Delete button. Deleting a message moves it to the Deleted Mail folder. You can retrieve deleted messages by opening this folder. To *really* delete a message, delete it from the Deleted Mail folder.

When deleting or performing other actions on messages in a list, you can select more than one message to operate on:

- With the mouse, hold down the Shift key while clicking each message.

- With the keyboard, press and hold down the Shift key while using ↑ and ↓ to select.

Saving Messages

You may want to save a message for future reference. To save a message, move it from the Inbox folder to another folder. You can also use this method to move a message from any open folder to another folder:

1. Select one or more messages in the message list.

2. Move the message in one of two ways:

- Drag it to the folder in which you want to save it. When a box appears around the desired folder, release the mouse button.

- Click the Move button, select the destination folder in the list that is displayed, and then click on the OK button.

> | OK |

> **N O T E**
>
> To copy a message to another folder, so that there will be a copy of the message in each folder, press and hold down the Ctrl key while dragging the message.

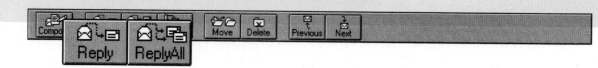

Replying to a Message

After reading a message you'll often want to send a reply. You can reply to an open message or one that is selected in a list. Here are the steps to follow:

1. Open the message, or select it in a list.

2. To reply to only the message sender, click on the Reply button, press Ctrl+R, or select <u>M</u>ail ➤ <u>R</u>eply. To reply to the sender and all individuals in the message's To and CC (Carbon Copy) boxes, click on the Reply All button.

3. A new message form is opened with the original message sender's address (and others, if you selected Reply All) in the To box, the subject in the Subject box, and the text of the original message in the message area.

4. Compose your reply. You can delete the original message text, or add comments to it, as desired.

5. Click on the Send button to send the message.

NOTE

When you reply to a message, any attachments that came with it are not included in the reply.

Forwarding a Message

You can forward a message that you received to another individual, either with or without comments.

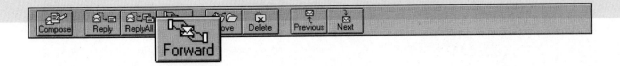

1. Open the message or select it in the Inbox list.

2. Click on the Forward button, press Ctrl+F, or select <u>M</u>ail ➤ <u>F</u>or-ward. A message form opens with the original message's text inserted.

3. Click on the Address button and specify the individual(s) to whom you want to forward the message.

4. If desired, add your own comments to the message.

5. Click on the Send button.

Retrieving Attachments

An *attachment* is a file that the sender has enclosed along with the message. An attachment can be a Word document, an Excel workbook, or any other kind of file. When a message includes an attachment it is indicated by an icon in the message. Figure 20.4 shows a message that has an attached file.

The icon will indicate the program that the attachment was created by. For example, an Excel workbook will display the Excel icon with the file name under it. You must have a copy of the original program—in this case, Microsoft Excel—in order to open and print the attached file. You do not need the program to simply save the attached file.

To open an attached file:

1. Display the message.

2. Double-click the attachment icon. The associated program will start and display the attached file.

FIGURE 20.4

An attached file is indicated by an icon in the message.

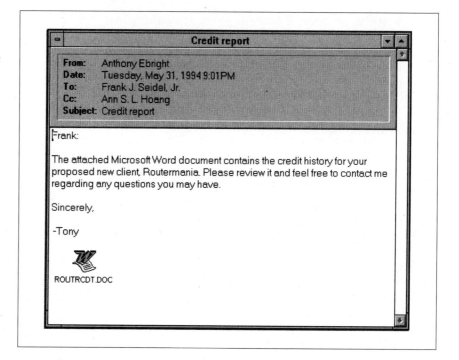

3. Use the program to edit, print, and save the attached file as needed. When you quit you will return to Mail.

When you receive an attachment, it remains part of the original message. If you delete the message, its attachments are deleted as well. If you want to save the attached file independent of the message, here's what to do:

1. Open or select the message with the attachment.

2. Select File ➤ Save Attachment. A dialog box is displayed listing the message's attachments.

3. To save a single attached file, select it in the Attached Files list.

4. If desired, enter a different name for the saved file in the File Name box.

5. Use the Drives and Directories lists to select the drive and directory in which you want to save the file(s).

6. To save the one selected attachment, click on the Save button. To save all attachments, click on the Save All button.

7. When you are finished, click on the Close button.

Creating and Sending a Message

To create and send a message:

1. Click on the Compose button. Mail displays the Send Note window, shown in Figure 20.5.

2. To specify the recipient(s) of the message, click on the Address button. Mail displays the Address dialog box, shown in Figure 20.6.

3. Specify one or more recipients as follows:

   - Select a recipient from the list by clicking; select more than one recipient by holding down the Shift key while clicking.

   - To select recipients from another address directory, click on the Directory button. Mail displays a list of other directories. Select the desired one and click the OK button. That directory's addresses will now be displayed in the Address list.

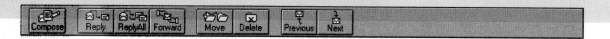

FIGURE 20.5

*You compose a message
to be sent in the Send
Note window.*

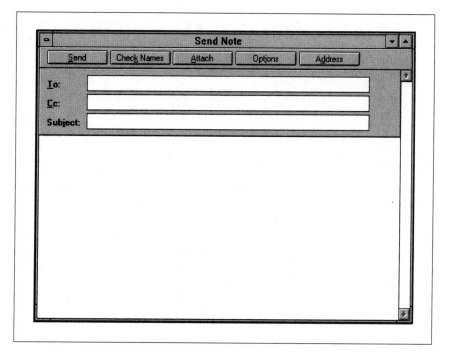

- To move the selected recipients to the To box, click on the To button. To move them to the CC box, click on the CC button.

- To remove a recipient from the To or CC boxes, select it and press Del.

4. When all recipients have been specified, click on the OK button to return to the message form.

5. To set message options, click on the Options button. Mail displays the dialog box shown in Figure 20.7.

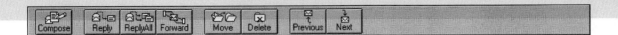

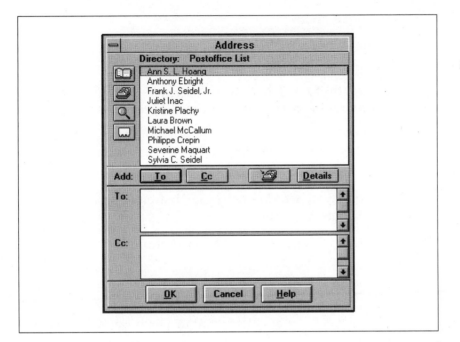

FIGURE 20.6

You select the address for the message in the Address dialog box.

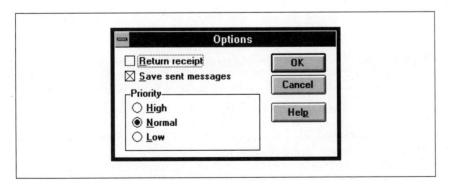

FIGURE 20.7

You set message options in the Options dialog box.

Set options as follows:

☐ **R**eturn receipt

- Select the Return Receipt option if you want to receive a receipt when the recipient opens the message.

☐ **S**ave sent messages

- Select the Save Sent Messages option if you want a copy of the message saved in the Sent Mail folder.

- Select High, Normal, or Low priority for the message. This setting controls how the message header is displayed in the recipient's Inbox.

OK

6. When options are set, click on the OK button or press ↵ to return to the message form.

Send

7. To send the message, click on the Send button.

Including Attachments in Messages

You can include any file as an attachment to a message. You can add attachments to messages you create and also to messages you forward.

Attach

1. While composing the message, click on the Attach button. Mail displays the Attach dialog box, shown in Figure 20.8.

2. Select the file to attach by clicking it in the File Name list.

List Files of **T**ype:

All Files (*.*)

3. To list only files of a certain type, such as Excel workbook files, pull down the List Files Of Type list and select the file type.

4. If necessary, use the Drives and Directories lists to select files from a different drive or directory.

Attach

5. Click on the Attach button to attach the file.

6. Repeat steps 2 though 5 to attach additional files, if desired.

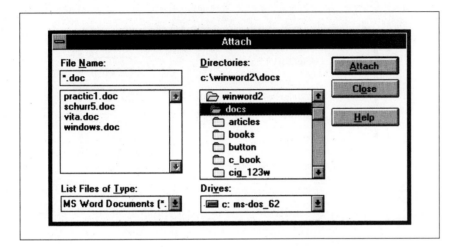

FIGURE 20.8

You specify files to attach to a message using the Attach dialog box.

7. Click on the Close button.

Each attached file is displayed as an icon in the message. To unattach a file, click on its icon and then press Del.

Printing Messages

You can print any messages, whether they are ones you sent or ones you received.

1. Select the message(s) to be printed.

2. Select File ➤ Print or press Ctrl+P. Mail displays the Print dialog box, shown in Figure 20.9.

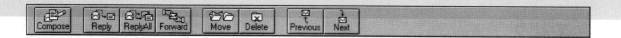

FIGURE 20.9

You use the Print dialog box to print selected messages.

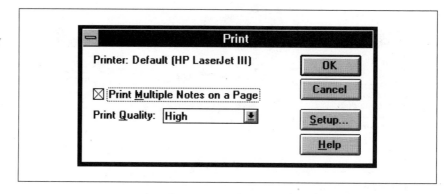

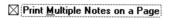

3. When printing multiple messages, clear the Print Multiple Notes On A Page option to have each message print on a separate page.

4. Click on the OK button or press ↵ to start printing.

Quitting Mail

There are two commands for quitting Mail. They will have the same effect unless you are running other mail-enabled applications—in other words, another program that uses your mailbox.

- To quit mail but remain signed in so that other mail-enabled applications can use your mailbox, select File ➤ Exit. If you later restart Mail you will not have to sign in.

- To quit mail and sign out from your mailbox, select File ➤ Exit and Sign Out.

# ndex

Note to the Reader: Boldfaced page numbers indicate primary discussions of a topic. *Italicized* page numbers indicate illustrations.

N

Instant Answers About Word 6 for Windows.

265 pp. ISBN: 1400-8

Get quick answers to your most pressing questions about the latest version of Word for Windows. Anything you'd possibly want to know about this program can be found here in the *Word 6 for Windows Instant Reference*.

This convenient pocket-sized reference features, clear explanations of all commands, step-by-step solutions to your Word for Windows problems and alphabetically organized entries that let you find what you need fast.

Suitable for beginners and veterans alike, the *Word 6 for Windows Instant Reference* is your best bet for plain-English guidance to the popular word-processing program.

SYBEX.
Shortcuts to Understanding.

SYBEX Inc.
2021 Challenger Drive
Alameda, CA 94501
1 (510) 523-8233
1 (800) 227-2346

SYBEX

Quick. Compact.
Complete.

A superbly organized index and intuitive cross-referencing are keys to the user-friendliness of this powerful, pocket-sized companion to the world's top selling spreadsheet for Windows. Contains all the new version 5 features.

Go from
zero to 60 on the
Information Superhighway—
in a flash!

What's a good modem? Isn't there some *simple* explanation of the "Internet?"
How is it different from Prodigy or CompuServe? What's the cost?

At last, here's *the* book on joining the online community, from SYBEX.

*Now available
wherever computer
books are sold.*

274 pages.
ISBN 1417-2

SYBEX

Shortcuts to Understanding.

SYBEX, Inc.
2021 Challenger Drive
Alameda, CA 94501
1-800-227-2346
1-510-523-8233

All the facts about WinFax.

Whether you got WinFax Lite free with your modem, or just went out and bought WinFax Pro 3.0 or 4.0, you'll appreciate the frank, troubleshooting approach of this companion for the popular Windows computer fax software.

Now available wherever computer books are sold.

376 pages.
ISBN 1462-8

SYBEX

Shortcuts to Understanding.

SYBEX, Inc.
2021 Challenger Drive
Alameda, CA 94501
1-800-227-2346
1-510-523-8233

GET A FREE CATALOG JUST FOR EXPRESSING YOUR OPINION.

Help us improve our books and get a *FREE* full-color catalog in the bargain. Please complete this form, pull out this page and send it in today. The address is on the reverse side.

Name _____   Company _____

Address _____   City _____ State ____ Zip _____

Phone (___) _____

1. **How would you rate the overall quality of this book?**
   - ❑ Excellent
   - ❑ Very Good
   - ❑ Good
   - ❑ Fair
   - ❑ Below Average
   - ❑ Poor

2. **What were the things you liked most about the book? (Check all that apply)**
   - ❑ Pace
   - ❑ Format
   - ❑ Writing Style
   - ❑ Examples
   - ❑ Table of Contents
   - ❑ Index
   - ❑ Price
   - ❑ Illustrations
   - ❑ Type Style
   - ❑ Cover
   - ❑ Depth of Coverage
   - ❑ Fast Track Notes

3. **What were the things you liked *least* about the book? (Check all that apply)**
   - ❑ Pace
   - ❑ Format
   - ❑ Writing Style
   - ❑ Examples
   - ❑ Table of Contents
   - ❑ Index
   - ❑ Price
   - ❑ Illustrations
   - ❑ Type Style
   - ❑ Cover
   - ❑ Depth of Coverage
   - ❑ Fast Track Notes

4. **Where did you buy this book?**
   - ❑ Bookstore chain
   - ❑ Small independent bookstore
   - ❑ Computer store
   - ❑ Wholesale club
   - ❑ College bookstore
   - ❑ Technical bookstore
   - ❑ Other _____

5. **How did you decide to buy this particular book?**
   - ❑ Recommended by friend
   - ❑ Recommended by store personnel
   - ❑ Author's reputation
   - ❑ Sybex's reputation
   - ❑ Read book review in _____
   - ❑ Other _____

6. **How did you pay for this book?**
   - ❑ Used own funds
   - ❑ Reimbursed by company
   - ❑ Received book as a gift

7. **What is your level of experience with the subject covered in this book?**
   - ❑ Beginner
   - ❑ Intermediate
   - ❑ Advanced

8. **How long have you been using a computer?**
   - years _____
   - months _____

9. **Where do you most often use your computer?**
   - ❑ Home
   - ❑ Work

   - ❑ Both
   - ❑ Other _____

10. **What kind of computer equipment do you have? (Check all that apply)**
    - ❑ PC Compatible Desktop Computer
    - ❑ PC Compatible Laptop Computer
    - ❑ Apple/Mac Computer
    - ❑ Apple/Mac Laptop Computer
    - ❑ CD ROM
    - ❑ Fax Modem
    - ❑ Data Modem
    - ❑ Scanner
    - ❑ Sound Card
    - ❑ Other _____

11. **What other kinds of software packages do you ordinarily use?**
    - ❑ Accounting
    - ❑ Databases
    - ❑ Networks
    - ❑ Apple/Mac
    - ❑ Desktop Publishing
    - ❑ Spreadsheets
    - ❑ CAD
    - ❑ Games
    - ❑ Word Processing
    - ❑ Communications
    - ❑ Money Management
    - ❑ Other _____

12. **What operating systems do you ordinarily use?**
    - ❑ DOS
    - ❑ OS/2
    - ❑ Windows
    - ❑ Apple/Mac
    - ❑ Windows NT
    - ❑ Other _____

13. On what computer-related subject(s) would you like to see more books?

_____

_____

_____

_____

14. Do you have any other comments about this book? (Please feel free to use a separate piece of paper if you need more room)

_____

_____

_____

_____

- - - - - - - - - - PLEASE FOLD, SEAL, AND MAIL TO SYBEX - - - - - - - - - -

SYBEX INC.
Department M
2021 Challenger Drive
Alameda, CA
94501

Your Pushbutton Roadmap to Microsoft Office
in a full-color, pull-out poster!

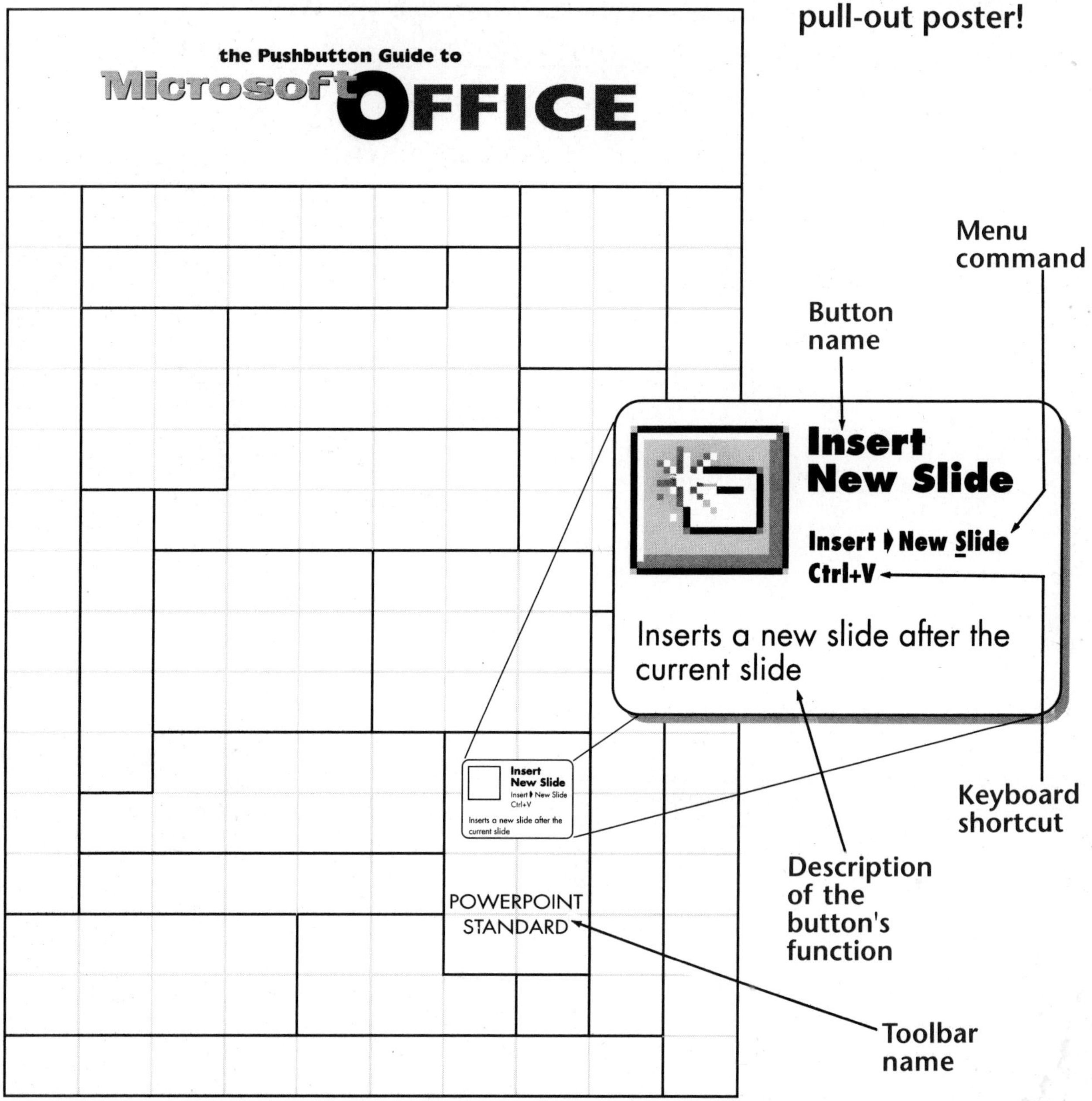

the Pushbutton Guide to
Microsoft OFFICE

Menu command

Button name

Insert New Slide

Insert ▸ New Slide
Ctrl+V

Inserts a new slide after the current slide

Keyboard shortcut

Insert New Slide
Insert ▸ New Slide
Ctrl+V

Inserts a new slide after the current slide

POWERPOINT STANDARD

Description of the button's function

Toolbar name